LangGraph LLM

Building the Future of Language Intelligence

Written By

Morgan Devline

copyright

Table of Contents

Preface

Introduction to the Book's Mission and Vision

This book is born from a shared passion for unlocking the transformative potential of language intelligence. At its core, our mission is to demystify LangGraph LLM, providing readers with a comprehensive and practical guide that bridges theoretical foundations and real-world applications. i aim to empower developers, researchers, and business leaders by offering:

- **In-Depth Research and Expertise:**
  An exploration grounded in extensive research, current advancements, and expert insights. The book provides not only detailed technical discussions on the architecture and operational principles of LangGraph LLM but also practical case studies and tutorials that highlight its application across diverse sectors.
- **Clear Structure and Organization:**
  A thoughtfully organized narrative that starts with the basics of language intelligence and progressively builds towards more advanced topics. This logical progression ensures that readers at all levels—from beginners to seasoned professionals—can engage with the content effectively. Each chapter concludes with summaries and key takeaways, reinforcing the learning and guiding readers through complex subjects with clarity.
- **Engaging and Accessible Content:**
  While rooted in technical detail, the writing style is designed to be engaging and accessible. Through storytelling, real-world examples, and practical illustrations, the book transforms abstract concepts into relatable insights. It is crafted to spark curiosity and inspire innovation, inviting readers to not only understand LangGraph LLM but also to envision its future possibilities.
- **Practical Applications and Problem-Solving:**
  Beyond theory, the book emphasizes hands-on learning. It offers tutorials, walkthroughs, and project ideas that allow readers to directly apply their knowledge. Through a series of case studies and expert interviews, we showcase how LangGraph LLM can be leveraged to solve contemporary challenges in fields ranging from healthcare to finance and beyond.
- **Innovative and Forward-Thinking Perspective:**
  Recognizing that technology is ever-evolving, this book also casts a forward-looking gaze. It discusses upcoming trends, ethical

considerations, and interdisciplinary applications that position LangGraph LLM within the broader narrative of artificial intelligence and digital transformation. The vision is to equip readers not only with current know-how but also with the foresight to drive future innovations.

In essence, this book is more than just a technical manual—it is a journey through the landscape of modern language intelligence. Whether you are seeking to enhance your technical skills, adopt new technologies in your enterprise, or simply stay informed about the latest developments in AI, our mission is to serve as your comprehensive resource and trusted guide in the evolving world of LangGraph LLM.

Acknowledgements

This book is the result of collective effort, deep collaboration, and the contributions of many individuals who generously shared their time, expertise, and insights.I extend my heartfelt thanks to everyone who played a role in shaping this work:

- **Industry Experts and Thought Leaders:**
  We are immensely grateful to the leading figures in artificial intelligence and natural language processing who provided invaluable guidance and expert reviews. Their feedback has ensured the technical rigor and innovative perspective that underpin this book.
- **Academic and Research Collaborators:**
  Special thanks to our academic partners and research colleagues, whose cutting-edge work and dedication to advancing language intelligence have inspired many of the ideas presented herein.
- **Case Study Contributors:**
  Our sincere appreciation goes to the professionals from various industries—healthcare, finance, technology, and beyond—who shared their real-world experiences. Their practical insights and case studies have enriched the narrative, demonstrating the broad applicability of LangGraph LLM.
- **Editorial and Peer Review Teams:**
  We are indebted to our editors and peer reviewers for their meticulous efforts in refining the content. Their commitment to excellence has helped shape this book into a resource that is both accessible and authoritative.
- **Supportive Community and Early Adopters:**
  A heartfelt thank you to the vibrant community of developers,

enthusiasts, and early adopters of LangGraph LLM. Your feedback, discussions, and shared projects have been instrumental in identifying key challenges and opportunities, which in turn have driven the practical focus of this work.

- **Family and Friends:**
  Finally, we acknowledge the unwavering support of our family and friends. Their encouragement and understanding have been the backbone of this journey, providing us with the inspiration to explore new frontiers in language intelligence.

Each contribution has played a vital role in making this book a comprehensive guide for both novices and experts alike. We are honored to share this work with you and hope it serves as a valuable resource in your journey through the evolving landscape of language intelligence.

How to Use This Book

This book is designed to serve as both a comprehensive reference and a practical guide for exploring LangGraph LLM. Here's how you can make the most of its content:

- **Sequential or Selective Reading:**
  You can start at the beginning to build a solid foundation in language intelligence, or jump directly to chapters that match your interests— whether that's technical deep dives, case studies, or hands-on tutorials.
- **Chapter Summaries and Key Takeaways:**
  At the end of each chapter, you'll find summaries and bullet-point key takeaways. These sections are perfect for quick reviews and to reinforce your learning.
- **Hands-On Tutorials and Code Walkthroughs:**
  For those who learn by doing, practical examples and coding tutorials are included throughout the book. Follow along with the step-by-step instructions to set up your environment and build your own LangGraph LLM projects.
- **Expert Interviews and Case Studies:**
  Real-world examples and expert insights are interwoven with the technical content. Use these sections to understand how LangGraph LLM is being implemented across various industries and what challenges have been overcome in practice.
- **Visual Aids and Diagrams:**
  The book includes diagrams, flowcharts, and code snippets to

visually explain complex ideas. These aids are designed to complement the written content and make abstract concepts more tangible.

- **Reference Materials and Appendices:**
  Appendices offer additional resources, glossaries, and FAQs. Bookmark these sections for quick reference as you dive deeper into the material.
- **Interactive and Self-Paced Learning:**
  Treat this book as a dynamic learning tool. Experiment with the code examples, challenge yourself with the exercises provided, and engage with the broader LangGraph community to further your understanding.
- **Continuous Updates:**
  Recognizing the fast-evolving nature of language intelligence, we encourage you to check for any online updates or supplementary materials referenced throughout the text. These resources are aimed at keeping your knowledge current with the latest trends and breakthroughs.

By navigating through this book in a way that suits your learning style and needs, you can effectively build a robust understanding of LangGraph LLM—from its theoretical foundations to its practical applications. Enjoy your journey into the future of language intelligence!

Chapter 1: Introduction to Language Intelligence

1.1. The Evolution of Language Models

The journey of language models began with the exploration of statistical methods and rule-based systems in the early days of natural language processing. Initially, researchers focused on harnessing patterns from text through frequency-based models, such as n-gram models, which relied on the probability of sequences of words occurring together. These early models, though limited in their understanding of context and nuance, laid the groundwork by demonstrating that language, with all its complexity, could be quantified and analyzed through data.

As computational power increased and algorithms became more sophisticated, the field witnessed a paradigm shift with the introduction of machine learning techniques. The advent of neural networks opened new avenues for language modeling. Early neural language models, such as feed-forward networks and recurrent neural networks (RNNs), began to capture dependencies over longer spans of text. However, these approaches still faced challenges, particularly in handling long-term dependencies and contextual understanding, which are essential for truly grasping the intricacies of human language.

The introduction of transformer architectures marked a revolutionary turning point. With the transformer model's self-attention mechanism, language models could now process entire sentences or even paragraphs simultaneously, allowing for a deeper and more coherent understanding of context. This innovation paved the way for models like BERT and GPT, which demonstrated unprecedented abilities in language understanding, text generation, and even tasks like translation and summarization. These models not only captured the statistical properties of language but also began to approximate a form of semantic comprehension that was previously out of reach.

In parallel with these developments, research into graph-based representations of language further expanded the horizons of what language models could achieve. By structuring information in a way that reflects the interconnected nature of language—where words, phrases, and concepts are linked in a complex web—graph-based methods added a new layer of understanding. This approach allowed models to incorporate relational information and contextual dependencies that traditional sequential models might overlook. Today, the integration of graph-based methods with transformer architectures is at the cutting edge of language intelligence, providing more robust, adaptable, and contextually aware models.

The evolution of language models is a testament to the rapid advancements in both theoretical research and practical applications. Each generation of models has built upon the successes and lessons of its predecessors, continuously pushing the boundaries of what is possible in language understanding and generation. As we delve deeper into the specifics of LangGraph LLM in later chapters, it is important to recognize this historical progression—not only as a narrative of technological achievement but as a foundation that informs the sophisticated design and innovative potential of modern language models.

1.1.1. Historical Perspective of NLP

The history of Natural Language Processing (NLP) is a fascinating journey that mirrors the evolution of computing and artificial intelligence. Early work in NLP began with rule-based systems that attempted to mimic human language processing through explicitly defined grammatical rules and heuristics. During this period, researchers focused on developing methods that could parse sentences, understand basic syntax, and even perform rudimentary translations based on handcrafted rules. These early systems, although limited by their rigidity, laid the conceptual foundation for the field by illustrating that language could be decomposed into formal structures.

As computational capabilities advanced, the field experienced a significant paradigm shift with the advent of statistical methods. In the mid-20th century, researchers began to leverage probability theory and large corpora of text to statistically model language. Techniques such as n-gram models emerged, which analyzed the frequency of word sequences to predict subsequent words. This approach allowed for a more flexible understanding of language compared to rigid rule-based systems, even though it still struggled with capturing long-range dependencies and nuanced meaning.

Key developments during this era include:

- The creation of probabilistic models that could handle ambiguities in language.

- The development of early machine translation systems, which, despite their crude performance, demonstrated the potential for automated language processing.
- The introduction of algorithms for part-of-speech tagging and syntactic parsing, which set the stage for more complex models.

The next major milestone in the evolution of NLP was the integration of machine learning techniques. With the emergence of statistical learning methods, researchers began to design algorithms that could learn from data. This period saw the rise of models based on Hidden Markov Models (HMMs) for tasks such as speech recognition and sequence labeling, along with the early use of neural networks for language tasks. Although these models were constrained by the computational limitations of their time, they marked an important shift towards data-driven approaches that could adapt and improve with more information.

The breakthrough came with the development of deep learning architectures, especially with the advent of recurrent neural networks (RNNs) and, later, the revolutionary transformer models. These new methods allowed for the capture of complex, long-range dependencies in text and transformed the landscape of NLP by enabling unprecedented levels of language understanding and generation. The introduction of attention mechanisms and transformers further refined the ability to model context, leading to the creation of state-of-the-art systems like BERT, GPT, and ultimately the innovative LangGraph LLM.

The historical evolution of NLP is a testament to the field's relentless progress. Each phase—rule-based systems, statistical methods, machine learning, and deep learning—contributed essential insights and techniques that built upon one another. Today, modern language models are capable of handling intricate tasks that were once thought to be the exclusive domain of human cognition, thanks to the cumulative advancements made over decades. This rich history not only provides context for current developments but also inspires future innovations as researchers continue to push the boundaries of what language intelligence can achieve.

1.1.2. Milestones in AI Language Processing

The evolution of AI language processing is punctuated by several groundbreaking milestones that have collectively transformed the field. These milestones represent key moments when significant advancements pushed the boundaries of what machines could understand and generate in natural language.

One of the earliest notable milestones was the development of conversational agents in the 1960s, exemplified by programs like ELIZA. ELIZA simulated a human-like conversation by employing pattern matching and scripted responses, capturing public imagination despite its simplistic design. This early work laid the groundwork for envisioning computers as interactive partners in dialogue.

During the subsequent decades, the shift from rule-based approaches to statistical methods marked another pivotal transformation. In the 1980s and 1990s, as researchers began harnessing the power of probability theory, models such as n-gram and Hidden Markov Models emerged. These statistical approaches allowed systems to predict word sequences based on observed frequencies, providing a more flexible and data-driven framework for language processing.

The turn of the millennium witnessed the integration of machine learning techniques into NLP. Algorithms that could learn from vast amounts of data began to replace handcrafted rules, leading to improved performance in tasks such as speech recognition, translation, and sentiment analysis. The incorporation of probabilistic models enabled systems to better handle the inherent ambiguities of human language.

The advent of deep learning in the 2000s heralded a new era for AI language processing. The development of recurrent neural networks (RNNs) and long short-term memory (LSTM) networks significantly improved the handling of sequential data, allowing models to capture long-range dependencies in text. This era also saw the rise of word embeddings like word2vec and GloVe, which transformed the representation of words into continuous vector spaces and captured semantic relationships in a powerful, computationally efficient manner.

A watershed moment occurred in 2017 with the introduction of the transformer architecture in the paper "Attention is All You Need." This innovation, with its self-attention mechanism, enabled models to process entire sentences simultaneously and capture complex contextual relationships without the limitations of sequential processing. The transformer model laid the foundation for subsequent breakthroughs, such as BERT and GPT, which have redefined the limits of language understanding and generation.

Recent years have continued this trend of rapid innovation. Large-scale language models now leverage billions of parameters, exhibit remarkable fluency, and tackle an ever-expanding range of tasks from text summarization to creative writing. These advancements are not only a product of improved algorithms and architectures but also the availability of vast datasets and enhanced computational power.

To summarize some of the key milestones:

- **1960s:** Introduction of conversational agents like ELIZA, marking the beginning of interactive language processing.
- **1980s-1990s:** Transition to statistical models, including n-gram and Hidden Markov Models, which harnessed data-driven insights.
- **2000s:** Emergence of machine learning and deep learning techniques, with RNNs and LSTMs enhancing sequential data processing.
- **2013-2014:** Development of word embeddings (e.g., word2vec, GloVe) that captured semantic relationships in continuous vector spaces.
- **2017:** Launch of the transformer architecture, revolutionizing the field with its self-attention mechanism.
- **2018-Present:** Proliferation of large-scale models like BERT, GPT-2, GPT-3, and beyond, leading to significant breakthroughs in natural language understanding and generation.

Each of these milestones reflects a step forward in our collective ability to teach machines the intricacies of human language, paving the way for the advanced systems we see today. The cumulative impact of these innovations has transformed not only how we interact with technology but also the very nature of communication in the digital age.

1.2. The Emergence of LangGraph LLM

LangGraph LLM emerged as a breakthrough in the landscape of language models, marking a distinct evolution in the integration of graph-based methodologies with modern deep learning architectures. This innovative approach was born out of the recognition that traditional transformer models, while incredibly powerful, sometimes struggle to capture the intricate relational structures inherent in human language. By embedding graph theory into the heart of its design, LangGraph LLM offers a more nuanced understanding of context and interconnectivity among words, phrases, and concepts.

The development of LangGraph LLM was driven by a convergence of academic research and practical needs. On one hand, pioneering studies in graph neural networks had demonstrated that representing data as interconnected nodes could vastly improve the performance of systems in domains ranging from social network analysis to molecular biology. On the other hand, the demand for more sophisticated language models was growing rapidly, as industries sought solutions that could not only process text but also infer and leverage the underlying relationships between disparate pieces of information. LangGraph LLM was conceived as a response to these dual imperatives—combining the depth of graph-based reasoning with the flexibility and scalability of transformer architectures.

In practical terms, LangGraph LLM distinguishes itself through several key innovations. First, it incorporates a dedicated module that constructs and refines a graph representation of input data, enabling the model to discern complex relationships that might be overlooked by sequential processing alone. This graph module operates alongside traditional transformer layers, feeding into a unified system that processes both linear and relational features of language. Additionally, the model employs advanced attention mechanisms that dynamically prioritize information based on the strength and relevance of these relationships, resulting in outputs that are more context-aware and semantically rich.

The emergence of LangGraph LLM also reflects broader trends in artificial intelligence. As researchers continue to push the boundaries of what language models can achieve, there is a growing emphasis on interdisciplinary approaches that borrow insights from fields such as network theory, cognitive science, and even sociology. By integrating these diverse perspectives, LangGraph LLM not only advances the technical capabilities of language models but also paves the way for applications that require a deeper understanding of context and nuance—whether in conversational agents, knowledge management systems, or data analytics platforms.

Ultimately, the launch of LangGraph LLM represents a significant milestone in the evolution of language intelligence. It embodies a thoughtful synthesis of traditional methodologies and cutting-edge innovations, setting the stage for the next generation of models that will continue to redefine our interaction with technology. As we explore this book further, we will delve into the technical underpinnings, practical applications, and forward-thinking innovations that define LangGraph LLM, highlighting how this model is poised to shape the future of language processing and artificial intelligence.

1.2.1. Defining LangGraph LLM

LangGraph LLM is a state-of-the-art language model that uniquely integrates the capabilities of graph-based reasoning with the advanced architectures of modern transformers. At its core, this model is designed to not only process sequential text data but also to understand and leverage the inherent relationships and structures within language. Unlike traditional models that primarily focus on the order of words, LangGraph LLM constructs a dynamic graph representation where words, phrases, and concepts are treated as interconnected nodes. This structure allows the model to capture both local and global context, making it exceptionally adept at discerning nuanced relationships and dependencies.

The defining characteristics of LangGraph LLM can be understood through its dual approach: it combines the robust pattern recognition capabilities of transformer-based models with the rich relational insights offered by graph theory. This integration results in several key innovations. First, the model employs a dedicated graph module that maps out the intricate web of connections between language elements, effectively highlighting semantic links that might be missed by linear models. Second, it utilizes advanced attention mechanisms that not only weigh the importance of individual words but also prioritize the relational significance between them. These features work in tandem to produce outputs that are more contextually aware and semantically enriched.

By defining language through a graph-based lens, LangGraph LLM opens up new possibilities for tackling complex tasks in natural language processing. It is particularly effective in applications where understanding the interplay between multiple pieces of information is crucial, such as in question answering, summarization, and conversational agents. Furthermore, its design reflects a broader trend in artificial intelligence toward embracing interdisciplinary approaches—drawing from fields like network theory, cognitive science, and linguistics—to create models that mirror the multifaceted nature of human language. In essence, LangGraph LLM is not just an incremental improvement over existing models; it represents a paradigm shift towards a more holistic and interconnected understanding of language intelligence.

1.2.2. Innovations and Differentiators

LangGraph LLM distinguishes itself from traditional language models through a series of groundbreaking innovations that redefine how machines understand and generate language. One of the primary innovations lies in its seamless integration of graph-based reasoning with transformer architectures. While conventional models excel at handling sequential information, LangGraph LLM goes a step further by mapping out the intricate relationships between words, phrases, and concepts as interconnected nodes. This graph-based representation empowers the model to capture both local nuances and broader, context-rich associations that are essential for complex language understanding.

Another key differentiator is the model's advanced attention mechanism. In traditional transformers, attention mechanisms primarily focus on the significance of words in relation to each other based on their positions in a sequence. LangGraph LLM enhances this by dynamically adjusting attention weights based on the strength and relevance of the relationships highlighted in its graph structure. This results in a more refined understanding of context, as the model can prioritize information that is semantically significant over information that is merely sequentially proximal.

LangGraph LLM also sets itself apart through its adaptability and versatility in real-world applications. Its ability to integrate relational data makes it particularly effective in environments where context is paramount—such as in nuanced conversational agents, comprehensive summarization tools, and sophisticated question-answering systems. The model's design ensures that it can handle both the predictable patterns of language and the unpredictable, emergent properties of human communication, thereby bridging the gap between static data processing and dynamic understanding.

Furthermore, the innovative architecture of LangGraph LLM has been influenced by interdisciplinary insights, drawing from advancements in network theory, cognitive science, and computational linguistics. This interdisciplinary approach not only enriches the model's theoretical foundation but also translates into tangible benefits, such as improved performance in detecting subtleties like sarcasm, idioms, and contextual shifts. The model's architecture is continuously refined to adapt to the rapidly evolving landscape of language intelligence, ensuring that it remains at the forefront of innovation.

In summary, the innovations and differentiators of LangGraph LLM are encapsulated in its dual approach to language processing, its dynamic attention mechanisms, and its interdisciplinary design philosophy. These features collectively provide a more comprehensive, nuanced, and adaptable framework for understanding language—a framework that is poised to address the challenges and harness the opportunities of the next generation of natural language processing applications.

1.3. Objectives and Scope of the Book

This book is designed to serve as a comprehensive resource that bridges the gap between theoretical foundations and practical implementations in the realm of language intelligence, with a specific focus on LangGraph LLM. Its objectives are twofold: to provide an in-depth exploration of the model's technical intricacies and to demonstrate its practical applications in real-world scenarios. In doing so, the book aims to empower a diverse audience—from developers and researchers to business leaders and technology enthusiasts—with the knowledge and skills needed to navigate and leverage the advanced capabilities of LangGraph LLM.

At the core of this work is a commitment to meticulous research and a thorough understanding of contemporary developments in natural language processing. The book is structured to guide readers progressively: it begins with foundational concepts and historical perspectives, moves through the sophisticated architectures and innovations embodied by LangGraph LLM, and ultimately culminates in hands-on projects, case studies, and future outlooks. This progression ensures that readers not only grasp the underlying theory but also appreciate how these ideas are translated into practical, high-impact applications.

The scope of the book is intentionally broad yet focused, covering multiple dimensions of LangGraph LLM:

- **Technical Foundations:**
  Readers will gain a detailed understanding of the underlying algorithms, architectures, and methodologies that form the backbone of LangGraph LLM. This includes discussions on graph theory, transformer architectures, and the latest trends in deep learning.
- **Practical Applications:**
  The text delves into real-world use cases and hands-on tutorials, offering step-by-step guides on how to implement and fine-tune the model. By examining case studies and expert interviews, the book highlights the tangible benefits and challenges of deploying LangGraph LLM in various industries.
- **Innovative Insights:**
  The book provides an interdisciplinary perspective that links

advancements in network theory, cognitive science, and computational linguistics. This broader context is crucial for understanding how LangGraph LLM fits within the evolving landscape of artificial intelligence and language processing.

- **Future Trends and Ethical Considerations:**
  In addition to current applications, the text explores emerging trends, potential future developments, and the ethical implications of using advanced language models. This forward-thinking approach is designed to equip readers with the foresight needed to adapt to future challenges and innovations.

Ultimately, the objectives and scope of this book are to demystify the complexities of LangGraph LLM, offer a balanced blend of theory and practice, and inspire readers to both apply and further innovate within the field of language intelligence. By providing a detailed and engaging roadmap, this work aims to become a definitive guide for anyone looking to understand or utilize the power of LangGraph LLM in today's rapidly evolving technological landscape.

1.4. Overview of Chapters and How to Navigate

This book is organized into a series of chapters that progressively build your understanding of LangGraph LLM—from its historical and theoretical roots to its modern applications and future prospects. The structure is designed to be both comprehensive and flexible, allowing you to either follow the chapters sequentially or to jump directly to topics that align with your specific interests or professional needs.

The early chapters lay a solid foundation by exploring the evolution of language models and the core principles of natural language processing. You will find an in-depth historical perspective that charts the journey from rule-based systems to advanced deep learning architectures. As you progress, the book introduces the emergence of LangGraph LLM, explaining its design philosophy, key innovations, and the specific ways it diverges from traditional models. This sets the stage for later chapters that delve into technical details, training methodologies, and practical implementations.

In the middle sections, the focus shifts to real-world applications. You will encounter detailed discussions on how LangGraph LLM is integrated into various industries, accompanied by practical tutorials, code walkthroughs, and case studies. These chapters are rich with expert insights and hands-on examples, making complex concepts accessible and directly applicable. If you are looking to build or refine your own projects, these sections provide a roadmap for setting up environments, troubleshooting common issues, and optimizing performance.

The latter chapters broaden the discussion to include innovative uses, ethical considerations, and future trends in language intelligence. These final parts are designed to inspire forward-thinking perspectives and encourage you to envision new possibilities for the technology. They not only review current challenges and solutions but also explore interdisciplinary applications and the evolving regulatory landscape.

Throughout the book, each chapter concludes with a summary that highlights the key takeaways, ensuring that you can quickly review the most important points before moving on. The layout is complemented by clear headings and subheadings, making navigation straightforward whether you are reading cover-to-cover or using the book as a reference tool for specific topics. This design ensures that the content is as practical as it is informative, equipping you with both the theoretical knowledge and the practical skills needed to master LangGraph LLM.

Chapter 2: Foundations of Modern Language Models

2.1. Fundamentals of Machine Learning in NLP

The field of Natural Language Processing (NLP) has evolved dramatically with the advent of machine learning, which has become the cornerstone of modern language models. Machine learning has allowed systems to learn patterns and extract meaning from large volumes of text data, transforming how we approach tasks such as translation, sentiment analysis, and text summarization.

At its core, machine learning in NLP involves training algorithms on vast corpora of language data so that they can identify underlying structures and generate predictions. Early NLP systems relied on hand-crafted rules and statistical models, which, while groundbreaking at the time, were limited by their inability to generalize well to new or unexpected inputs. Machine learning methods address these limitations by enabling models to learn from examples rather than relying solely on predefined rules.

One of the key approaches in machine learning for NLP is supervised learning, where models are trained on labeled datasets. In supervised learning, the model learns to map inputs (such as sentences or documents) to specific outputs (like sentiment labels or translation equivalents). This approach has been instrumental in developing systems that can accurately classify text, recognize named entities, or even translate languages with a high degree of accuracy.

Unsupervised learning is another fundamental approach, where models learn patterns from unstructured, unlabeled data. Techniques such as clustering and dimensionality reduction help in discovering hidden structures within the data. These methods have paved the way for innovations like word embeddings, where words are represented as vectors in a continuous space. Embeddings such as word2vec and GloVe capture semantic relationships between words, enabling models to understand context and similarity in a way that traditional methods could not.

Another milestone in the application of machine learning to NLP is the development of deep learning models. Deep learning, particularly through neural networks, has significantly advanced the field by allowing for the modeling of complex, non-linear relationships within data. Early neural network models, like feed-forward networks and recurrent neural networks (RNNs), demonstrated that it was possible to learn language patterns directly from raw text. However, these models often struggled with long-term dependencies in text.

The introduction of advanced architectures such as Long Short-Term Memory (LSTM) networks and, more recently, transformer models, has revolutionized how machines process language. LSTM networks, with their ability to retain information over long sequences, improved upon the limitations of standard RNNs. Meanwhile, transformers leverage self-attention mechanisms to capture relationships between all elements in a sequence simultaneously, making them particularly effective for tasks requiring a deep contextual understanding.

To summarize, the fundamentals of machine learning in NLP encompass several critical concepts and approaches:

- **Supervised Learning:** Training models on labeled datasets to perform specific tasks, such as text classification or translation.
- **Unsupervised Learning:** Discovering inherent patterns in unstructured data, crucial for techniques like word embeddings.
- **Deep Learning:** Using neural network architectures, including RNNs, LSTMs, and transformers, to capture complex language patterns and long-range dependencies.

These techniques have not only enhanced the capabilities of language models but also laid the foundation for more advanced systems like LangGraph LLM. By leveraging machine learning, NLP has transitioned from a rule-based discipline to one where models can adapt, learn, and evolve with exposure to new data. This evolution is central to understanding the technological advancements discussed in the subsequent chapters, where we explore how these fundamental methods are integrated and extended in modern language models.

2.1.1. Key Concepts and Terminology

Understanding the key concepts and terminology in machine learning for NLP is essential to grasp the evolution and functionality of modern language models. At the heart of these models lies a vocabulary of technical terms and foundational principles that enable machines to process and generate language effectively.

One of the fundamental concepts is **tokenization**, which involves breaking down text into smaller units, such as words or subwords, that can be processed by a machine. This step is crucial because it converts raw text into a format that models can work with, enabling them to analyze and understand linguistic structure.

Another core idea is **embeddings**, which are mathematical representations of words and phrases in continuous vector space. Embeddings like word2vec, GloVe, and contextualized representations produced by transformers allow models to capture semantic relationships and similarities between words. By converting text into vectors, embeddings enable the model to perform complex operations like similarity comparisons and analogical reasoning.

Supervised learning is a pivotal approach in machine learning where models are trained on labeled datasets. Here, each input—such as a sentence—is paired with an expected output, like a category or translation. This method allows models to learn a mapping from inputs to outputs through techniques like classification or regression. In contrast, **unsupervised learning** involves training on unlabeled data to uncover hidden patterns and structures. Techniques such as clustering and dimensionality reduction fall under this category and are fundamental for creating meaningful word embeddings.

Deep learning has revolutionized the field of NLP through the use of neural networks—computational models inspired by the human brain. These networks, particularly **Recurrent Neural Networks (RNNs)** and their successors like **Long Short-Term Memory (LSTM) networks**, have historically been used to model sequences of data. However, the advent of the **transformer architecture** has dramatically shifted the landscape. Transformers utilize **self-attention mechanisms**, which allow the model to weigh the importance of different parts of the input text simultaneously, capturing context and dependencies more efficiently than sequential models.

Additional key terminologies include:

- **Backpropagation:** The algorithm used to train neural networks by updating model parameters based on the error rate obtained in the previous epoch.

- **Gradient Descent:** An optimization technique that minimizes the loss function by iteratively adjusting the model's parameters.
- **Loss Function:** A measure of how far the model's predictions are from the actual target values, guiding the training process.
- **Hyperparameters:** Configurable parameters such as learning rate, number of layers, and batch size, which are not learned from the data but are critical to model performance.

These concepts form the backbone of modern NLP techniques and are instrumental in the development of sophisticated models like LangGraph LLM. By combining tokenization, embeddings, and advanced deep learning techniques, these models can capture the intricate patterns of human language, enabling applications ranging from machine translation to conversational agents. This foundational knowledge sets the stage for exploring how these elements are integrated and enhanced in subsequent chapters, where we delve into the architecture and innovations that define cutting-edge language models.

2.1.2. Statistical vs. Neural Approaches

The evolution of natural language processing can be largely divided into two significant paradigms: statistical methods and neural approaches. Each of these paradigms has contributed unique strengths and limitations to the way we model and understand language.

Statistical methods emerged as the first robust approach to NLP. These methods rely on probability theory to model language, primarily using techniques that count the frequency of words and phrases in large corpora. Models such as n-grams and Hidden Markov Models (HMMs) became popular because they could predict the likelihood of a word appearing based on the preceding words. This probabilistic framework allowed for the effective handling of language variations and ambiguities, albeit in a somewhat limited capacity. Statistical approaches are generally characterized by their reliance on hand-crafted features and predefined rules, which means that while they can perform well on specific tasks, they often struggle to capture the deeper contextual relationships inherent in human language.

In contrast, neural approaches to NLP, particularly those involving deep learning, have revolutionized the field by learning representations directly from raw text data. Neural models, such as recurrent neural networks (RNNs) and, more recently, transformer architectures, do not depend on manually defined features. Instead, they automatically learn complex patterns and contextual relationships from data through training on massive datasets. The use of embeddings—continuous vector representations of words—enables these models to understand semantic similarities and differences more naturally. Neural approaches have the distinct advantage of handling long-range dependencies and subtle linguistic nuances, which are often challenging for statistical models. However, this comes at the cost of requiring large amounts of data and substantial computational resources to train effectively.

To highlight the key differences:

- **Feature Engineering:**
  Statistical methods typically require extensive manual feature engineering to capture language nuances, whereas neural approaches learn these features automatically through data-driven training.
- **Contextual Understanding:**
  While statistical models provide a good approximation based on frequency and probability, neural models—especially those employing transformers—excel at understanding the broader context and intricate relationships within text.
- **Scalability and Adaptability:**
  Neural models are highly scalable and adaptable to different tasks, benefiting from transfer learning and fine-tuning techniques. Statistical models, though simpler, often require re-engineering when applied to different contexts or domains.

The shift from statistical to neural methods represents a major leap forward in NLP, enabling the development of more sophisticated and accurate language models. This evolution underpins modern systems such as LangGraph LLM, which combine the strengths of both approaches by incorporating deep neural architectures alongside insights from traditional methods to achieve a more nuanced understanding of language.

2.2. Deep Learning and Transformer Architectures

Deep learning has fundamentally transformed the landscape of natural language processing by introducing models that can learn intricate patterns from vast amounts of unstructured data. This paradigm shift is largely attributable to neural network architectures that are capable of capturing non-linear relationships and long-term dependencies in text. Early deep learning models, such as feed-forward networks and recurrent neural networks (RNNs), laid the groundwork by demonstrating that a model could learn meaningful representations directly from raw language data. However, these models often encountered challenges in managing the complexity and length of natural language, prompting researchers to seek more robust solutions.

The breakthrough came with the advent of the transformer architecture, which redefined how models process sequences of text. Unlike RNNs that operate sequentially, transformers process all input tokens simultaneously, allowing for more efficient and parallelized computation. This is made possible through the innovative self-attention mechanism, which enables the model to weigh the importance of each word in relation to every other word in a sentence, regardless of their positional distance. In doing so, transformers can capture contextual relationships with far greater nuance and precision than previous models.

Key aspects of transformer architectures include:

- **Self-Attention Mechanism:**
  This mechanism allows the model to dynamically adjust the focus on different parts of the input sequence, ensuring that each word's representation is enriched with information from all other words. This results in a comprehensive contextual understanding that is crucial for tasks like translation, summarization, and question answering.
- **Parallel Processing:**
  By eliminating the sequential constraints of RNNs, transformers can process entire sentences or even larger blocks of text in parallel. This not only speeds up training and inference times but also enables the model to scale effectively with larger datasets.
- **Layered Structure and Multi-Head Attention:**
  Transformers are composed of multiple layers, each incorporating several attention heads. This multi-head attention allows the model to learn different types of relationships in the data concurrently, providing a richer and more diverse representation of language.
- **Positional Encoding:**
  Since transformers do not inherently process sequential data in order, positional encodings are added to the input embeddings to retain information about the order of words. This ensures that the model understands the sequence in which words appear, maintaining the integrity of the language structure.

The adoption of transformer architectures has led to a dramatic improvement in a wide range of NLP applications. Models such as BERT, GPT, and their successors have set new benchmarks in language understanding, generation, and even reasoning tasks. Their success is not only a result of the architectural innovations but also due to their ability to be pre-trained on extensive datasets and fine-tuned for specific applications. This transfer learning approach has significantly lowered the barrier for entry into high-performance NLP, making advanced language models accessible for diverse applications.

In summary, the evolution from traditional deep learning models to transformer architectures represents a monumental leap in NLP. By harnessing the power of self-attention, parallel processing, and sophisticated layered structures, transformers have redefined what is possible in language modeling. This advancement underpins modern systems like LangGraph LLM, which build upon these foundations to offer even deeper insights into language through the integration of graph-based reasoning and contextual analysis.

2.2.1. Overview of Neural Networks

Neural networks form the foundational building blocks of deep learning, inspired by the structure and function of the human brain. At their core, these computational models consist of layers of interconnected nodes, often referred to as neurons, that work together to transform input data into meaningful outputs. Each neuron receives input signals, processes them using mathematical functions, and passes the results on to the next layer. This architecture allows the network to learn complex patterns and relationships from data.

In a typical neural network, the data first enters through an input layer, which is then passed through one or more hidden layers before reaching the output layer. The hidden layers are where most of the processing happens, as they apply various weights and activation functions to capture non-linear relationships in the data. The process of adjusting these weights during training, guided by an algorithm called backpropagation, enables the network to gradually improve its predictions or classifications.

There are several key types of neural networks that have been developed to handle different kinds of data and tasks. For example, feed-forward neural networks, one of the simplest forms, process data in a single pass from input to output without cycles or feedback loops. In contrast, recurrent neural networks (RNNs) introduce loops that allow information to persist, making them particularly well-suited for sequential data such as text. More recent innovations, such as transformer architectures, have built upon these concepts by incorporating mechanisms like self-attention, which enable models to consider the entire context of a sequence simultaneously.

In summary, neural networks are versatile computational frameworks capable of learning intricate patterns from data. Their layered structure, combined with powerful training methods, has paved the way for significant breakthroughs in fields such as natural language processing, computer vision, and beyond. As we progress through the book, this foundational understanding of neural networks will be critical for appreciating how advanced models like LangGraph LLM harness these principles to push the boundaries of language intelligence.

2.2.2. Transformer Models: Theory and Practice

Transformer models represent a transformative approach to handling natural language, marking a significant departure from earlier architectures such as recurrent neural networks. At the theoretical level, transformers are built on the concept of self-attention, a mechanism that allows the model to weigh the importance of each word in a sequence relative to every other word. This contrasts with traditional sequential models, which process text one word at a time and often struggle with long-range dependencies. The self-attention mechanism provides a holistic view of the entire input, enabling the model to capture nuanced relationships and contextual dependencies that are vital for understanding language.

Central to the transformer architecture is the idea of multi-head attention. Instead of computing a single attention score for each pair of words, the transformer divides the attention process into several "heads." Each head learns to focus on different aspects or relationships within the text. This multi-faceted attention approach enriches the representation of the input by capturing a diverse set of features simultaneously. Additionally, transformers incorporate positional encoding—a technique to inject information about the order of words into the model. Since self-attention treats the input as a set of tokens without any inherent order, positional encodings ensure that the model is aware of sequence and structure, which is critical for tasks where word order influences meaning.

From a practical standpoint, transformer models have become the backbone of many state-of-the-art systems in natural language processing. Their design enables extensive parallelization during training, significantly reducing computational time compared to sequential models like RNNs. This efficiency, combined with their ability to scale to enormous datasets, has allowed transformers to excel in pre-training and fine-tuning paradigms. Models such as BERT and GPT, which are based on transformer architectures, have set new benchmarks in tasks like text generation, translation, summarization, and sentiment analysis.

In practice, transformers are typically pre-trained on vast corpora in an unsupervised manner to learn general language representations. This pre-training phase equips the model with a robust understanding of language patterns and structures. Once pre-trained, the model can be fine-tuned on specific tasks with relatively little additional data, making it versatile for a wide range of applications. The success of this approach has led to a surge in applications across diverse domains, from conversational agents and recommendation systems to complex question-answering platforms and beyond.

To summarize key points:

- **Self-Attention:**
  Enables the model to consider relationships between all tokens simultaneously, ensuring a rich, context-aware representation of language.
- **Multi-Head Attention:**
  Divides the attention mechanism into multiple heads, each capturing different aspects of the text, thereby providing a comprehensive and nuanced understanding.
- **Positional Encoding:**
  Introduces order and structure into the token representations, allowing the model to maintain the sequential context necessary for coherent language processing.
- **Parallel Processing and Scalability:**
  Facilitates efficient training on large datasets and supports the pre-training and fine-tuning approach, making transformers highly adaptable to various NLP tasks.

The theoretical innovations of transformer models, when combined with practical implementation strategies, have led to a new era in language processing. Their design not only addresses the limitations of previous models but also opens up unprecedented opportunities for innovation, as exemplified by advanced systems like LangGraph LLM. This synthesis of theory and practice is fundamental to the progress in language intelligence, setting the stage for even more sophisticated models in the future.

2.3. Graph-Based Approaches in AI

Graph-based approaches in artificial intelligence leverage the inherent structure of data by representing information as networks of interconnected nodes and edges. This method mirrors the way humans often conceptualize relationships—through a network of associations rather than linear sequences. At its essence, a graph is a mathematical representation where nodes (or vertices) represent entities and edges denote the relationships between them. This framework allows AI systems to capture complex interdependencies, making it particularly suited for tasks where context and relational data play a critical role.

The application of graph-based techniques in AI has evolved alongside other advances in machine learning and deep learning. Early efforts in this domain were primarily focused on simpler graph traversal algorithms and heuristics that could identify patterns within structured data. Over time, these methods have been refined and integrated with neural network architectures to create more powerful models known as Graph Neural Networks (GNNs). GNNs are designed to operate directly on graph structures, learning representations that encapsulate both the features of individual nodes and the topology of the entire graph. This dual focus enables the extraction of rich, relational information that traditional sequence-based models might overlook.

One of the significant advantages of graph-based approaches is their flexibility in modeling a wide variety of data types. For instance, in social network analysis, graphs can represent users as nodes and their interactions as edges, allowing algorithms to identify community structures, influence patterns, and anomalous behaviors. In the realm of natural language processing, graphs are used to capture the syntactic and semantic relationships between words, phrases, and sentences. By integrating these representations, models can more effectively understand the context and infer meaning beyond what linear models typically capture.

Key benefits of employing graph-based methods in AI include:

- **Enhanced Contextual Understanding:**
  Graphs provide a natural framework to model complex relationships and dependencies, enabling AI systems to consider broader context when making decisions.
- **Robust Handling of Non-Sequential Data:**
  Unlike traditional models that rely on sequential inputs, graph-based

approaches are adept at managing data that does not inherently follow a linear order, such as social networks, molecular structures, or knowledge graphs.

- **Improved Interpretability:**
  The structure of a graph can offer more intuitive insights into how data points are related, which can be valuable for understanding model behavior and for troubleshooting.

In recent years, the integration of graph-based methods with transformer architectures has led to innovative models that harness the strengths of both approaches. By embedding graph structures within the framework of transformers, modern systems like LangGraph LLM are able to capture both sequential and relational information, leading to a more nuanced and comprehensive understanding of language. This hybrid approach is particularly powerful in scenarios where understanding the relationships between entities is as important as understanding the entities themselves.

In summary, graph-based approaches in AI represent a critical evolution in how machines process and interpret data. By moving beyond linear representations and embracing the interconnected nature of information, these methods have opened up new avenues for research and practical applications across a diverse array of fields—from natural language processing and recommendation systems to bioinformatics and social network analysis. As AI continues to evolve, the integration of graph-based reasoning will likely play an increasingly central role in developing more intelligent, context-aware systems.

2.3.1. Introduction to Graph Theory

Graph theory is a branch of mathematics that studies the relationships between objects, offering a powerful framework for modeling complex networks. At its most fundamental level, a graph consists of a collection of nodes (also known as vertices) and the connections between them, referred to as edges. This simple yet versatile structure can represent a wide range of real-world scenarios, from social networks and transportation systems to the intricate web of relationships within language.

To illustrate these concepts in a practical setting, imagine a social network where each person is represented by a node. If two individuals are friends, a connection (edge) is drawn between their nodes. This visual and conceptual representation makes it easier to analyze and understand the dynamics of the network, such as identifying influential individuals or communities.

Practical Example: Representing a Social Network

Consider a small social network comprising four individuals: Alice, Bob, Charlie, and Diana. The relationships are as follows:

- Alice is friends with Bob and Diana.
- Bob is friends with Alice and Charlie.
- Charlie is friends with Bob.
- Diana is friends with Alice.

This network can be represented as a graph where:

- **Nodes:** Alice, Bob, Charlie, Diana.
- **Edges:** (Alice-Bob), (Alice-Diana), (Bob-Charlie).

In a programming context, we can represent this graph using an **adjacency list** or an **adjacency matrix**. Here's a simple Python example using an adjacency list representation:

```python
 code
# Define the graph using an adjacency list
social_network = {
    "Alice": ["Bob", "Diana"],
    "Bob": ["Alice", "Charlie"],
    "Charlie": ["Bob"],
    "Diana": ["Alice"]
}

# Display the social network graph
for person, friends in social_network.items():
    print(f"{person} is connected to: {',
'.join(friends)}")
```

When you run this code, it prints out the relationships, offering a clear, hands-on view of how the graph is structured.

Graph Representations and Their Applications

There are two common methods to represent graphs in a computational setting:

- **Adjacency List:**
  Each node has a list of adjacent nodes. This is memory efficient and particularly useful for sparse graphs. In our social network example, the dictionary above serves as an adjacency list.
- **Adjacency Matrix:**
  A two-dimensional array where each cell (i, j) indicates whether there is an edge between node i and node j. For a small network, this representation can be demonstrated with a simple 2D list in Python.

Here's a brief example using an adjacency matrix for the same network:

```python
 code
# Define the nodes in order
nodes = ["Alice", "Bob", "Charlie", "Diana"]

# Initialize a 4x4 matrix with zeros
adjacency_matrix = [[0]*4 for _ in range(4)]

# Define the edges by updating the matrix
edges = [("Alice", "Bob"), ("Alice", "Diana"),
("Bob", "Charlie")]

# Helper function to get the index of a node
def index(name):
    return nodes.index(name)

# Populate the adjacency matrix (assuming an
undirected graph)
for u, v in edges:
    i, j = index(u), index(v)
    adjacency_matrix[i][j] = 1
    adjacency_matrix[j][i] = 1  # since the graph
is undirected

# Display the matrix
print("Adjacency Matrix:")
for row in adjacency_matrix:
    print(row)
```

This code sets up a matrix where a 1 indicates the presence of an edge between nodes, allowing you to see the full connectivity in a tabular form.

Hands-On Application: Analyzing Graph Properties

Beyond just representing data, graph theory provides tools to analyze network properties. For example, you might want to determine if the graph is connected—that is, if there is a path between every pair of nodes. This type of analysis is critical in many applications:

- **Social Networks:** Identify isolated communities or influential nodes.
- **Transportation Networks:** Find the shortest path between locations.
- **Natural Language Processing:** Model relationships between words or concepts.

A simple hands-on task could be to implement a breadth-first search (BFS) algorithm to check for connectivity. Here's a conceptual outline in Python:

```python
 code
def bfs(graph, start):
    visited = set()
    queue = [start]

    while queue:
        vertex = queue.pop(0)
        if vertex not in visited:
            visited.add(vertex)
            queue.extend([neighbor for neighbor in
graph[vertex] if neighbor not in visited])
    return visited

# Check connectivity starting from 'Alice'
visited_nodes = bfs(social_network, "Alice")
print("Nodes reachable from Alice:", visited_nodes)
```

This function explores all nodes reachable from the starting node, demonstrating a basic yet powerful application of graph theory.

Graph theory not only provides the theoretical underpinnings for understanding complex networks but also offers practical tools and techniques that are directly applicable in real-world scenarios. Whether you're analyzing social networks, optimizing transportation routes, or modeling relationships in language, graph theory offers a structured, intuitive way to represent and explore data. The examples and code snippets provided here are intended to give you a hands-on introduction to these concepts, bridging the gap between theory and practice.

2.3.2. Applications in Language Modeling

Graph-based approaches have significantly broadened the horizons of language modeling by offering methods to capture complex interdependencies that go beyond linear sequences. In language modeling, graphs are used to represent various layers of linguistic structure, including syntactic dependencies, semantic relationships, and even discourse-level connections.

One of the most prominent applications of graph-based techniques in language modeling is in dependency parsing. In this approach, sentences are transformed into graphs where each word is a node, and edges represent syntactic relationships such as subject-verb or modifier-noun links. This graphical representation enables models to better understand the grammatical structure of sentences, making them more robust in tasks like machine translation and information extraction.

Another important application is in semantic role labeling, where the relationships between predicates and their corresponding arguments are mapped out in a graph. By modeling these semantic connections, language models can achieve a deeper understanding of the underlying meaning in text, which is essential for tasks like summarization and question answering.

Practical Example: Building a Dependency Graph

To illustrate these concepts in a hands-on manner, consider the following Python example using the **networkx** library. In this example, we simulate a simplified dependency graph for the sentence: "Alice quickly reads the book." In this graph, each word is a node, and the edges denote the grammatical relationships between them.

```python
code
import networkx as nx
import matplotlib.pyplot as plt
```

```python
# Create a directed graph to represent dependencies
dependency_graph = nx.DiGraph()

# Define nodes for each word in the sentence
words = ["Alice", "quickly", "reads", "the",
"book"]
for word in words:
    dependency_graph.add_node(word)

# Add edges to represent dependency relationships
# For instance, "reads" is the main verb, "Alice"
is its subject, "quickly" is an adverb modifying
"reads",
# "book" is the object of "reads", and "the"
modifies "book"
dependency_graph.add_edge("reads", "Alice")    #
subject relation
dependency_graph.add_edge("reads", "quickly")    #
adverbial modifier
dependency_graph.add_edge("reads", "book")        #
object relation
dependency_graph.add_edge("book", "the")          #
determiner relation

# Draw the dependency graph
pos = nx.spring_layout(dependency_graph)
nx.draw(dependency_graph, pos, with_labels=True,
node_color='lightblue', arrowstyle='->',
arrowsize=15)
plt.title("Dependency Graph for 'Alice quickly
reads the book.'")
plt.show()
```

In this code snippet, we construct a directed graph where each directed edge indicates a dependency from a head word to its dependent. By visualizing the graph, you can easily see how the sentence structure is captured in a non-linear format. Such representations can be further utilized in language models to improve syntactic and semantic analysis.

Applications in Advanced Language Models

Beyond basic dependency parsing, graph-based methods are also integral to more advanced language models. For instance, graph neural networks (GNNs) are increasingly used to process the structured information contained in semantic graphs. These networks propagate information across the graph, allowing the model to learn rich representations that integrate both local word information and broader contextual relationships.

Integrating graph-based embeddings with transformer architectures is another innovative application. In such hybrid models, graph representations can enhance the self-attention mechanism by incorporating explicit relational knowledge. This combination allows models like LangGraph LLM to achieve superior performance on tasks that require deep contextual understanding, such as complex question answering, nuanced text summarization, and even creative content generation.

Hands-On Experiment: Graph Convolutional Networks for Language Tasks

A practical experiment might involve using a graph convolutional network (GCN) to process a dependency graph extracted from a sentence and then use the resulting embeddings to improve sentiment analysis. While a complete implementation would involve extensive preprocessing and integration with deep learning frameworks, the core idea is to treat the dependency graph as an input to a GCN, which refines node representations based on their neighbors. These refined representations are then fed into a classifier that predicts sentiment.

This hands-on approach demonstrates how graph-based methods can bridge the gap between structural linguistic knowledge and the statistical learning capabilities of modern neural networks. By incorporating explicit relational structures, language models become better equipped to handle the complexities of human language.

In summary, graph-based approaches in language modeling provide a robust framework to capture syntactic and semantic relationships that are often lost in linear representations. From dependency parsing and semantic role labeling to the integration of GNNs and transformers, these methods enhance language models by offering richer, more context-aware representations. The practical examples presented here are just a starting point, illustrating the potential of graph-based techniques to transform the way we model and understand language.

2.4. Evaluation Metrics and Benchmarking

Evaluating language models is crucial to both measure their performance and guide their further development. This process involves a combination of quantitative metrics and qualitative assessments that together provide a comprehensive picture of a model's strengths and weaknesses. In this section, we explore the common metrics used to assess language models, along with practical examples to illustrate how these metrics are applied.

Quantitative Evaluation Metrics

Several key metrics are widely used in the field of natural language processing to evaluate the performance of language models. These metrics provide numerical scores that help compare models and assess improvements over time.

One of the fundamental metrics in language modeling is **perplexity**, which measures how well a probability model predicts a sample. A lower perplexity score indicates that the model is better at predicting the next word in a sequence. This metric is particularly useful during the training phase of language models.

For tasks such as machine translation or summarization, metrics like **BLEU (Bilingual Evaluation Understudy)** and **ROUGE (Recall-Oriented Understudy for Gisting Evaluation)** are commonly used. BLEU measures the overlap between the model's output and one or more reference texts, while ROUGE evaluates the quality of summaries by comparing the generated summary to a set of reference summaries.

Another critical evaluation aspect involves **accuracy** for classification tasks and **F1 scores** for tasks where class imbalance might be an issue. These metrics help gauge the precision and recall of a model's predictions.

Practical Example: Evaluating with BLEU Score

Consider a scenario where you are using a language model for machine translation. The BLEU score is a standard metric to evaluate the quality of the translations. Below is a simple Python example using the NLTK library to compute a BLEU score for a set of translated sentences:

```python
python
```

```
 code
import nltk
from nltk.translate.bleu_score import sentence_bleu

# Reference translation(s) for the test sentence
reference = [['the', 'cat', 'is', 'on', 'the',
'mat']]
# Candidate translation generated by the model
candidate = ['the', 'cat', 'is', 'on', 'the',
'mat']

# Calculate the BLEU score
bleu_score = sentence_bleu(reference, candidate)
print("BLEU Score:", bleu_score)
```

This example demonstrates how to evaluate the translation quality by comparing the candidate translation against the reference using the BLEU score. Although this is a simplified case, in practice, you would compute BLEU scores over a large corpus to obtain a robust evaluation.

Benchmarking Language Models

Benchmarking involves comparing a model's performance against established datasets and tasks. Common benchmarks in NLP include datasets like GLUE, SuperGLUE, and SQuAD for various language understanding tasks. These benchmarks provide standardized test suites that allow researchers and developers to gauge how well their models perform relative to the state-of-the-art.

For instance, when evaluating a model like LangGraph LLM, you might run it through a series of benchmark tests on tasks such as sentiment analysis, question answering, and text summarization. The results are then compared to published scores from other models. This process not only validates the model's capabilities but also helps identify areas for further improvement.

Hands-On Experiment: Evaluating Perplexity

To provide another practical example, consider evaluating a language model using perplexity. The following Python code snippet demonstrates a basic calculation of perplexity for a model's output:

```
python
```

```
code
import math

def calculate_perplexity(probabilities):
    """
    Calculate perplexity given a list of
probabilities for the correct next word.
    :param probabilities: List of probabilities for
the correct word in a sequence.
    :return: Perplexity score.
    """
    # Avoid log(0) by ensuring all probabilities
are greater than zero
    log_prob_sum = sum(math.log(prob, 2) for prob
in probabilities if prob > 0)
    avg_log_prob = log_prob_sum /
len(probabilities)
    perplexity = 2 ** (-avg_log_prob)
    return perplexity

# Example probabilities for a sequence of words
predicted by the model
example_probabilities = [0.1, 0.2, 0.05, 0.3, 0.15]
perplexity =
calculate_perplexity(example_probabilities)
print("Perplexity:", perplexity)
```

This example shows how you can take a series of probabilities that your model assigns to the correct words in a sequence and compute a perplexity score. A lower perplexity indicates that the model is more confident in its predictions, which is generally desirable in language modeling.

Integrating Qualitative Analysis

While quantitative metrics are invaluable, they are often complemented by qualitative assessments. Human evaluation plays a critical role in understanding aspects of language models that numbers alone cannot capture, such as fluency, coherence, and creativity. Expert reviews and user studies provide insights into how well a model performs in real-world applications and whether it meets the nuanced expectations of human communication.

Evaluation metrics and benchmarking provide a multi-faceted framework for assessing language models. From perplexity and BLEU scores to human evaluations, these methods ensure that models like LangGraph LLM are not only technically sound but also practically effective. By combining quantitative metrics with qualitative insights, developers can iteratively refine models to achieve higher performance and more natural language understanding. This rigorous evaluation process is essential for advancing the state-of-the-art in language intelligence and ensuring that innovations translate into real-world improvements.

2.4.1. Common Metrics in NLP

Evaluating the performance of NLP systems requires a variety of metrics tailored to the specific tasks at hand. These metrics offer quantitative ways to measure how well a model processes, generates, or understands language. In this section, we examine several common metrics in NLP, exploring both their theoretical underpinnings and practical applications.

One of the most fundamental metrics is **perplexity**, which is used primarily in language modeling. Perplexity quantifies how well a probability model predicts a sample; a lower perplexity indicates that the model is better at anticipating the next word in a sequence. In practice, perplexity is calculated as the exponential of the average negative log-likelihood of a test set. For example, when evaluating a language model, you might compute the perplexity over a corpus to determine if the model is confident in its predictions.

For tasks involving text generation or translation, **BLEU (Bilingual Evaluation Understudy)** is widely used. BLEU measures the overlap between the model's output and one or more reference texts. It does this by calculating n-gram precision while applying a brevity penalty to avoid overly short outputs. In a practical setting, you might use BLEU to evaluate the quality of machine-translated sentences by comparing them against high-quality human translations.

Another critical metric for summarization and other generative tasks is **ROUGE (Recall-Oriented Understudy for Gisting Evaluation)**. Unlike BLEU, ROUGE emphasizes recall and measures how much of the reference content is captured in the generated text. ROUGE is particularly useful when evaluating the completeness of a summary or when ensuring that key points are not omitted.

For classification tasks, **accuracy** is a straightforward metric that represents the percentage of correct predictions made by the model. However, in scenarios where data is imbalanced, **precision**, **recall**, and the **F1 score** provide a more nuanced view. Precision measures the correctness of positive predictions, recall assesses the model's ability to capture all positive instances, and the F1 score combines these into a single metric that balances both concerns.

Additionally, metrics like **METEOR** and **CIDEr** have been developed for tasks such as image captioning and other language generation applications, further expanding the toolkit available to researchers and developers.

Practical Illustrations

- **Perplexity Example:**
  Imagine training a language model on a corpus of news articles. By calculating the perplexity on a held-out test set, you might find that the model achieves a perplexity of 45, indicating moderate confidence in predicting subsequent words. If improvements in model architecture lower the perplexity to 30, this suggests a better grasp of language patterns.
- **BLEU Score in Machine Translation:**
  Consider a scenario where you are translating English sentences into French. After generating translations, you compare them to expert human translations. A BLEU score of 0.65 (on a scale from 0 to 1) might be considered competitive, indicating that a significant portion of the n-grams in your translation match those in the reference translations. This quantitative assessment is further supported by qualitative human evaluations.
- **ROUGE in Summarization:**
  When evaluating a summarization model, you might compute ROUGE scores to determine how much of the essential content is captured by the summary. For instance, a ROUGE-1 score (measuring unigram overlap) of 0.70 suggests that 70% of the words in the reference summary appear in the generated summary, reflecting good content coverage.
- **F1 Score in Text Classification:**
  For a sentiment analysis model tasked with classifying reviews as positive or negative, you may observe that while the overall accuracy is high, the F1 score for the minority class is lower. This indicates that the model might be missing some positive instances or incorrectly labeling negatives. An F1 score of 0.80 for positive

reviews, compared to 0.90 for negative reviews, suggests an area for targeted improvement.

These common metrics—perplexity, BLEU, ROUGE, accuracy, precision, recall, and F1 score—each offer valuable insights into different aspects of language model performance. By combining these quantitative measures with qualitative assessments, researchers and practitioners can develop a well-rounded understanding of a model's capabilities and areas for improvement. This multi-metric approach is essential for refining NLP systems and ensuring that models like LangGraph LLM are not only theoretically robust but also practically effective in real-world applications.

2.4.2. Challenges in Evaluation

Evaluating NLP models, particularly in the context of language generation and understanding, presents a range of challenges that go beyond simply calculating numerical scores. One of the primary hurdles is the inherent subjectivity of language. Unlike more deterministic tasks, language processing often involves nuances, context, and cultural subtleties that are difficult to capture with standard quantitative metrics.

For example, metrics like BLEU and ROUGE rely on n-gram overlaps between generated text and reference texts. While these metrics provide a useful baseline, they can fail to capture the full richness of meaning or the stylistic qualities that might make a translation or summary effective. A translation might use different words that are equally valid, yet the n-gram overlap could be low, resulting in a misleading evaluation. This subjectivity is compounded when the task involves creative language generation, where multiple valid outputs exist.

Another significant challenge is the evaluation of context and coherence over longer passages. Models may generate text that is locally coherent—meaning that each sentence seems reasonable on its own—while the overall narrative may lack a consistent theme or logical progression. Traditional metrics might not adequately penalize such inconsistencies, as they focus on word-level similarities rather than global coherence. Practical testing often requires human evaluation to determine whether the text makes sense as a whole.

Additionally, the diversity of language tasks themselves introduces complexity. Different tasks, such as sentiment analysis, machine translation, summarization, or dialogue generation, each have distinct evaluation criteria. For instance, while accuracy and F1 scores might suffice for classification tasks, evaluating conversational agents requires assessing interactivity, engagement, and appropriateness of responses—qualities that are inherently qualitative and subjective.

A further challenge arises from the limitations of available benchmark datasets. Many benchmarks, although widely adopted, may not reflect the diversity of real-world language use. They can be biased towards certain styles, topics, or language registers, leading to models that perform well on benchmarks but struggle with broader applications. This gap between benchmark performance and real-world utility is a persistent issue that researchers continue to address.

Finally, computational and practical constraints also play a role in evaluation challenges. Running extensive human evaluations or maintaining large-scale benchmark tests can be resource-intensive and time-consuming. This often necessitates a trade-off between the depth of evaluation and the practical feasibility of implementing these assessments during iterative model development.

In summary, the evaluation of NLP models is challenged by:

- **Subjectivity in Language:**
  Variations in valid outputs and stylistic choices make it difficult to rely solely on quantitative metrics.
- **Context and Coherence Issues:**
  Standard metrics may miss the overall narrative quality or thematic consistency, requiring complementary human judgment.
- **Task-Specific Requirements:**
  Different NLP tasks demand tailored evaluation strategies, complicating the development of universal benchmarks.
- **Benchmark Limitations:**
  Existing datasets may not capture the full diversity of language, leading to a gap between benchmark performance and real-world effectiveness.
- **Resource Constraints:**
  Comprehensive evaluations, especially those involving human assessors, are often expensive and time-consuming.

Addressing these challenges requires a multi-faceted evaluation approach, combining quantitative metrics with qualitative analysis and continuous refinement of benchmarks. This integrated strategy is essential to ensure that models like LangGraph LLM not only achieve impressive scores on paper but also deliver practical, context-aware language understanding and generation in real-world applications.

Chapter 3: LangGraph LLM Architecture

3.1. Core Design Principles

The architecture of LangGraph LLM is built upon a synthesis of established neural network frameworks and innovative graph-based reasoning techniques. At its core, the design philosophy emphasizes the need to capture both the sequential patterns of language and the complex relationships that exist among linguistic elements. This dual approach is achieved through the integration of transformer models and graph representations, setting the stage for a new generation of language models.

One of the primary principles is modularity. The architecture is divided into distinct modules that handle specific tasks, such as input processing, graph construction, attention-based context aggregation, and output generation. This modularity not only simplifies the design but also allows for targeted improvements. For instance, the graph module is responsible for constructing a relational map of the input text, identifying dependencies and semantic links between words, phrases, and even entire sentences. This module works in tandem with transformer layers, which excel at capturing long-range dependencies through their self-attention mechanisms.

Scalability is another cornerstone of LangGraph LLM. The design is crafted to handle large-scale datasets and complex linguistic tasks without compromising performance. The parallel processing capabilities of transformer architectures are complemented by efficient graph algorithms that allow for rapid construction and traversal of large graphs. This ensures that even as the volume and complexity of input data grow, the model maintains its effectiveness and speed.

Adaptability and flexibility are also central to the design principles. LangGraph LLM is engineered to be versatile, allowing for fine-tuning and adaptation across different domains and tasks. Whether the goal is machine translation, summarization, or conversational AI, the architecture is designed to be easily customized. This is achieved through well-defined interfaces between modules and the incorporation of transfer learning techniques, ensuring that the model can leverage pre-trained knowledge and adjust to new contexts with minimal retraining.

Interpretability is an important yet often challenging aspect of modern language models. By integrating graph-based reasoning, LangGraph LLM provides an additional layer of transparency. The explicit graph representations help in understanding how the model connects various language elements, offering insights into the decision-making process. For example, when analyzing a sentence, the graph module highlights the syntactic and semantic relationships that the model deems important, making it easier for developers and researchers to interpret the model's behavior and debug potential issues.

To illustrate these design principles in a practical context, consider a simplified scenario where the model processes a sentence to generate a dependency graph and then uses this graph to enhance its attention mechanism. In a typical workflow:

- **Input Processing:** The sentence is tokenized and converted into embeddings, providing a numerical representation of each word.
- **Graph Construction:** A graph module takes these embeddings and constructs a network where nodes represent words, and edges represent syntactic or semantic relationships, such as subject-verb or modifier-noun connections.
- **Attention Augmentation:** The transformer layers integrate the graph information, using it to adjust the attention weights. This ensures that the model focuses on the most relevant relationships, improving context understanding.
- **Output Generation:** The refined representations are then used to generate the final output, be it a translation, summary, or response in a dialogue system.

Each of these steps is meticulously designed to interact with the others in a cohesive manner, reflecting the overarching goal of creating a robust and context-aware language model. The architecture of LangGraph LLM exemplifies how the convergence of traditional neural network techniques and graph-based methodologies can lead to significant advancements in language processing capabilities. This approach not only enhances performance on standard benchmarks but also paves the way for innovative applications in various real-world scenarios.

3.1.1. System Overview and Objectives

LangGraph LLM is designed as a next-generation language model that unites the robust capabilities of transformer architectures with the rich relational insights offered by graph-based reasoning. The system is architected in a modular fashion, where each component is specialized to address a specific aspect of language processing, yet they interoperate seamlessly to deliver enhanced contextual understanding and performance.

At the highest level, the system comprises several core modules:

- **Input Processing Module:**
  This module is responsible for converting raw text into meaningful numerical representations. It tokenizes the input, applies embedding techniques, and prepares the data for further processing. The goal is to capture the subtle nuances of language right from the start, ensuring that subsequent modules operate on a rich, informative base.
- **Graph Construction Module:**
  Here, the system translates the sequential input into a structured graph format. Each token or phrase is represented as a node, and edges capture syntactic and semantic relationships—such as subject-verb or modifier-noun connections. This transformation is pivotal in allowing the model to see beyond mere word order, instead focusing on the underlying structure of the language.
- **Transformer and Attention Integration Module:**
  The core of LangGraph LLM leverages transformer layers that incorporate a self-attention mechanism. However, this module is uniquely augmented by the graph-derived insights. By integrating graph information into the attention process, the model can dynamically adjust its focus to emphasize relational contexts, thus achieving a more nuanced understanding of the input text.
- **Output Generation Module:**
  Finally, the refined representations are used to generate the desired output, whether that be a translated sentence, a summary, or a response in a dialogue system. The output module is designed to ensure that the enriched context derived from both sequential and relational data is effectively translated into high-quality text generation.

The objectives of LangGraph LLM are multi-fold:

- **Enhanced Contextual Understanding:**
  By marrying the strengths of transformers with graph-based representations, the system is engineered to capture both local word-level information and broader relational structures. This duality enables more accurate predictions and richer text generation.
- **Improved Interpretability:**
  The explicit graph module offers a window into the model's

decision-making process. Developers can visualize and analyze the constructed graphs, gaining insights into how specific relationships in the input influence the model's outputs. This transparency is critical for debugging and fine-tuning model behavior.

- **Scalability and Adaptability:**
  The modular design ensures that LangGraph LLM can scale efficiently to handle large datasets and complex language tasks. It is also adaptable, capable of being fine-tuned for various domains—from technical documentation to creative writing—without needing to overhaul the entire architecture.

- **Practical Integration:**
  Beyond theoretical excellence, LangGraph LLM is built with real-world applications in mind. The system is designed to integrate smoothly with existing workflows and to be extensible through APIs and customizable modules. This ensures that organizations can leverage the model's advanced capabilities for diverse applications such as machine translation, sentiment analysis, and conversational AI.

Practical Example: End-to-End Processing

Consider a practical scenario where LangGraph LLM processes the sentence, "The innovative research team quickly solved the complex problem." In this workflow:

1. **Input Processing:**
   The sentence is tokenized into individual words and converted into embeddings, capturing their semantic meanings.
2. **Graph Construction:**
   The model constructs a dependency graph where "research team" is connected to "innovative" (modifier relationship), "solved" is identified as the core action, and "complex problem" is established as the object of that action.
3. **Transformer Integration:**
   The self-attention mechanism, now enriched by the graph structure, focuses on the relationship between "innovative" and "research team" as well as between "solved" and "complex problem." This enables a deeper understanding of the sentence's intent.
4. **Output Generation:**
   Using the combined information, the model generates output that might be a summarized version or a translation, while preserving the nuanced relationships uncovered during processing.

In summary, the system overview of LangGraph LLM showcases an architecture built on modularity, scalability, and integrative intelligence. Its core design principles and objectives focus on delivering a model that not only achieves state-of-the-art performance but also provides clarity and flexibility for practical applications. This approach marks a significant evolution in language model design, paving the way for more sophisticated and context-aware AI systems.

3.1.2. Innovations in Architecture

LangGraph LLM distinguishes itself through a series of innovations that push beyond conventional language modeling techniques. At the heart of these innovations is the seamless integration of graph-based reasoning with transformer architectures, enabling the model to capture not only the sequential patterns of language but also the rich, non-linear relationships among words, phrases, and concepts.

One of the key breakthroughs is the incorporation of a dedicated graph module that transforms traditional input data into a structured graph representation. This module analyzes the input text to identify syntactic and semantic dependencies, effectively constructing a network where each node represents a linguistic element and each edge denotes a relationship such as a subject-verb or modifier-noun link. By doing so, LangGraph LLM is able to recognize contextual cues that might be overlooked by standard transformer models.

Another innovative aspect is the dynamic integration of graph insights into the transformer's self-attention mechanism. In traditional transformers, attention weights are computed based solely on token embeddings. LangGraph LLM, however, augments this process by incorporating relational information derived from the graph structure. This means that when the model assigns attention scores, it takes into account both the positional and relational importance of tokens, resulting in more nuanced context awareness. In practical terms, this enhanced attention mechanism improves tasks such as machine translation, summarization, and question answering by ensuring that relevant relationships within the input are emphasized during processing.

Additional innovations include:

- **Adaptive Graph Construction:**
  The model continuously refines its graph representation as it

50

processes text, allowing it to adjust to the specific context of each input. This dynamic approach ensures that even subtle language cues are captured effectively.

- **Multi-Modal Fusion:**
  By combining sequential transformer representations with graph-derived features, LangGraph LLM achieves a more holistic understanding of language. This fusion enables the model to excel in both language comprehension and generation tasks, making it highly versatile for various applications.
- **Enhanced Interpretability:**
  The explicit use of graph structures not only boosts performance but also provides greater transparency. Developers can visualize the constructed graphs to gain insights into the decision-making process of the model, facilitating easier debugging and fine-tuning.

Practical Example: Integrating Graph Data into Attention

Imagine a scenario where the model processes the sentence, "The dedicated team swiftly resolved the critical issue." The graph module identifies that "dedicated team" is closely related and that "swiftly" acts as an intensifier for "resolved," while "critical issue" forms the object of the resolution. In the transformer layers, this graph-based context is used to adjust the attention weights. Instead of treating each word independently based solely on sequential proximity, the model increases the attention weight between "team" and "dedicated," as well as between "resolved" and "critical issue." This targeted focus enables the model to generate outputs that more accurately reflect the intended meaning and nuance of the sentence.

In summary, the innovations in the LangGraph LLM architecture lie in its ability to merge graph-based insights with advanced transformer mechanisms. This combination leads to superior contextual understanding, enhanced interpretability, and versatile applicability across a range of language tasks. These innovations set the stage for next-generation language processing, where models are not only statistically powerful but also capable of deeply understanding the intricate web of relationships that underpin human language.

3.2. Detailed Component Analysis

This section serves as a comprehensive guide to the individual components that make up LangGraph LLM. Each component is designed to handle specific tasks, and together they create a robust, context-aware language model. Below is a step-by-step breakdown of the core components and their functions, presented in a clear and structured format.

1. Input Processing Module

- **Purpose:**
  Transform raw text into a numerical format suitable for further analysis.
- **Key Steps:**
  - **Tokenization:**
    Breaks the text into individual tokens (words or subwords).
    Example: Converting "The skilled engineer" into ["The", "skilled", "engineer"].
  - **Embedding:**
    Converts tokens into dense vectors that capture semantic meaning.
    Example: Using contextualized embeddings to ensure even rare words have a rich representation.
- **Outcome:**
  A set of numerical representations that form the basis for subsequent processing.

2. Graph Construction Module

- **Purpose:**
  Build a structured graph that maps the syntactic and semantic relationships within the text.
- **Key Steps:**
  - **Node Creation:**
    Each token becomes a node in the graph.
  - **Edge Establishment:**
    Identify and connect tokens based on their relationships (e.g., subject-verb, modifier-noun).
    Example: In the sentence "The skilled engineer meticulously designed the innovative system," an edge connects "engineer" with "skilled" to denote a modifier relationship.
  - **Graph Visualization (Optional):**
    Utilize libraries like NetworkX to visualize the graph for better understanding and debugging.

- **Outcome:**
  A dependency or semantic graph that adds an extra layer of context beyond sequential information.

3. Transformer and Attention Integration Module

- **Purpose:**
  Merge the sequential representations with graph-derived insights to create enriched context-aware representations.
- **Key Steps:**
  - **Self-Attention Mechanism:**
    Compute attention weights that reflect the importance of each token relative to others.
  - **Graph-Augmented Attention:**
    Adjust the standard attention process by integrating signals from the constructed graph.
    Example: Enhancing the connection between "designed" and "innovative system" based on graph data.
  - **Multi-Head Attention:**
    Use multiple attention heads to capture diverse aspects of the text's relationships.
- **Outcome:**
  Enhanced representations that capture both sequential context and relational dependencies.

4. Output Generation Module

- **Purpose:**
  Convert the enriched, integrated representations back into coherent, human-readable text.
- **Key Steps:**
  - **Decoding:**
    Use strategies such as beam search or sampling to generate text.
    Example: Producing a translation, summary, or response in a dialogue system.
  - **Quality Assurance:**
    Ensure that the generated text accurately reflects the nuanced context derived from previous modules.
- **Outcome:**
  The final output text that is fluent, context-aware, and aligned with the intended task (e.g., translation, summarization).

Practical Workflow Example

Scenario: Processing the sentence "The skilled engineer meticulously designed the innovative system."

1. **Input Processing:**
   - Tokenize the sentence into ["The", "skilled", "engineer", "meticulously", "designed", "the", "innovative", "system"].
   - Convert these tokens into embeddings that capture their semantic properties.
2. **Graph Construction:**
   - Build a graph where:
     - "engineer" is connected to "skilled" (modifier relationship).
     - "designed" is identified as the central action, linking to "meticulously" (adverbial modifier) and "innovative system" (object relationship).
3. **Transformer and Attention Integration:**
   - Apply the self-attention mechanism, then enhance it by integrating the relational insights from the graph.
   - Adjust attention weights to emphasize the relationship between "designed" and "innovative system" as well as between "meticulously" and "designed".
4. **Output Generation:**
   - Decode the integrated representations to generate the final text output, ensuring that all relational nuances are preserved in the output.

Summary

This detailed component analysis provides a step-by-step guide to understanding how LangGraph LLM processes text:

- **Input Processing** lays the groundwork by converting text into a numerical form.
- **Graph Construction** adds context by mapping relationships.
- **Transformer and Attention Integration** fuses sequential and relational data.
- **Output Generation** converts the enriched data back into human-readable form.

Each component plays a critical role in ensuring that LangGraph LLM not only understands language at a surface level but also grasps the intricate relationships that underpin its meaning. This guidebook approach is intended to provide clear, actionable insights for both developers and researchers interested in the inner workings of advanced language models.

3.2.1. Input Processing and Data Embedding

This section provides a clear, step-by-step guide to the initial phase of LangGraph LLM: transforming raw text into numerical representations that can be further processed. The process involves two main tasks: input processing (including tokenization) and data embedding. Each step is critical for capturing the semantic and syntactic nuances of the language.

Objectives

- **Convert Raw Text into Structured Data:**
  Transform unstructured text into a format that the model can understand and process.
- **Capture Semantic Nuances:**
  Generate dense vector representations (embeddings) that encode the meaning of each token, enabling the model to recognize subtle linguistic differences.

Step-by-Step Breakdown

1. Tokenization

- **Purpose:**
  Break the input text into individual tokens (words or subwords) to facilitate further analysis.
- **Process:**
  - **Segmentation:**
    Split sentences into individual tokens using whitespace and punctuation as natural delimiters.
    Example: Converting the sentence "The skilled engineer" into the list `["The", "skilled", "engineer"]`.
  - **Subword Tokenization:**
    For complex or rare words, apply methods like Byte-Pair Encoding (BPE) to break tokens into smaller, more frequent sub-units.

55

Example: Splitting "unbelievable" into subword units such as `["un", "believ", "able"]`.

- **Outcome:**
  A sequence of tokens that preserves the structure and meaning of the original text.

2. Data Embedding

- **Purpose:**
  Transform tokens into dense vectors that capture their semantic properties and relationships with other tokens.
- **Process:**
  - **Static Embeddings:**
    Utilize pre-trained embeddings (e.g., word2vec, GloVe) that assign each token a fixed vector based on global corpus statistics.
    Limitation: These do not capture context-specific nuances.
  - **Contextualized Embeddings:**
    Apply transformer-based models (e.g., BERT, GPT) to generate embeddings that change based on the token's context within a sentence.
    Example: The word "bank" will have different embeddings when used in "river bank" versus "savings bank."
  - **Fine-Tuning:**
    Adjust the embedding layer during model training to better capture domain-specific nuances or to adapt to new vocabulary.
- **Outcome:**
  A set of dense vectors corresponding to each token, ready for further processing by subsequent modules (e.g., graph construction and transformer layers).

Practical Workflow Example

Scenario: Process the sentence "The skilled engineer meticulously designed the innovative system."

1. **Tokenization:**
   - **Input Sentence:** "The skilled engineer meticulously designed the innovative system."

- o **Tokenized Output:** `["The", "skilled",
  "engineer", "meticulously", "designed",
  "the", "innovative", "system"]`
- o **Subword Consideration:** For words that might be rare or compound, subword tokenization is applied to ensure robust representation.

2. **Data Embedding:**
   - o **Static Embedding Example:**
     Each token is mapped to a pre-trained vector from a resource like GloVe.
   - o **Contextualized Embedding Example:**
     Using a transformer model, the word "designed" receives a context-aware embedding that considers the influence of "meticulously" and "innovative system."
   - o **Fine-Tuning:**
     During training, these embeddings are refined to capture specific patterns relevant to the task at hand.

Summary

- **Tokenization:**
  Breaks text into manageable units, ensuring that even compound words are effectively segmented.
- **Data Embedding:**
  Converts tokens into vectors that encode semantic meaning, with options for both static and contextualized representations.

By following these clear steps, LangGraph LLM lays a solid foundation for deeper language understanding. This guide ensures that both the raw input and its subsequent embedding capture the nuances necessary for advanced processing, ultimately leading to more accurate and context-aware outputs in tasks such as translation, summarization, and dialogue generation.

3.2.2. Graph-Based Reasoning Modules

This section provides a structured guide to the Graph-Based Reasoning Modules within LangGraph LLM. These modules are designed to enhance the model's understanding of linguistic relationships by capturing the structural and relational information that exists between tokens. By representing language as a graph, the model can identify and utilize dependencies that go beyond simple sequential patterns.

Objectives

- **Enhance Contextual Representation:**
  Capture syntactic and semantic relationships among tokens that improve the overall contextual understanding.
- **Facilitate Relationship Modeling:**
  Provide explicit representations of linguistic structures (e.g., dependency relations) to support downstream processing in transformer layers.

Step-by-Step Breakdown

1. Graph Construction

- **Purpose:**
  Transform the tokenized input into a graph that explicitly represents the relationships between words.
- **Process:**
  - **Node Identification:**
    Each token from the input text is treated as a node.
  - **Edge Definition:**
    Establish connections (edges) based on linguistic relationships, such as:
    - **Syntactic Relationships:**
      Subject-verb, object-verb, modifier-noun, etc.
    - **Semantic Relationships:**
      Connections based on meaning, such as synonyms or related concepts.
  - **Graph Representation:**
    The constructed graph may be represented using common data structures (e.g., adjacency lists or matrices) or specialized graph libraries (e.g., NetworkX).
- **Outcome:**
  A structured graph that visually and numerically maps out how words in a sentence are interrelated, providing a richer context for further processing.

2. Graph Embedding

- **Purpose:**
  Convert the structured graph into vector representations that can be integrated with the transformer's processing.

- **Process:**
  - **Node Feature Encoding:**
    Each node is assigned a feature vector that encapsulates its embedding as derived from the Input Processing Module.
  - **Edge Feature Encoding:**
    Edges can also be encoded with weights or features that indicate the strength or type of relationship.
  - **Graph Neural Networks (GNNs):**
    Apply GNN architectures (such as Graph Convolutional Networks) to propagate information across nodes, refining their representations based on their neighborhood structure.
- **Outcome:**
  Enhanced node embeddings that incorporate relational information from the entire graph, thereby enriching the context available to subsequent modules.

3. Integration with Transformer Layers

- **Purpose:**
  Fuse graph-derived embeddings with the transformer's self-attention mechanism to create a unified, context-aware representation.
- **Process:**
  - **Attention Augmentation:**
    Modify the standard self-attention mechanism to factor in graph-based relationships. This may involve:
    - Adjusting attention weights based on the strength of connections in the graph.
    - Incorporating graph embeddings directly into the attention computation.
  - **Fusion Strategy:**
    Combine the sequential token embeddings and graph-enhanced embeddings through concatenation, addition, or more complex fusion techniques to create a richer representation.
- **Outcome:**
  A harmonized representation that leverages both sequential and relational context, leading to improved performance in tasks requiring nuanced language understanding.

Practical Workflow Example

Scenario: Process the sentence "The skilled engineer meticulously designed the innovative system."

1. **Graph Construction:**
   - **Nodes:**
     Create nodes for each token: "The", "skilled", "engineer", "meticulously", "designed", "the", "innovative", "system."
   - **Edges:**
     Define edges based on relationships:
     - "engineer" ← "skilled" (modifier relationship)
     - "designed" connects to "meticulously" (adverbial modification)
     - "designed" → "system" (object relationship)
     - "system" ← "innovative" (modifier relationship)
   - **Graph Representation:**
     Use an adjacency list or matrix to represent these connections.
2. **Graph Embedding:**
   - **Node Features:**
     Initialize node features using embeddings from the Input Processing Module.
   - **GNN Processing:**
     Apply a graph convolutional network to refine these features, where each node's new representation is a function of its own features and those of its connected neighbors.
3. **Integration with Transformer Layers:**
   - **Attention Augmentation:**
     Modify the self-attention scores to boost the connection between "designed" and "system" based on the edge weight in the graph.
   - **Fusion:**
     Merge the graph-enhanced embeddings with the original token embeddings, resulting in a comprehensive representation that captures both sequence and structure.

Summary

- **Graph Construction:**
  Converts tokenized text into a graph, defining nodes and edges based on linguistic relationships.

- **Graph Embedding:**
  Uses GNNs to refine node representations by incorporating relational information from the graph.
- **Integration with Transformer Layers:**
  Enhances the self-attention mechanism by integrating graph-based context, resulting in a unified, context-rich representation.

By following these steps, LangGraph LLM leverages graph-based reasoning to capture complex inter-token relationships. This guidebook-style approach provides a clear and structured framework for understanding how the model enhances language understanding through the integration of graph-derived insights.

3.2.3. Integration with Transformer Layers

This section serves as a step-by-step guide on how LangGraph LLM integrates graph-derived information with transformer layers to produce enhanced, context-aware representations. The goal is to fuse the relational insights from the graph-based reasoning modules with the sequential processing strengths of the transformer's self-attention mechanism.

Objectives

- **Combine Sequential and Relational Context:**
  Merge token embeddings with graph-enhanced features for richer representations.
- **Enhance Self-Attention:**
  Adjust attention weights in transformer layers based on the relationships captured in the graph.
- **Improve Downstream Performance:**
  Leverage the integrated context to generate more accurate outputs in tasks like translation, summarization, and question answering.

Step-by-Step Breakdown

1. Preparation of Embeddings

- **Token Embeddings:**
  Begin with embeddings produced during the Input Processing phase. These embeddings represent each token's semantic properties.
- **Graph-Enhanced Embeddings:**
  Refine these embeddings using the Graph Construction and Graph

Embedding modules. Each token now has an additional representation that encapsulates its relationships with other tokens, as determined by the graph.

2. Adjusting the Self-Attention Mechanism

- **Standard Self-Attention Recap:**
  In traditional transformer layers, each token's representation is updated by computing attention scores with every other token in the sequence. These scores are derived solely from the token embeddings.
- **Incorporating Graph Information:**
  Enhance the attention computation by integrating the graph-based embeddings:
  - **Attention Weight Modification:**
    Adjust the attention scores to reflect the strength and type of relationships identified in the graph. For example, if the graph indicates a strong dependency between two tokens (e.g., a subject-verb relationship), the attention score between these tokens is boosted.
  - **Fusion of Embeddings:**
    Merge the standard token embeddings with the graph-enhanced embeddings. This can be done through:
    - **Concatenation:** Combine the two sets of features and pass them through a projection layer.
    - **Addition:** Element-wise addition of the embeddings to create a unified representation.
- **Multi-Head Attention with Graph Signals:**
  Each attention head can learn different aspects of the graph-enhanced context. By integrating graph-derived adjustments across multiple heads, the model captures a diverse set of relational features.

3. Updating Representations

- **Integrated Representation Generation:**
  After modifying the attention weights, the transformer layer produces an updated representation for each token that now reflects both its sequential context and its relational context from the graph.
- **Layer Stacking:**
  These integrated representations are passed through successive transformer layers, with each layer further refining the context by

combining signals from both sources. This iterative process deepens the model's understanding and improves overall performance.

Practical Workflow Example

Scenario: Integrate graph-based reasoning for the sentence "The skilled engineer meticulously designed the innovative system."

1. **Initial Embeddings:**
   o Tokens such as "engineer," "designed," and "system" are converted into embeddings during the Input Processing stage.
2. **Graph-Enhanced Embeddings:**
   o The Graph Construction Module identifies that "engineer" is modified by "skilled" and that "designed" has an object "system" modified by "innovative."
   o A Graph Neural Network refines the embeddings, encoding these relationships.
3. **Attention Adjustment:**
   o During the self-attention calculation in a transformer layer, the model adjusts the attention score between "designed" and "system" to be higher, reflecting their strong dependency.
   o The token embeddings are merged with the graph-enhanced embeddings using a fusion strategy (e.g., concatenation followed by a linear transformation).
4. **Final Representation:**
   o The resulting token representations capture both the sequential flow and the detailed relational context, improving the quality of the output generated in subsequent modules.

Summary

- **Preparation:**
  Start with standard token embeddings and refine them with graph-based reasoning.
- **Attention Enhancement:**
  Modify the transformer's self-attention mechanism to factor in graph-derived relationships, using techniques such as attention weight modification and embedding fusion.
- **Unified Representation:**
  The final integrated representations combine sequential and relational information, paving the way for superior performance in downstream NLP tasks.

By integrating graph-based insights with transformer layers, LangGraph LLM creates a more comprehensive and context-aware representation of language. This guidebook approach clarifies each step, providing actionable insights into how the model fuses two powerful methodologies to advance the state-of-the-art in language understanding.

3.3. Scalability and Performance Optimization

In this section, we provide a detailed guide on the techniques and strategies used to ensure that LangGraph LLM can efficiently scale and maintain high performance, even as the volume of data and model complexity increases. The focus here is on both architectural and algorithmic optimizations that enable the model to handle large datasets and complex language tasks without compromising speed or accuracy.

Objectives

- **Ensure Efficient Resource Utilization:**
  Optimize the model's architecture to make the best use of computational resources such as memory and processing power.
- **Enable Scalability:**
  Design the system so that it can scale to handle large-scale datasets and high-throughput environments, whether in training or inference.
- **Maintain High Performance:**
  Optimize both the latency and throughput of the model during real-world deployment.

Step-by-Step Breakdown

1. Architectural Optimizations

- **Modular Design:**
  The model's architecture is designed in a modular fashion, allowing individual components to be scaled or replaced independently. For instance, the transformer layers can be increased in number to boost capacity without impacting the graph-based modules.
- **Parallel Processing:**
  Leverage the inherent parallelism in transformer architectures, which processes tokens simultaneously, and optimize graph computations using parallel algorithms where possible.

- **Distributed Training:**
  Utilize techniques like data and model parallelism to distribute the training process across multiple GPUs or machines. This not only speeds up the training but also allows the model to learn from larger datasets.

2. Algorithmic Optimizations

- **Efficient Attention Mechanisms:**
  Implement strategies such as sparse attention or low-rank approximations to reduce the computational cost of the self-attention mechanism. This is crucial when processing long sequences.
- **Graph Sampling and Pruning:**
  For the graph-based modules, use graph sampling techniques to focus on the most relevant relationships and prune redundant edges. This reduces the complexity of graph computations without sacrificing essential context.
- **Caching and Precomputation:**
  Cache frequently used embeddings or intermediate computations, and precompute certain graph structures when the input data is known to have a stable structure. This can significantly reduce inference latency.

3. Practical Techniques for Performance Optimization

- **Batch Processing:**
  Process inputs in batches rather than individually, which allows for more efficient use of hardware accelerators like GPUs.
- **Mixed Precision Training:**
  Use lower-precision arithmetic (e.g., FP16) during training and inference to speed up computations and reduce memory usage while maintaining acceptable accuracy.
- **Hyperparameter Tuning:**
  Systematically adjust parameters such as learning rate, batch size, and the number of attention heads to find an optimal balance between performance and computational cost.

Practical Workflow Example

Scenario: Optimizing LangGraph LLM for a large-scale translation task.

1. **Distributed Training Setup:**

- o **Implementation:**
  Set up data parallelism across multiple GPUs using frameworks like PyTorch's DistributedDataParallel.
- o **Outcome:**
  Training time is reduced, and the model can handle larger batches of data.

2. **Efficient Attention:**
   - o **Implementation:**
     Integrate a sparse attention mechanism in the transformer layers to limit the number of computations by focusing on the most important token interactions.
   - o **Outcome:**
     Reduced memory usage and faster processing of long sequences without significant loss in model performance.

3. **Graph Optimization:**
   - o **Implementation:**
     Use graph sampling to select only the most relevant edges in the graph-based reasoning module, and precompute common graph structures for recurrent text patterns.
   - o **Outcome:**
     Lower computational overhead during inference, resulting in faster response times.

4. **Mixed Precision and Caching:**
   - o **Implementation:**
     Enable mixed precision training and inference via frameworks like NVIDIA's Apex, and cache intermediate token embeddings during batch processing.
   - o **Outcome:**
     Further acceleration of model computations while preserving accuracy.

Summary

- **Architectural Optimizations:**
  Modular design, parallel processing, and distributed training enable the model to scale efficiently.
- **Algorithmic Optimizations:**
  Techniques such as efficient attention mechanisms, graph sampling, and caching reduce computational overhead.
- **Practical Techniques:**
  Batch processing, mixed precision, and hyperparameter tuning help maintain high performance during training and inference.

By following these detailed steps and techniques, LangGraph LLM achieves robust scalability and optimized performance, ensuring that it can handle large-scale, complex language tasks in real-world applications. This guidebook-style approach provides clear, actionable strategies for both developers and researchers looking to implement or improve performance in advanced language models.

3.4. Comparative Analysis with Other LLMs

This section provides a structured guide to comparing LangGraph LLM with other large language models (LLMs) currently available in the field. The comparative analysis is essential for understanding the unique strengths and trade-offs of LangGraph LLM in relation to conventional models. Below, we outline key criteria and steps for a comprehensive comparison, along with practical examples and discussion points.

Objectives

- **Highlight Key Differentiators:**
  Identify the unique features of LangGraph LLM, such as graph-based reasoning and enhanced attention mechanisms.
- **Benchmark Performance:**
  Compare accuracy, efficiency, scalability, and resource requirements against other LLMs.
- **Assess Interpretability and Flexibility:**
  Evaluate how well each model supports debugging, transparency, and adaptability to various tasks.

Step-by-Step Comparative Framework

1. Architectural Differences

- **Graph Integration:**
  - *LangGraph LLM:* Incorporates graph-based modules to capture syntactic and semantic relationships explicitly.
  - *Traditional LLMs (e.g., GPT, BERT):* Rely primarily on sequential transformer architectures with self-attention.
- **Attention Mechanism:**
  - *LangGraph LLM:* Enhances self-attention by adjusting weights based on graph-derived insights, offering deeper contextual understanding.

o   *Other Models:* Use standard self-attention without explicit relational cues, which may limit nuanced understanding in complex language structures.

2. Performance and Efficiency

- **Accuracy and Contextual Understanding:**
  o   ***LangGraph LLM:*** Typically shows improved performance on tasks requiring deep contextual analysis, such as summarization and question answering.
  o   *Other LLMs:* Often achieve high accuracy on benchmark datasets but may struggle with tasks that involve intricate relational reasoning.
- **Computational Efficiency:**
  o   *Optimization Strategies:*
      LangGraph LLM leverages model pruning, quantization, and optimized graph processing to balance performance with resource utilization.
  o   *Comparative Considerations:*
      Traditional models may require larger architectures to achieve similar levels of accuracy, leading to increased computational costs.

3. Scalability and Flexibility

- **Modular Design:**
  o   ***LangGraph LLM:*** The modular approach enables independent optimization and scaling of components (e.g., graph module, transformer layers), offering flexibility for domain-specific applications.
  o   *Other Models:* While scalable, many traditional LLMs have less modularity, making it challenging to adapt specific components without reengineering the entire system.
- **Adaptability to Different Tasks:**
  o   ***LangGraph LLM:*** Shows promise in fine-tuning for specialized applications due to its integrated graph reasoning, which can capture domain-specific relational nuances.
  o   *Other LLMs:* Generally adaptable through transfer learning but might require extensive retraining to handle tasks that benefit from explicit relationship modeling.

4. Interpretability and Transparency

- **Model Debugging and Analysis:**
  - *LangGraph LLM:* Provides enhanced interpretability through its explicit graph structures. Developers can visualize these graphs to understand decision-making and improve debugging.
  - *Other Models:* Often operate as "black boxes," with interpretability relying on indirect methods (e.g., attention visualization) that may not fully explain the underlying reasoning.

5. Practical Example: Benchmarking Scenario

Scenario: Evaluate performance on a complex summarization task.

- **LangGraph LLM:**
  - **Approach:** Uses graph-based analysis to capture relationships between key phrases and contextual elements.
  - **Result:** Tends to produce summaries that are not only accurate but also maintain a coherent structure and contextual flow.
- **Traditional LLM (e.g., GPT-3):**
  - **Approach:** Relies on massive pre-training and standard self-attention.
  - **Result:** Generates summaries with high fluency but sometimes misses nuanced relational context, especially in documents with complex structures.

Summary of Comparative Analysis

- **Unique Strengths of LangGraph LLM:**
  - Integration of graph-based reasoning for enhanced relational understanding.
  - Improved interpretability through explicit graph visualizations.
  - Optimized performance via modular design and advanced attention mechanisms.
- **Considerations for Other LLMs:**
  - Often achieve state-of-the-art performance on benchmark datasets using extensive transformer architectures.

- May require larger model sizes to capture context, which can increase computational demands.
- Interpretability can be limited due to their predominantly sequential processing.

By following this structured guide, developers and researchers can comprehensively assess the strengths and trade-offs of LangGraph LLM compared to other language models. This analysis not only informs the selection of the right model for a specific application but also highlights potential areas for further innovation and optimization in the design of future LLMs.

Chapter 4: Training and Fine-Tuning LangGraph LLM

4.1. Data Collection and Preprocessing

This section provides a comprehensive guide to the crucial first steps in training LangGraph LLM: collecting the right data and preprocessing it effectively. These steps are essential to ensure that the model learns from high-quality, representative examples and that the subsequent training process is both efficient and effective.

Objectives

- **Gather High-Quality Data:**
  Ensure that the dataset reflects the language, context, and diversity needed for the model's intended applications.
- **Clean and Standardize Input:**
  Remove noise and inconsistencies to provide a consistent learning base for the model.
- **Prepare Data for Embedding and Modeling:**
  Transform raw text into structured, numerical formats suitable for input into the model.

Step-by-Step Breakdown

1. Data Collection

- **Define Data Sources:**
  Identify and select a diverse set of sources that are relevant to the model's domain. Examples include:
  - **Text Corpora:** News articles, books, research papers.
  - **Web Scraping:** Curated content from reputable websites.
  - **Specialized Datasets:** Domain-specific datasets for tasks such as legal text analysis or medical records.
- **Ensure Diversity and Representativeness:**
  Collect data that captures a wide range of language styles, topics, and dialects. This helps the model generalize better and reduces the risk of bias.
- **Data Licensing and Ethics:**
  Verify that all collected data complies with legal and ethical

standards. Ensure proper licensing, data privacy, and consent where necessary.

2. Data Cleaning

- **Remove Noise and Redundancy:**
  Clean the dataset by eliminating irrelevant content such as advertisements, boilerplate text, or duplicate entries.
  - *Example:* Use regular expressions to filter out HTML tags or URLs from web-scraped data.
- **Standardize Text:**
  Normalize the text to a consistent format. This may include:
  - Converting text to lowercase.
  - Removing extraneous whitespace.
  - Correcting misspellings and punctuation errors.
- **Language Filtering:**
  If the model is intended for a specific language, filter out content in other languages to maintain consistency.

3. Preprocessing for Tokenization and Embedding

- **Tokenization:**
  Split the cleaned text into tokens (words or subwords).
  - *Example:* Use a tokenizer that implements Byte-Pair Encoding (BPE) to handle rare or compound words effectively.
- **Handling Special Tokens:**
  Identify and appropriately tag special tokens, such as:
  - Sentence delimiters.
  - Unknown tokens (tokens that do not appear in the vocabulary).
  - Padding tokens for batch processing.
- **Text Segmentation:**
  Divide long documents into manageable segments or sentences to improve the efficiency of training and downstream processing.

4. Data Augmentation (Optional)

- **Synthetic Data Generation:**
  In cases where data is scarce, consider augmenting the dataset by generating synthetic examples. Techniques include:
  - Paraphrasing sentences.

- Back-translation (translating text to another language and back to the original).
- **Balancing the Dataset:**
  Ensure that the data distribution is balanced across different classes or topics to prevent model bias.

Practical Workflow Example

Scenario: Preparing a dataset for training LangGraph LLM on news article summarization.

1. **Data Collection:**
   - **Sources:** Scrape reputable news websites and use existing news corpora.
   - **Diversity:** Ensure the dataset covers a variety of topics such as politics, technology, and health.
2. **Data Cleaning:**
   - **Noise Removal:** Use scripts to strip out advertisements, HTML tags, and duplicate articles.
   - **Standardization:** Convert all text to lowercase and normalize punctuation.
3. **Preprocessing:**
   - **Tokenization:** Apply a BPE-based tokenizer to the cleaned text.
   - **Segmentation:** Divide articles into individual sentences or paragraphs.
   - **Special Tokens:** Insert sentence boundary tokens where needed to help the model understand structure.
4. **Data Augmentation (Optional):**
   - Use paraphrasing tools to expand the dataset, especially for underrepresented topics.
   - Balance the dataset by ensuring each topic is proportionally represented.

Summary

- **Data Collection:**
  Identify diverse, high-quality sources while adhering to legal and ethical guidelines.
- **Data Cleaning:**
  Remove noise, standardize the text, and ensure consistency across the dataset.

- **Preprocessing:**
  Tokenize the text, handle special tokens, and segment long documents to prepare for embedding.
- **Optional Augmentation:**
  Generate synthetic data and balance the dataset to enhance the learning process.

Following these steps will provide a robust foundation for training LangGraph LLM, ensuring that the model has access to clean, well-structured, and representative data. This guidebook approach is designed to deliver clear, actionable insights that support both novice and experienced practitioners in preparing data effectively for large language model training.

4.1.1. Data Sources and Quality Considerations

This section is designed as a practical guide for selecting and evaluating data sources when preparing your dataset for training LangGraph LLM. By carefully choosing high-quality, diverse sources and following rigorous cleaning practices, you ensure that your model is built on a solid foundation. Below, we outline key steps and provide hands-on examples to illustrate each concept.

1. Identifying Data Sources

A. Text Corpora

- **Books and Literature:**
  Use open-source collections like Project Gutenberg.
  Example: Download classic novels for rich narrative styles.
- **News Articles:**
  Utilize established news datasets (e.g., Reuters, BBC).
  Example: Reuters Corpus can be accessed via academic channels.
- **Research Papers:**
  Explore repositories like arXiv or PubMed for technical and formal language content.

B. Web Scraping

- **Reputable Websites:**
  Scrape content from verified news sites or official blogs.
  Example: Use Python's `requests` and `BeautifulSoup` libraries to extract articles.

C. Specialized Datasets

- **Domain-Specific Data:**
  For legal, medical, or technical applications, source data from specialized repositories that meet your domain requirements.

2. Quality Considerations

A. Representativeness and Diversity:

- Ensure your dataset includes multiple perspectives, dialects, and topics.
- **Practical Tip:** Create a spreadsheet to log sources and check that no single category dominates your data.

B. Data Cleanliness:

- Remove irrelevant content (e.g., ads, HTML tags) and duplicates.
- **Hands-On Example:**

```python
 code
import re

def clean_text(text):
    # Remove HTML tags
    clean = re.compile('<.*?>')
    text = re.sub(clean, '', text)
    # Remove URLs
    text = re.sub(r'http\S+', '', text)
    # Normalize whitespace
    text = ' '.join(text.split())
    return text

sample_text = "<p>Check out our website: http://example.com</p>"
print("Cleaned Text:",
clean_text(sample_text))
```

C. Validity and Reliability:

- Prioritize data from credible, authoritative sources.

- **Practical Tip:** Use domain experts or pre-verified datasets when possible.

D. Ethical and Legal Compliance:

- Verify licensing terms and ensure data usage complies with privacy standards.
- **Practical Tip:** Maintain a document listing licensing details and consent information for each dataset.

Practical Workflow Example

Scenario: Preparing a dataset for training a news summarization module.

1. **Data Collection:**
   o **Sources:**
      - **Text Corpora:** Use a pre-existing news dataset like Reuters.
      - **Web Scraping:** Extract additional articles using BeautifulSoup:

```python
 code
import requests
from bs4 import BeautifulSoup

url = "https://www.example-news-
site.com/latest-news"
response = requests.get(url)
soup = BeautifulSoup(response.text,
'html.parser')

# Extract all paragraph text
articles = soup.find_all('p')
article_text = "
".join([para.get_text() for para in
articles])
print("Extracted Article:",
article_text)
```

   o **Diversity Check:** Ensure topics span politics, technology, health, etc.

2. **Data Cleaning:**
   o Remove HTML tags, advertisements, and boilerplate text using the `clean_text` function shown above.
   o Normalize text to lowercase, remove duplicates, and standardize punctuation.
3. **Quality Verification:**
   o **Manual Inspection:** Review a random sample of articles to ensure content quality.
   o **Automated Checks:** Write scripts to detect outliers in text length or unusual characters.
4. **Documentation:**
   o Keep records of each data source, including URL, publication date, and licensing information.

Summary

- **Data Sources:**
  Combine diverse sources such as books, news articles, research papers, and domain-specific repositories.
- **Quality Considerations:**
  Ensure data representativeness, cleanliness, and validity while complying with ethical and legal standards.
- **Practical Implementation:**
  Use Python scripts for cleaning and web scraping, and maintain thorough documentation of your data sources.

By following these practical, step-by-step guidelines and incorporating the hands-on examples, you can build a robust, high-quality dataset for training LangGraph LLM. This structured approach not only improves model performance but also ensures that your dataset is ethically sourced and representative of real-world language use.

4.1.2. Cleaning and Preparing Datasets

This section serves as a practical guide to cleaning and preparing your datasets for training LangGraph LLM. Proper data preparation is essential for model performance, ensuring that the text is clean, standardized, and ready for tokenization and embedding. The following steps outline a clear, actionable process with hands-on examples.

Objectives

- **Eliminate Noise:**
  Remove irrelevant or erroneous information that could mislead the model.
- **Standardize Format:**
  Ensure consistency in text formatting, punctuation, and case.
- **Prepare for Tokenization:**
  Transform the text into a format that facilitates effective tokenization and subsequent embedding.

Step-by-Step Breakdown

1. Remove Unwanted Content

- **HTML and Markup Removal:**
  Use regular expressions to strip out HTML tags and other markup elements.

  Example:

  python

  ```python
  import re

  def remove_html(text):
      html_pattern = re.compile('<.*?>')
      return re.sub(html_pattern, '', text)

  sample_text = "<div>Welcome to <b>LangGraph
  LLM</b> training!</div>"
  cleaned_text = remove_html(sample_text)
  print("After HTML Removal:", cleaned_text)
  ```

  Outcome: The output text no longer contains any HTML tags.

- **Eliminate URLs and Special Characters:**
  Filter out URLs and extraneous symbols that do not contribute to the language model's learning.

  Example:

  python

```python
def remove_urls(text):
    return re.sub(r'http\S+', '', text)

text_with_url = "Visit https://example.com for more info!"
cleaned_text = remove_urls(text_with_url)
print("After URL Removal:", cleaned_text)
```

Outcome: URLs are removed to focus on the core textual content.

2. Normalize and Standardize Text

- **Case Conversion:**
  Convert all text to lowercase to maintain uniformity.

  Example:

  python

  ```python
  def normalize_text(text):
      return text.lower()

  sample_text = "LangGraph LLM Is Revolutionary."
  normalized_text = normalize_text(sample_text)
  print("Normalized Text:", normalized_text)
  ```

  Outcome: All characters are converted to lowercase for consistency.

- **Whitespace and Punctuation:**
  Remove redundant whitespace and standardize punctuation.

  Example:

  python

  ```python
  def standardize_whitespace(text):
      return ' '.join(text.split())

  messy_text = "This    is    an    example sentence."
  ```

```python
standardized_text =
standardize_whitespace(messy_text)
print("Standardized Whitespace:",
standardized_text)
```

Outcome: Extra spaces are removed, resulting in a clean sentence.

3. Handle Special Cases

- **Remove Duplicate Entries:**
  Identify and eliminate duplicate sentences or documents.

  Example:

  python

  ```python
  def remove_duplicates(data_list):
      return list(set(data_list))

  texts = ["This is a sentence.", "This is a
  sentence.", "Another sentence."]
  unique_texts = remove_duplicates(texts)
  print("Unique Texts:", unique_texts)
  ```

  Outcome: Only unique texts remain for training.

- **Correct Common Errors:**
  Use spell-checking libraries (e.g., pyspellchecker) or custom dictionaries to correct misspellings.

  Example (Conceptual):

  python

  ```python
  from spellchecker import SpellChecker

  spell = SpellChecker()
  text = "Ths is an exmple of a splelling eror."
  corrected_text = "
  ".join([spell.correction(word) for word in
  text.split()])
  print("Corrected Text:", corrected_text)
  ```

Outcome: Common spelling errors are corrected, improving data quality.

4. Preparing Data for Tokenization

- **Text Segmentation:**
  Divide longer texts into sentences or paragraphs to facilitate effective tokenization.

  Example:

  python

  ```python
  import nltk
  nltk.download('punkt')
  from nltk.tokenize import sent_tokenize

  long_text = "LangGraph LLM is a powerful tool.
  It revolutionizes language processing. Prepare
  your data well."
  sentences = sent_tokenize(long_text)
  print("Sentences:", sentences)
  ```

  Outcome: The text is segmented into individual sentences for easier processing.

- **Handling Special Tokens:**
  Identify tokens for sentence boundaries, unknown words, or padding, ensuring consistency across the dataset.

  Practical Tip: Define a vocabulary that includes special tokens like [PAD], [UNK], [CLS], and [SEP] before tokenization begins.

Summary

- **Eliminate Noise:**
  Remove HTML, URLs, and extraneous characters using regular expressions.
- **Standardize Format:**
  Normalize text by converting to lowercase, standardizing punctuation, and removing extra whitespace.

- **Handle Special Cases:**
  Remove duplicates, correct errors, and segment text into manageable units.
- **Prepare for Tokenization:**
  Ensure that the data is segmented and special tokens are properly identified for effective embedding.

By following these hands-on steps and utilizing the provided code snippets, you can efficiently clean and prepare your dataset for training LangGraph LLM. This guidebook approach ensures that the input data is of high quality and uniformly formatted, paving the way for a more effective training process and ultimately leading to better model performance.

4.2. Training Methodologies

This section serves as a comprehensive guide on the various training methodologies used to develop LangGraph LLM. It covers the approaches for training large language models, including supervised, unsupervised, and reinforcement learning strategies, as well as the techniques used for distributed training and optimization. The following guide explains each methodology with clear steps and practical examples to help you implement these strategies effectively.

Objectives

- **Leverage Multiple Learning Paradigms:**
  Combine supervised, unsupervised, and reinforcement learning approaches to enhance model performance.
- **Efficiently Train on Large Datasets:**
  Utilize distributed training techniques to handle the scale and complexity of training data.
- **Optimize Training Processes:**
  Apply optimization strategies to balance speed, resource usage, and model accuracy.

Step-by-Step Breakdown

1. Supervised Learning

- **Purpose:**
  Train the model on labeled datasets where each input has an

associated output. This method is especially useful for tasks like classification, translation, or summarization.

- **Process:**
  - **Data Preparation:**
    Ensure that the dataset is clean and labeled correctly. For instance, in a translation task, each source sentence should have a corresponding target sentence.
  - **Loss Function:**
    Define a loss function (e.g., cross-entropy loss) that measures the difference between the model's predictions and the actual labels.
  - **Optimization:**
    Use gradient descent algorithms (like Adam or SGD) to minimize the loss over training iterations.
- **Practical Example:**
  Suppose you have a dataset for machine translation. In Python using PyTorch, a simplified training loop might look like:

```python
import torch
import torch.nn as nn
import torch.optim as optim

# Assume model, dataloader, and loss_fn are
predefined
optimizer = optim.Adam(model.parameters(),
lr=0.001)

for epoch in range(num_epochs):
    for batch in dataloader:
        inputs, targets = batch   # inputs:
source sentences, targets: target sentences
        optimizer.zero_grad()
        outputs = model(inputs)
        loss = loss_fn(outputs, targets)
        loss.backward()
        optimizer.step()
    print(f"Epoch {epoch+1}/{num_epochs},
Loss: {loss.item()}")
```

Outcome: The model learns to predict the correct translation by minimizing the loss.

2. Unsupervised Learning

- **Purpose:**
  Train the model using large amounts of unlabeled data to learn language patterns and structures. This is crucial for pre-training models to capture general language representations.
- **Process:**
  - **Pre-Training Objectives:**
    Use tasks such as Masked Language Modeling (MLM) or Next Sentence Prediction (NSP) to enable the model to learn contextual relationships.
  - **Data Utilization:**
    Leverage vast, unlabeled corpora to expose the model to diverse linguistic patterns.
- **Practical Example:**
  In an unsupervised setting, a transformer model might use MLM. Here's a conceptual code snippet:

```python
# Assume 'model' is a transformer and 'inputs'
are tokenized text with some tokens masked
outputs = model(inputs)
# loss_fn calculates loss only on the masked
tokens
loss = loss_fn(outputs, targets)
loss.backward()
optimizer.step()
```

Outcome: The model learns to predict missing words, thereby acquiring a broad understanding of language structure.

3. Reinforcement Learning

- **Purpose:**
  Fine-tune the model using feedback from its own outputs to improve performance in tasks where the quality of generated text matters (e.g., dialogue systems).
- **Process:**

- o **Reward Function:**
  Define a reward mechanism that quantifies the quality of the model's output. Rewards can be based on human feedback or automated metrics.
- o **Policy Optimization:**
  Use reinforcement learning algorithms such as Proximal Policy Optimization (PPO) to update the model based on the rewards received.
- **Practical Example:**
  In a dialogue generation task, the model's response might be evaluated by a reward function. A high-level pseudocode example is:

```python
# Generate a response using the current model
response = model.generate(input_text)
# Compute reward (this could be based on user
feedback or automated evaluation)
reward = compute_reward(response)
# Update model parameters using a
reinforcement learning algorithm (e.g., PPO)
loss = compute_rl_loss(response, reward)
loss.backward()
optimizer.step()
```

Outcome: The model learns to generate more appropriate and engaging responses based on reward signals.

4. Distributed Training and Optimization

- **Purpose:**
  Scale the training process across multiple GPUs or machines to handle large datasets and complex models efficiently.
- **Process:**
  - o **Data Parallelism:**
    Split the training data across multiple GPUs so that each processes a subset of the batch.
  - o **Model Parallelism:**
    Distribute different parts of the model across multiple devices, beneficial when the model is too large for a single GPU.

- o **Mixed Precision Training:**
  Use lower-precision arithmetic (e.g., FP16) to speed up training and reduce memory usage without sacrificing model accuracy.
- **Practical Example:**
  Using PyTorch's DistributedDataParallel:

```python
import torch
import torch.distributed as dist
from torch.nn.parallel import
DistributedDataParallel as DDP

# Initialize the process group
dist.init_process_group(backend='nccl')
model = model.to(device)
ddp_model = DDP(model)

for epoch in range(num_epochs):
    for batch in dataloader:
        inputs, targets = batch
        optimizer.zero_grad()
        outputs = ddp_model(inputs)
        loss = loss_fn(outputs, targets)
        loss.backward()
        optimizer.step()
```

Outcome: Training is accelerated by leveraging multiple GPUs, enabling the model to process larger batches and reduce training time.

Summary

- **Supervised Learning:**
  Train the model on labeled data using loss functions and optimization techniques.
- **Unsupervised Learning:**
  Pre-train the model on large unlabeled corpora using objectives like MLM to learn general language representations.

- **Reinforcement Learning:**
  Fine-tune the model using reward signals to improve the quality of generated outputs in interactive tasks.
- **Distributed Training:**
  Utilize data and model parallelism, along with mixed precision training, to efficiently scale the training process.

By following these step-by-step training methodologies, you can effectively train LangGraph LLM to achieve state-of-the-art performance across various language tasks. This guidebook-style approach ensures that each training method is clearly explained and practically demonstrated, providing actionable insights for both novice and experienced practitioners.

4.2.1. Supervised, Unsupervised, and Reinforcement Learning

This section serves as a comprehensive guide to the three primary learning paradigms used in training LangGraph LLM: supervised, unsupervised, and reinforcement learning. Each approach plays a unique role in building and refining the model's language capabilities. Below, we break down each method with clear steps, practical examples, and code snippets where applicable.

A. Supervised Learning

Purpose:
Train the model using labeled datasets where each input has a corresponding output. This is particularly effective for tasks such as translation, summarization, and classification.

Key Steps:

1. **Data Preparation:**
   - Ensure the dataset is clean and correctly labeled.
   - For a translation task, every source sentence should have an accurate target sentence.
2. **Loss Function:**
   - Define a loss function (e.g., cross-entropy loss) to quantify the difference between predicted outputs and actual labels.
3. **Optimization:**

- o Use gradient-based optimization methods (like Adam or SGD) to update model parameters and minimize the loss.

Practical Example (Python with PyTorch):

python

```
import torch
import torch.nn as nn
import torch.optim as optim

# Assume 'model' is a predefined LangGraph LLM
model and 'dataloader' is set up with source-target
pairs.
loss_fn = nn.CrossEntropyLoss()
optimizer = optim.Adam(model.parameters(),
lr=0.001)
num_epochs = 5

for epoch in range(num_epochs):
    for batch in dataloader:
        inputs, targets = batch   # inputs: source
text, targets: expected outputs
        optimizer.zero_grad()
        outputs = model(inputs)   # forward pass
        loss = loss_fn(outputs, targets)
        loss.backward()   # backpropagation
        optimizer.step()   # update weights
    print(f"Epoch {epoch+1}/{num_epochs}, Loss:
{loss.item():.4f}")
```

Outcome: The model gradually learns to produce accurate outputs by minimizing the loss between its predictions and the true labels.

B. Unsupervised Learning

Purpose:
Leverage large amounts of unlabeled data to learn general language representations. This pre-training phase is essential for capturing broad linguistic patterns.

Key Steps:

1. **Pre-Training Objectives:**
   - o Implement tasks such as Masked Language Modeling (MLM) or Next Sentence Prediction (NSP) to let the model learn contextual relationships.
2. **Data Utilization:**
   - o Use extensive unlabeled corpora to expose the model to a wide variety of language constructs.

Practical Example (Conceptual Code Snippet):

python

```
# Assume 'model' is a transformer-based component
of LangGraph LLM
# 'inputs' are tokenized text with certain tokens
masked, and 'targets' contain the correct tokens
for masked positions.
outputs = model(inputs)
loss = loss_fn(outputs, targets)  # loss computed
only for the masked tokens
loss.backward()
optimizer.step()
```

Outcome: The model learns to predict masked words, thereby developing a robust understanding of language context and structure without relying on explicit labels.

C. Reinforcement Learning

Purpose:
Fine-tune the model by optimizing it based on reward signals, particularly useful for tasks involving interactive dialogue or generative content where qualitative measures are important.

Key Steps:

1. **Define a Reward Function:**

o   Create a reward mechanism that evaluates the quality of the model's outputs. Rewards may be based on user feedback or automated quality metrics.

2. **Policy Optimization:**
   o   Apply reinforcement learning algorithms, such as Proximal Policy Optimization (PPO), to update the model in response to the rewards received.

Practical Example (High-Level Pseudocode):

python

```python
# Generate a response for a given input
response = model.generate(input_text)

# Compute reward based on the quality of the
response
reward = compute_reward(response)

# Compute reinforcement learning loss using a
policy gradient approach
rl_loss = compute_rl_loss(response, reward)

# Update model parameters based on the
reinforcement learning objective
rl_loss.backward()
optimizer.step()
```

Outcome: The model adjusts its behavior based on the reward feedback, gradually enhancing its ability to produce contextually appropriate and engaging outputs.

Summary

- **Supervised Learning:**
  Uses labeled data, defined loss functions, and gradient descent to guide the model in learning specific tasks.
- **Unsupervised Learning:**
  Pre-trains the model on unlabeled data using objectives like MLM, enabling it to grasp general language patterns.

- **Reinforcement Learning:**
  Fine-tunes the model by rewarding outputs that meet qualitative criteria, particularly useful for interactive and generative tasks.

By integrating these three learning paradigms, LangGraph LLM benefits from both a solid foundation in general language understanding and the ability to specialize in task-specific applications. This comprehensive guidebook approach ensures that each methodology is clearly explained and practically demonstrated, providing actionable insights for practitioners at all levels.

4.2.2. Distributed Training and Optimization

This section provides a clear, step-by-step guide for scaling the training of LangGraph LLM using distributed training and optimization techniques. By leveraging multiple GPUs or machines, you can significantly reduce training time and handle larger datasets and more complex models. Below are the objectives, key steps, practical examples, and a summary to help you implement distributed training effectively.

Objectives

- **Accelerate Training:**
  Utilize parallel processing across multiple GPUs or machines to reduce overall training time.
- **Handle Large Models:**
  Distribute the workload to manage models that are too large for a single device.
- **Optimize Resource Utilization:**
  Employ techniques such as mixed precision training and data/model parallelism to maximize computational efficiency.

Step-by-Step Breakdown

1. Data Parallelism

- **Purpose:**
  Split the training data across multiple GPUs so that each GPU processes a different subset of the data in parallel.
- **Key Steps:**

- o **Initialize Process Group:**
  Use a backend (e.g., NCCL for GPUs) to set up communication between processes.
- o **Wrap Model with DistributedDataParallel (DDP):**
  This PyTorch module synchronizes gradients and updates across all GPUs.
- o **Partition Data:**
  Use a DistributedSampler to ensure each GPU receives a unique portion of the dataset.

2. Model Parallelism

- **Purpose:**
  Split the model itself across multiple devices when it is too large to fit into the memory of a single GPU.
- **Key Steps:**
  - o **Partition the Model:**
    Divide the model into sub-components that can be allocated to different devices.
  - o **Manage Inter-Device Communication:**
    Ensure efficient data transfer between GPUs during forward and backward passes.

3. Mixed Precision Training

- **Purpose:**
  Use lower-precision arithmetic (e.g., FP16) to reduce memory usage and speed up computations while preserving model accuracy.
- **Key Steps:**
  - o **Implement AMP (Automatic Mixed Precision):**
    Use tools like NVIDIA's Apex or PyTorch's native AMP package.
  - o **Monitor Model Accuracy:**
    Validate that the reduced precision does not significantly impact the model's performance.

4. Practical Example: Distributed Data Parallel Training with PyTorch

Below is an example of setting up distributed training using PyTorch's DistributedDataParallel (DDP):

```python
import os
import torch
import torch.distributed as dist
import torch.nn as nn
import torch.optim as optim
from torch.nn.parallel import
DistributedDataParallel as DDP
from torch.utils.data import DataLoader,
DistributedSampler
from torchvision import datasets, transforms

def setup_distributed_training():
    # Initialize the process group for distributed
training
    dist.init_process_group(backend='nccl')
    local_rank = int(os.environ['LOCAL_RANK'])
    torch.cuda.set_device(local_rank)
    return local_rank

def cleanup():
    dist.destroy_process_group()

def main():
    local_rank = setup_distributed_training()

    # Define a simple model (for demonstration
purposes)
    model = nn.Sequential(
        nn.Linear(784, 512),
        nn.ReLU(),
        nn.Linear(512, 10)
    ).to(local_rank)

    # Wrap the model with DistributedDataParallel
    ddp_model = DDP(model, device_ids=[local_rank])

    # Prepare the dataset and DistributedSampler
```

```python
    transform =
transforms.Compose([transforms.ToTensor(),
transforms.Normalize((0.5,), (0.5,))])
    dataset = datasets.MNIST(root='./data',
train=True, download=True, transform=transform)
    sampler = DistributedSampler(dataset)
    dataloader = DataLoader(dataset, batch_size=64,
sampler=sampler)

    # Define loss function and optimizer
    loss_fn = nn.CrossEntropyLoss()
    optimizer = optim.Adam(ddp_model.parameters(),
lr=0.001)

    num_epochs = 3
    for epoch in range(num_epochs):
        sampler.set_epoch(epoch)   # Ensure
different shuffling in each epoch
        for batch_idx, (data, target) in
enumerate(dataloader):
            data, target = data.to(local_rank),
target.to(local_rank)
            optimizer.zero_grad()
            outputs =
ddp_model(data.view(data.size(0), -1))   # Flatten
MNIST images
            loss = loss_fn(outputs, target)
            loss.backward()
            optimizer.step()

            if batch_idx % 100 == 0:
                print(f"Epoch {epoch+1}, Batch
{batch_idx}, Loss: {loss.item():.4f}")

    cleanup()

if __name__ == "__main__":
    main()
```

Explanation:

- **Process Group Initialization:**
  The script initializes a distributed process group using NCCL, setting the correct GPU device for each process.
- **Model Wrapping:**
  The model is wrapped in `DistributedDataParallel`, ensuring that gradients are synchronized across GPUs.
- **Data Partitioning:**
  A `DistributedSampler` splits the MNIST dataset among the processes, so each GPU processes a unique subset.
- **Training Loop:**
  The model is trained over several epochs, with each process handling its portion of the data. Loss values are printed periodically for monitoring.

5. Additional Optimization Techniques

- **Hyperparameter Tuning:**
  Experiment with different learning rates, batch sizes, and number of epochs to find the optimal configuration for distributed training.
- **Monitoring and Profiling:**
  Use tools like NVIDIA's Nsight or PyTorch's built-in profiler to monitor GPU utilization and optimize bottlenecks.
- **Checkpointing:**
  Save intermediate models regularly to ensure progress is not lost in case of interruptions, and to facilitate fine-tuning later.

Summary

- **Data Parallelism:**
  Splits the training data across multiple GPUs, utilizing a DistributedSampler and wrapping the model in DDP.
- **Model Parallelism:**
  Distributes the model across devices if it exceeds a single GPU's capacity.
- **Mixed Precision Training:**
  Reduces memory usage and speeds up computation by leveraging lower-precision arithmetic.
- **Practical Implementation:**
  The provided code snippet demonstrates a working setup for

distributed training using PyTorch, which you can adapt and expand for your specific tasks.

By following these detailed steps and practical examples, you can effectively implement distributed training and optimization for LangGraph LLM. This guidebook approach ensures that the process is clear and actionable, helping you achieve faster, more efficient training on large-scale datasets and complex models.

4.3. Fine-Tuning Strategies

This section provides a step-by-step guide to fine-tuning LangGraph LLM for specific tasks and domains. Fine-tuning is the process of adapting a pre-trained model to a targeted application by training it further on a specialized dataset. This guide outlines various strategies, practical tips, and hands-on examples to help you optimize LangGraph LLM for your particular needs.

Objectives

- **Customize the Model:**
  Adapt the pre-trained model to a specific task (e.g., sentiment analysis, summarization, or dialogue generation) with minimal additional data.
- **Enhance Performance:**
  Improve model accuracy and relevance by focusing on domain-specific data and objectives.
- **Optimize Resource Usage:**
  Efficiently use training time and computational resources during the fine-tuning process.

Step-by-Step Breakdown

1. Preparing the Fine-Tuning Dataset

- **Select Domain-Specific Data:**
  Choose a dataset that closely matches the target application.
  Example: For a legal document summarization task, gather a corpus of legal texts and summaries.
- **Data Cleaning and Preprocessing:**
  Apply the same cleaning steps used during initial training—remove noise, normalize text, and tokenize—ensuring consistency.

- **Labeling and Annotation (if needed):**
  If fine-tuning on a supervised task, verify that labels are accurate and representative of the desired output.

2. Configuring the Fine-Tuning Process

- **Learning Rate Adjustments:**
  Often, a lower learning rate is used during fine-tuning to prevent large updates that might overwrite pre-trained knowledge.
- **Batch Size and Epochs:**
  Select a batch size and number of epochs that balance training speed with convergence.
  Tip: Start with a small number of epochs and monitor validation performance to avoid overfitting.
- **Optimizer Selection:**
  Use adaptive optimizers like Adam or AdamW that work well for fine-tuning tasks.

3. Fine-Tuning Strategies

- **Full Model Fine-Tuning:**
  Update all model parameters on the new dataset. This is useful when ample domain-specific data is available.
- **Partial Fine-Tuning:**
  Freeze lower layers (which capture general language features) and only fine-tune the upper layers or task-specific heads.
  Benefit: Reduces training time and prevents overfitting, particularly with limited data.
- **Adapter Modules:**
  Introduce small, trainable modules (adapters) between the pre-trained layers. These adapters learn task-specific adjustments without modifying the entire model.
  Advantage: Maintains the stability of the pre-trained model while enabling customization.
- **Multi-Task Fine-Tuning:**
  Fine-tune the model on several related tasks simultaneously to improve generalization and performance on a broader range of inputs.

4. Practical Example: Fine-Tuning for Sentiment Analysis

Below is a practical example of fine-tuning LangGraph LLM on a sentiment analysis dataset using PyTorch. In this example, we perform partial fine-tuning, freezing the lower layers and only training the final classification head.

python

```python
import torch
import torch.nn as nn
import torch.optim as optim
from torch.utils.data import DataLoader, Dataset

# Assume 'LangGraphLLM' is the pre-trained model
class and 'SentimentDataset' is a custom dataset
for sentiment analysis
class SentimentDataset(Dataset):
    def __init__(self, texts, labels, tokenizer,
max_length=128):
        self.texts = texts
        self.labels = labels
        self.tokenizer = tokenizer
        self.max_length = max_length

    def __len__(self):
        return len(self.texts)

    def __getitem__(self, idx):
        encoded = self.tokenizer(self.texts[idx],
max_length=self.max_length, padding='max_length',
truncation=True, return_tensors="pt")
        item = {key: encoded[key].squeeze(0) for
key in encoded}
        item['labels'] =
torch.tensor(self.labels[idx], dtype=torch.long)
        return item

# Load the pre-trained LangGraph LLM model
model = LangGraphLLM.from_pretrained("langgraph-
llm-base")
tokenizer = model.tokenizer

# Freeze lower layers (example: freeze first 10
layers)
```

```
for i, layer in
enumerate(model.transformer_layers):
    if i < 10:
        for param in layer.parameters():
            param.requires_grad = False

# Add a classification head for sentiment analysis
(if not already present)
model.classifier = nn.Linear(model.hidden_size, 2)
# Assuming binary sentiment classification

# Prepare the dataset and dataloader
train_dataset = SentimentDataset(train_texts,
train_labels, tokenizer)
train_dataloader = DataLoader(train_dataset,
batch_size=32, shuffle=True)

# Define loss function and optimizer
loss_fn = nn.CrossEntropyLoss()
optimizer = optim.AdamW(filter(lambda p:
p.requires_grad, model.parameters()), lr=2e-5)

# Fine-tuning loop
num_epochs = 3
model.train()
for epoch in range(num_epochs):
    for batch in train_dataloader:
        optimizer.zero_grad()
        outputs =
model(input_ids=batch['input_ids'],

attention_mask=batch['attention_mask'])
        logits = model.classifier(outputs)
        loss = loss_fn(logits, batch['labels'])
        loss.backward()
        optimizer.step()
    print(f"Epoch {epoch+1}/{num_epochs}, Loss:
{loss.item():.4f}")
```

Outcome:
The model adapts its higher-level representations for sentiment analysis
while preserving general language knowledge in the frozen lower layers.

5. Monitoring and Evaluation

- **Validation:**
  Regularly evaluate performance on a validation set to monitor overfitting and adjust hyperparameters as needed.
- **Learning Rate Scheduling:**
  Optionally employ learning rate schedulers to gradually reduce the learning rate as fine-tuning progresses.
- **Early Stopping:**
  Consider early stopping strategies if the model's performance on the validation set stops improving.

Summary

- **Dataset Preparation:**
  Select and preprocess domain-specific data.
- **Process Configuration:**
  Adjust learning rates, batch sizes, and optimizer settings for fine-tuning.
- **Fine-Tuning Strategies:**
  Choose between full fine-tuning, partial fine-tuning, adapter modules, or multi-task approaches based on data availability and task requirements.
- **Practical Implementation:**
  The provided code example demonstrates partial fine-tuning for a sentiment analysis task.
- **Monitoring:**
  Continuously evaluate model performance and adjust strategies as needed.

By following these structured fine-tuning strategies and practical examples, you can effectively customize LangGraph LLM for your specific applications, ensuring optimal performance and efficient resource use. This guidebook approach offers clear, actionable insights for practitioners at all levels.

4.3.1. Transfer Learning and Domain Adaptation

This section offers a clear, step-by-step guide to leveraging transfer learning and domain adaptation for fine-tuning LangGraph LLM on specialized tasks. Transfer learning allows you to build on a model's pre-trained knowledge, while domain adaptation tailors that knowledge to specific domains or applications. Below, we outline practical strategies, actionable steps, and provide hands-on examples to help you effectively implement these techniques.

Objectives

- **Leverage Pre-Trained Knowledge:**
  Utilize the strengths of a pre-trained LangGraph LLM model to reduce training time and improve performance on domain-specific tasks.
- **Adapt to Specialized Domains:**
  Fine-tune the model to work effectively with domain-specific language, jargon, and data patterns.
- **Optimize Resource Usage:**
  Achieve high performance even with limited domain-specific data by efficiently adapting pre-trained weights.

Step-by-Step Breakdown

1. Model Initialization

- **Start with a Pre-Trained Model:**
  Load a pre-trained version of LangGraph LLM that has been trained on general language data. This model serves as your starting point.
- **Assess Compatibility:**
  Verify that the pre-trained model's architecture and vocabulary are suitable for your target domain.
  Practical Tip: Check if the model covers key domain-specific terms.

2. Fine-Tuning Strategy

- **Full vs. Partial Fine-Tuning:**
  - *Full Fine-Tuning:* Update all model parameters on your domain-specific dataset.
  - *Partial Fine-Tuning:* Freeze lower layers that capture general language features and update only higher layers or the task-specific head.
    Recommendation: With limited domain data, partial fine-tuning often yields better generalization.
- **Adapter Modules:**
  Optionally, insert small adapter modules between existing layers to learn domain-specific features without modifying the entire model.

3. Domain Adaptation Techniques

- **Data Collection:**
  Gather a representative dataset from your target domain, such as medical reports, legal documents, or technical articles.
- **Data Preprocessing:**
  Clean and prepare the domain-specific dataset, ensuring consistency with the pre-trained model's input format.
- **Gradual Unfreezing:**
  Consider gradually unfreezing layers from the top down during training. This strategy helps maintain the stability of pre-trained representations while adapting to new data.
- **Learning Rate Scheduling:**
  Use a lower learning rate during fine-tuning to make subtle updates to the pre-trained weights, preventing overfitting to the new domain.

4. Practical Example: Domain Adaptation for Medical Text Summarization

Below is a practical example using PyTorch to adapt LangGraph LLM for summarizing medical texts.

python

```
import torch
import torch.nn as nn
import torch.optim as optim
from torch.utils.data import DataLoader, Dataset

# Assume LangGraphLLM is a pre-trained model with a
compatible tokenizer.
from langgraph_llm import LangGraphLLM

# Custom dataset for medical text summarization
class MedicalSummaryDataset(Dataset):
    def __init__(self, texts, summaries, tokenizer,
max_length=256):
        self.texts = texts
        self.summaries = summaries
        self.tokenizer = tokenizer
        self.max_length = max_length
```

```python
    def __len__(self):
        return len(self.texts)

    def __getitem__(self, idx):
        text = self.texts[idx]
        summary = self.summaries[idx]
        encoded_text = self.tokenizer(text,
max_length=self.max_length, padding='max_length',
truncation=True, return_tensors="pt")
        encoded_summary = self.tokenizer(summary,
max_length=self.max_length, padding='max_length',
truncation=True, return_tensors="pt")
        item = {
            'input_ids':
encoded_text['input_ids'].squeeze(0),
            'attention_mask':
encoded_text['attention_mask'].squeeze(0),
            'labels':
encoded_summary['input_ids'].squeeze(0)
        }
        return item

# Load the pre-trained LangGraph LLM model
model = LangGraphLLM.from_pretrained("langgraph-
llm-base")
tokenizer = model.tokenizer

# Freeze lower layers for partial fine-tuning
(example: freeze first 8 transformer layers)
for i, layer in
enumerate(model.transformer_layers):
    if i < 8:
        for param in layer.parameters():
            param.requires_grad = False

# Create a DataLoader for your domain-specific
dataset
train_dataset = MedicalSummaryDataset(train_texts,
train_summaries, tokenizer)
train_dataloader = DataLoader(train_dataset,
batch_size=16, shuffle=True)
```

```python
# Define the loss function and optimizer
loss_fn =
nn.CrossEntropyLoss(ignore_index=tokenizer.pad_toke
n_id)
optimizer = optim.AdamW(filter(lambda p:
p.requires_grad, model.parameters()), lr=2e-5)

# Fine-tuning loop with gradual unfreezing
(simplified)
num_epochs = 3
model.train()
for epoch in range(num_epochs):
    for batch in train_dataloader:
        optimizer.zero_grad()
        outputs =
model(input_ids=batch['input_ids'],
attention_mask=batch['attention_mask'])
        # Assume outputs are logits for each token
        loss = loss_fn(outputs.view(-1,
outputs.size(-1)), batch['labels'].view(-1))
        loss.backward()
        optimizer.step()
    print(f"Epoch {epoch+1}/{num_epochs}, Loss:
{loss.item():.4f}")

    # Optional: Gradually unfreeze one additional
layer per epoch
    if epoch < len(model.transformer_layers):
        for param in
model.transformer_layers[epoch].parameters():
            param.requires_grad = True
```

Outcome:
In this example, the pre-trained LangGraph LLM is fine-tuned for the task of medical text summarization. By freezing the lower layers and gradually unfreezing additional layers, the model adapts to domain-specific language while preserving its general language understanding.

Summary

- **Leverage Pre-Trained Models:**
  Begin with a well-trained LangGraph LLM and evaluate its suitability for your domain.
- **Choose a Fine-Tuning Strategy:**
  Decide between full fine-tuning, partial fine-tuning, or using adapter modules, based on your data volume and task requirements.
- **Adapt to the Domain:**
  Collect and preprocess domain-specific data, and consider gradual unfreezing and learning rate scheduling to maintain stability.
- **Implement and Monitor:**
  Fine-tune using a clear training loop, monitor performance on validation data, and adjust hyperparameters as needed.

By following these structured steps and practical examples, you can effectively apply transfer learning and domain adaptation to LangGraph LLM. This guidebook approach ensures that even with limited domain-specific data, you can achieve high performance and tailor the model to meet specialized needs.

4.3.2. Hyperparameter Optimization

This section provides a clear, step-by-step guide to hyperparameter optimization for fine-tuning LangGraph LLM. Hyperparameters—such as learning rate, batch size, and number of epochs—are crucial settings that affect model performance. Optimizing these parameters helps you achieve better accuracy, faster convergence, and more efficient resource usage.

Objectives

- **Improve Model Performance:**
  Identify the optimal hyperparameters that lead to the best validation accuracy and generalization.
- **Accelerate Training:**
  Adjust settings to reduce training time while ensuring model stability.
- **Efficient Resource Utilization:**
  Optimize parameters to achieve a balance between computational cost and performance.

Step-by-Step Breakdown

1. Identify Key Hyperparameters

- **Learning Rate:**
  Controls the magnitude of weight updates during training.
- **Batch Size:**
  Determines how many samples are processed simultaneously.
- **Number of Epochs:**
  Specifies how many times the entire dataset is used during training.
- **Optimizer Parameters:**
  Settings for optimizers (e.g., AdamW's weight decay, beta values).
- **Dropout Rate:**
  Helps prevent overfitting by randomly deactivating neurons during training.

2. Choose an Optimization Strategy

- **Grid Search:**
  Define a range of values for each hyperparameter and evaluate every possible combination.
- **Random Search:**
  Randomly sample hyperparameter combinations from predefined distributions.
- **Bayesian Optimization:**
  Use probabilistic models to intelligently explore the hyperparameter space and converge on optimal values faster.

3. Implementing Hyperparameter Optimization

A. Grid Search Example

Below is a simple example using Python with PyTorch to perform a grid search over learning rate and batch size:

```python

import torch
import torch.nn as nn
import torch.optim as optim
from torch.utils.data import DataLoader
from itertools import product

# Hypothetical dataset and model
```

```python
# Assume train_dataset is pre-defined and
model_class is LangGraphLLM class
learning_rates = [1e-5, 2e-5, 5e-5]
batch_sizes = [16, 32]
num_epochs = 3

def train_model(model, dataloader, optimizer,
num_epochs):
    model.train()
    loss_fn =
nn.CrossEntropyLoss(ignore_index=tokenizer.pad_toke
n_id)
    for epoch in range(num_epochs):
        for batch in dataloader:
            optimizer.zero_grad()
            outputs =
model(input_ids=batch['input_ids'],
attention_mask=batch['attention_mask'])
            loss = loss_fn(outputs.view(-1,
outputs.size(-1)), batch['labels'].view(-1))
            loss.backward()
            optimizer.step()
    return loss.item()

best_loss = float('inf')
best_params = {}

for lr, bs in product(learning_rates, batch_sizes):
    print(f"Training with learning rate: {lr},
batch size: {bs}")
    dataloader = DataLoader(train_dataset,
batch_size=bs, shuffle=True)
    model =
LangGraphLLM.from_pretrained("langgraph-llm-base")
# Reset model
    optimizer = optim.AdamW(model.parameters(),
lr=lr)
    loss = train_model(model, dataloader,
optimizer, num_epochs)
    print(f"Resulting Loss: {loss:.4f}")
    if loss < best_loss:
        best_loss = loss
```

```
        best_params = {'learning_rate': lr,
'batch_size': bs}

print("Best Hyperparameters:", best_params, "with
Loss:", best_loss)
```

Outcome:
This grid search evaluates various combinations of learning rate and batch size, allowing you to choose the combination that results in the lowest training loss.

B. Random Search and Bayesian Optimization

For more complex or larger hyperparameter spaces, consider using libraries like Optuna or Ray Tune that support random search and Bayesian optimization:

```python
import optuna

def objective(trial):
    lr = trial.suggest_loguniform('learning_rate',
1e-6, 1e-4)
    bs = trial.suggest_categorical('batch_size',
[16, 32, 64])

    dataloader = DataLoader(train_dataset,
batch_size=bs, shuffle=True)
    model =
LangGraphLLM.from_pretrained("langgraph-llm-base")
    optimizer = optim.AdamW(model.parameters(),
lr=lr)

    loss = train_model(model, dataloader,
optimizer, num_epochs)
    return loss

study = optuna.create_study(direction='minimize')
study.optimize(objective, n_trials=20)

print("Best hyperparameters:", study.best_params)
```

Outcome:
This approach automatically explores the hyperparameter space and converges to optimal settings using Bayesian methods.

4. Evaluate and Monitor

- **Validation Set:**
  Always monitor model performance on a separate validation set to avoid overfitting to the training data.
- **Learning Curves:**
  Plot training and validation loss over epochs to visually assess convergence and stability.
- **Hyperparameter Tuning Logs:**
  Keep detailed logs of experiments, hyperparameters, and outcomes for reproducibility and further analysis.

Summary

- **Identify Key Hyperparameters:**
  Focus on learning rate, batch size, number of epochs, and optimizer settings.
- **Optimization Strategies:**
  Utilize grid search, random search, or Bayesian optimization to explore the hyperparameter space.
- **Practical Implementation:**
  Use code examples to run experiments, monitor performance, and select the best hyperparameters.
- **Evaluate:**
  Validate results on a dedicated validation set and analyze learning curves to ensure effective tuning.

By following these detailed steps and leveraging practical examples, you can systematically optimize the hyperparameters for LangGraph LLM. This guidebook approach ensures that the tuning process is clear, actionable, and reproducible, enabling you to achieve the best performance for your specific applications.

4.4. Overcoming Common Training Challenges

Training large language models like LangGraph LLM comes with a variety of challenges that can impact performance, convergence, and overall model quality. In this section, we provide a guidebook-style approach to addressing these issues, with practical tips and hands-on examples to help you navigate and overcome common training hurdles.

Objectives

- **Identify and Mitigate Training Issues:**
  Understand the common pitfalls during training and apply strategies to resolve them.
- **Ensure Stable and Efficient Training:**
  Improve convergence, prevent overfitting, and manage computational resources effectively.
- **Enhance Model Robustness:**
  Develop practices that lead to a more reliable and generalizable model.

Step-by-Step Strategies

1. Preventing Overfitting

- **Regularization Techniques:**
  Use dropout layers, weight decay, or early stopping to avoid overfitting.
  - *Example:*
    In PyTorch, add a dropout layer in your model architecture:

```python
import torch.nn as nn

class ExampleModel(nn.Module):
    def __init__(self, input_dim, hidden_dim, output_dim):
        super(ExampleModel, self).__init__()
        self.fc1 = nn.Linear(input_dim, hidden_dim)
```

```python
        self.dropout = nn.Dropout(p=0.5)
# 50% dropout
        self.fc2 = nn.Linear(hidden_dim,
output_dim)

    def forward(self, x):
        x = torch.relu(self.fc1(x))
        x = self.dropout(x)
        x = self.fc2(x)
        return x
```

- o **Early Stopping:**
  Monitor the validation loss and stop training when it begins to increase.
- **Data Augmentation:**
  Increase data variability by applying transformations or generating synthetic examples.

2. Stabilizing the Learning Rate

- **Learning Rate Scheduling:**
  Reduce the learning rate gradually during training using schedulers.
  - o *Example:*

```python
python

from torch.optim.lr_scheduler import
StepLR

optimizer =
optim.AdamW(model.parameters(), lr=2e-5)
scheduler = StepLR(optimizer,
step_size=2, gamma=0.5)   # Halve the LR
every 2 epochs

for epoch in range(num_epochs):
    for batch in dataloader:
        optimizer.zero_grad()
```

```
        outputs =
model(batch['input_ids'],
attention_mask=batch['attention_mask'])
        loss = loss_fn(outputs.view(-1,
outputs.size(-1)), batch['labels'].view(-
1))
        loss.backward()
        optimizer.step()
    scheduler.step()  # Update learning
rate
    print(f"Epoch {epoch+1}, Loss:
{loss.item():.4f}, LR:
{scheduler.get_last_lr()[0]}")
```

- **Warm-Up Period:**
  Begin training with a lower learning rate and gradually increase it
  during the initial steps.

3. Handling Vanishing/Exploding Gradients

- **Gradient Clipping:**
  Limit the gradients to prevent them from becoming too large.
  - *Example:*

  ```
  python
  ```

  ```
  torch.nn.utils.clip_grad_norm_(model.para
  meters(), max_norm=1.0)
  ```

- **Proper Weight Initialization:**
  Use initialization methods (e.g., Xavier or He initialization) that
  maintain gradient flow.

4. Managing Computational Resources

- **Mixed Precision Training:**
  Use FP16 precision to speed up training and reduce memory usage.
  - *Example with PyTorch AMP:*

  ```
  python
  ```

```python
from torch.cuda.amp import autocast,
GradScaler

scaler = GradScaler()

for epoch in range(num_epochs):
    for batch in dataloader:
        optimizer.zero_grad()
        with autocast():
            outputs =
model(batch['input_ids'],
attention_mask=batch['attention_mask'])
            loss = loss_fn(outputs.view(-
1, outputs.size(-1)),
batch['labels'].view(-1))
        scaler.scale(loss).backward()
        scaler.step(optimizer)
        scaler.update()
```

- **Efficient Batch Processing:**
  Use appropriate batch sizes to balance GPU memory usage and training speed.

5. Debugging Distributed Training

- **Synchronize Gradients:**
  Ensure that gradients are correctly synchronized across GPUs using frameworks like PyTorch's DistributedDataParallel (DDP).
- **Monitor Inter-GPU Communication:**
  Use profiling tools (e.g., NVIDIA Nsight) to detect bottlenecks in communication.
- **Log and Visualize:**
  Implement logging of training metrics and use visualization tools (e.g., TensorBoard) to monitor the training process across devices.

6. Addressing Data-Related Challenges

- **Data Imbalance:**
  If certain classes or topics are underrepresented, consider oversampling or using class-weighted loss functions.

- **Noisy Data:**
  Enhance data cleaning processes to remove or correct mislabeled or irrelevant data points.
- **Consistent Preprocessing:**
  Ensure that the data preprocessing pipeline is consistently applied to both training and validation datasets.

Summary

- **Overfitting Prevention:**
  Use dropout, early stopping, and data augmentation to ensure the model generalizes well.
- **Learning Rate Stabilization:**
  Employ learning rate schedulers, warm-up strategies, and gradient clipping to maintain steady training progress.
- **Resource Management:**
  Leverage mixed precision training and efficient batch processing to optimize computational resources.
- **Distributed Training Debugging:**
  Ensure synchronization and monitor inter-device communication for efficient distributed training.
- **Data Quality Assurance:**
  Address data imbalance and noise through careful preprocessing and augmentation.

By applying these step-by-step strategies and practical examples, you can effectively overcome common training challenges in LangGraph LLM. This guidebook approach is designed to provide actionable insights, ensuring a stable, efficient, and high-performing training process for your language model.

4.5. Case Studies in Training Efficiency

This section provides real-world examples that illustrate how various training strategies and optimizations have been applied to improve training efficiency for LangGraph LLM. These case studies highlight practical challenges and solutions, offering actionable insights for practitioners.

Case Study 1: Accelerating Training with Distributed Data Parallelism

Objective:
Reduce training time for a large-scale translation task by distributing the workload across multiple GPUs.

Approach and Implementation:

1. **Problem Identification:**
   Training on a massive translation dataset was taking several days on a single GPU, leading to delayed iterations and resource bottlenecks.
2. **Solution Strategy:**
   o **Data Parallelism:**
      Split the dataset among multiple GPUs using PyTorch's DistributedDataParallel (DDP) framework.
   o **Implementation:**
      Set up a distributed training environment where each GPU processes a unique subset of the data and synchronizes gradients after each batch.
3. **Key Steps:**
   o Initialize the process group using NCCL.
   o Wrap the LangGraph LLM model with DDP.
   o Use a DistributedSampler to ensure each GPU receives a distinct data slice.
   o Monitor training progress with logging and visualization tools like TensorBoard.
4. **Outcome:**
   Training time was reduced by approximately 70%, allowing faster experimentation and model iterations. This case demonstrates the value of distributed training for scaling efficiency.

Practical Example Code Snippet:

```python
python

import os
import torch
import torch.distributed as dist
from torch.nn.parallel import
DistributedDataParallel as DDP
from torch.utils.data import DataLoader,
DistributedSampler

def setup_distributed():
```

```
    dist.init_process_group(backend='nccl')
    local_rank = int(os.environ['LOCAL_RANK'])
    torch.cuda.set_device(local_rank)
    return local_rank

local_rank = setup_distributed()
model = LangGraphLLM.from_pretrained("langgraph-
llm-base").to(local_rank)
ddp_model = DDP(model, device_ids=[local_rank])
# Assume train_dataset is defined
sampler = DistributedSampler(train_dataset)
dataloader = DataLoader(train_dataset,
batch_size=32, sampler=sampler)
# Training loop proceeds as described in previous
examples...
```

Case Study 2: Enhancing Convergence with Learning Rate Warm-Up and Scheduling

Objective:
Improve model convergence and stability during fine-tuning on a domain-specific summarization task.

Approach and Implementation:

1. **Problem Identification:**
   Fine-tuning a pre-trained model on a small domain-specific dataset resulted in unstable training, with high variance in loss values and occasional divergence.
2. **Solution Strategy:**
   o **Warm-Up Period:**
     Start training with a low learning rate to allow the model to adjust gradually.
   o **Learning Rate Scheduler:**
     Gradually increase the learning rate during the warm-up period, then decay it using a scheduler such as StepLR or Cosine Annealing.
3. **Key Steps:**
   o Implement an initial warm-up phase for the first few epochs.
   o Use a learning rate scheduler to adjust the learning rate dynamically based on epoch count.

o   Monitor learning curves to ensure steady convergence.

4. **Outcome:**

The training loss stabilized, and convergence was achieved in fewer epochs, enhancing overall efficiency. This approach helped avoid early divergence and improved final performance.

Practical Example Code Snippet:

```python
from torch.optim.lr_scheduler import
CosineAnnealingLR

optimizer = optim.AdamW(model.parameters(), lr=1e-
5)
# Warm-up: gradually increase learning rate over
first 1000 steps (conceptual)
for step in range(1000):
    lr = 1e-5 * (step / 1000)
    for param_group in optimizer.param_groups:
        param_group['lr'] = lr

scheduler = CosineAnnealingLR(optimizer, T_max=10)
# T_max in epochs
for epoch in range(num_epochs):
    for batch in dataloader:
        optimizer.zero_grad()
        outputs = model(batch['input_ids'],
attention_mask=batch['attention_mask'])
        loss = loss_fn(outputs.view(-1,
outputs.size(-1)), batch['labels'].view(-1))
        loss.backward()
        optimizer.step()
    scheduler.step()
    print(f"Epoch {epoch+1}, Loss:
{loss.item():.4f}, LR:
{scheduler.get_last_lr()[0]:.8f}")
```

Case Study 3: Reducing Memory Footprint with Mixed Precision Training

Objective:
Decrease GPU memory usage and accelerate training without compromising model accuracy during pre-training.

Approach and Implementation:

1. **Problem Identification:**
   Training LangGraph LLM on large datasets was limited by GPU memory constraints, slowing down training and reducing batch sizes.
2. **Solution Strategy:**
   o **Mixed Precision Training:**
     Utilize FP16 precision with PyTorch's Automatic Mixed Precision (AMP) to reduce memory usage and increase computational throughput.
3. **Key Steps:**
   o Integrate AMP into the training loop.
   o Use a GradScaler to manage dynamic loss scaling.
   o Validate that training with mixed precision produces comparable accuracy to full precision.
4. **Outcome:**
   Memory usage was reduced by nearly 50%, allowing larger batch sizes and faster training iterations while maintaining model accuracy. This efficiency gain enabled the use of more complex models and larger datasets.

Practical Example Code Snippet:

```python
from torch.cuda.amp import autocast, GradScaler

scaler = GradScaler()
for epoch in range(num_epochs):
    for batch in dataloader:
        optimizer.zero_grad()
        with autocast():
            outputs = model(batch['input_ids'],
attention_mask=batch['attention_mask'])
            loss = loss_fn(outputs.view(-1,
outputs.size(-1)), batch['labels'].view(-1))
        scaler.scale(loss).backward()
        scaler.step(optimizer)
```

```
    scaler.update()
    print(f"Epoch {epoch+1}, Loss:
{loss.item():.4f}")
```

Summary

- **Distributed Data Parallelism:**
  Significantly reduces training time by dividing data among multiple GPUs.
- **Learning Rate Strategies:**
  Warm-up periods and dynamic learning rate scheduling lead to stable and faster convergence.
- **Mixed Precision Training:**
  Optimizes memory usage and computational speed, enabling larger batch sizes and complex models.

These case studies demonstrate practical solutions to common training challenges, providing actionable strategies that can be applied to optimize LangGraph LLM's training efficiency. By following these guidebook-style examples, practitioners can adapt similar methods to their own training environments, leading to faster, more efficient, and scalable language model development.

Chapter 5: Practical Applications and Implementations

5.1. Industry Applications of LangGraph LLM

This section serves as a practical guide to understanding how LangGraph LLM can be applied across various industries. By leveraging its advanced language understanding and graph-based reasoning capabilities, LangGraph LLM opens up new opportunities for innovation in multiple sectors. Below is a structured breakdown of industry applications, accompanied by concrete examples and actionable insights.

Objectives

- **Demonstrate Versatility:**
  Illustrate how LangGraph LLM can be adapted for diverse industry needs.
- **Highlight Practical Use Cases:**
  Provide real-world examples and step-by-step scenarios to show the model's impact.
- **Guide Implementation:**
  Offer actionable recommendations for integrating LangGraph LLM into existing systems and workflows.

Step-by-Step Industry Applications

1. Healthcare

- **Clinical Documentation and Summarization:**
  - **Application:** Automate the summarization of patient records, clinical notes, and research articles.
  - **Practical Benefit:** Reduces administrative burden on healthcare professionals and speeds up information retrieval.
  - **Example:** LangGraph LLM can be fine-tuned to extract key clinical insights from electronic health records (EHRs), generating concise summaries for rapid review by medical staff.

- **Medical Question Answering Systems:**
  - **Application:** Develop systems that provide accurate, context-aware responses to clinical queries.
  - **Practical Benefit:** Enhances decision-making by providing clinicians with quick access to relevant medical literature and treatment guidelines.
  - **Example:** A chatbot powered by LangGraph LLM can help doctors find answers to questions about drug interactions or diagnostic criteria by leveraging both sequential and relational data from medical texts.

2. Finance

- **Market Analysis and Trend Summarization:**
  - **Application:** Automate the summarization of financial reports, news articles, and market trends.

- **Practical Benefit:** Allows financial analysts to quickly grasp market sentiments and make informed decisions.
- **Example:** Fine-tune LangGraph LLM to analyze earnings calls transcripts and generate summary reports that highlight critical financial indicators and market trends.
- **Customer Service and Chatbots:**
  - **Application:** Develop intelligent customer support systems for banking and financial services.
  - **Practical Benefit:** Improves customer satisfaction by providing timely and accurate responses.
  - **Example:** A chatbot using LangGraph LLM can handle common queries about account balances, transaction details, and product information, while also escalating complex issues to human agents.

3. Legal

- **Document Analysis and Contract Review:**
  - **Application:** Automate the extraction of key clauses and terms from lengthy legal documents.
  - **Practical Benefit:** Reduces manual review time and minimizes the risk of oversight.
  - **Example:** LangGraph LLM can be fine-tuned to analyze contracts, identify risk factors, and generate summaries that highlight important legal obligations and rights.
- **Legal Research:**
  - **Application:** Assist in finding precedents and relevant case law based on legal queries.
  - **Practical Benefit:** Enhances the efficiency of legal research and supports faster case preparation.
  - **Example:** An application built on LangGraph LLM can provide lawyers with summaries of similar cases, including the reasoning behind judgments and key legal arguments.

4. Technology and Software Development

- **Code Documentation and Generation:**
  - **Application:** Automatically generate documentation for software projects and assist with code completion.
  - **Practical Benefit:** Increases developer productivity and ensures up-to-date documentation.

- **Example:** LangGraph LLM can be integrated into IDEs to provide context-aware code suggestions and generate explanations for complex code segments.
- **Customer Support for Tech Products:**
  - **Application:** Build AI-driven support systems to resolve technical issues and answer product-related questions.
  - **Practical Benefit:** Enhances user experience by reducing the time to resolution.
  - **Example:** A support chatbot can use LangGraph LLM to parse technical queries and provide detailed, step-by-step troubleshooting instructions.

5. Marketing and Media

- **Content Generation and Personalization:**
  - **Application:** Create tailored content for marketing campaigns, social media, and blog posts.
  - **Practical Benefit:** Increases engagement by delivering content that resonates with target audiences.
  - **Example:** Fine-tune LangGraph LLM to generate product descriptions, social media posts, or personalized newsletters that align with brand voice and current trends.
- **Sentiment Analysis and Brand Monitoring:**
  - **Application:** Analyze customer reviews, social media mentions, and public sentiment.
  - **Practical Benefit:** Helps companies monitor brand reputation and quickly respond to negative feedback.
  - **Example:** LangGraph LLM can be deployed to scan and summarize vast amounts of user-generated content, providing insights into public sentiment and emerging issues.

Summary

- **Healthcare:**
  Automate clinical documentation, summarization, and question answering to support medical decision-making.
- **Finance:**
  Enhance market analysis, trend summarization, and customer service through automated report generation and intelligent chatbots.
- **Legal:**
  Streamline document analysis, contract review, and legal research to reduce manual workload and increase accuracy.

- **Technology:**
  Boost developer productivity with automated code documentation, generation, and efficient customer support systems.
- **Marketing:**
  Personalize content creation and perform sentiment analysis to improve engagement and brand monitoring.

By leveraging these practical examples and step-by-step implementations, LangGraph LLM can be adapted to meet the unique needs of various industries. This guidebook approach provides actionable insights that enable organizations to harness advanced language understanding and graph-based reasoning, driving innovation and efficiency across their operations.

5.1.1. Healthcare, Finance, and Beyond

This section offers a guidebook-style overview of how LangGraph LLM can be applied in key industries such as healthcare and finance—and extend to other sectors. We detail practical use cases, implementation tips, and real-world examples to demonstrate the model's versatility.

Healthcare Applications

- **Clinical Documentation and Summarization:**
  - o **Objective:** Automate the summarization of electronic health records (EHRs), clinical notes, and research articles.
  - o **Practical Implementation:**
    Fine-tune LangGraph LLM on a corpus of clinical texts to extract key medical information, such as patient history, diagnosis, and treatment plans.
  - o **Example Use Case:**
    A hospital implements a system that automatically generates concise summaries of patient visits, reducing the administrative burden on clinicians and speeding up patient care.
- **Medical Question Answering:**
  - o **Objective:** Provide accurate, context-aware responses to clinical queries.
  - o **Practical Implementation:**
    Integrate LangGraph LLM into a chatbot platform to allow clinicians to ask questions about drug interactions, treatment guidelines, or diagnostic criteria.

- o **Example Use Case:**
  A virtual assistant for doctors that references medical literature and clinical guidelines to deliver timely and relevant answers during busy shifts.

Finance Applications

- **Market Analysis and Trend Summarization:**
  - o **Objective:** Streamline the process of analyzing financial reports, market trends, and news articles.
  - o **Practical Implementation:**
    Fine-tune LangGraph LLM on financial data to automatically generate summaries of earnings calls, stock market trends, or economic indicators.
  - o **Example Use Case:**
    Financial analysts receive daily briefings generated by the model, highlighting key movements and trends, which enables faster and more informed decision-making.
- **Customer Service and Chatbots:**
  - o **Objective:** Enhance customer support by deploying intelligent chatbots capable of handling routine queries.
  - o **Practical Implementation:**
    Integrate the model with a customer service platform to answer questions about account details, transaction histories, or product information.
  - o **Example Use Case:**
    A banking chatbot reduces call center volume by handling common inquiries, freeing human agents to manage more complex issues.

Beyond Healthcare and Finance

- **Legal Sector:**
  - o **Objective:** Automate contract analysis and legal document summarization.
  - o **Practical Implementation:**
    Adapt LangGraph LLM to extract key clauses, obligations, and risks from lengthy legal documents, aiding lawyers in quick reviews and due diligence.
- **Technology and Software Development:**

- o **Objective:** Enhance developer productivity by automating code documentation and generating context-aware code completions.
- o **Practical Implementation:**
  Integrate the model into development environments to assist with generating documentation and providing code suggestions tailored to the project context.
- **Marketing and Media:**
  - o **Objective:** Generate personalized content and monitor brand sentiment.
  - o **Practical Implementation:**
    Utilize LangGraph LLM to craft tailored marketing messages, social media posts, and customer communications that resonate with target audiences, as well as analyze customer reviews and social media chatter to gauge brand perception.

Summary

- **Healthcare:**
  Leverage LangGraph LLM to automate clinical documentation, summarize patient records, and build medical Q&A systems that support clinical decision-making.
- **Finance:**
  Apply the model to distill complex financial data into actionable summaries, facilitate market analysis, and power customer service chatbots to enhance client experiences.
- **Beyond:**
  Extend the model's capabilities to legal analysis, technology support, and marketing content creation—demonstrating its adaptability across a range of domains.

By following these practical applications and implementation strategies, organizations in healthcare, finance, and various other sectors can harness the advanced capabilities of LangGraph LLM to drive innovation, reduce operational costs, and improve decision-making processes. This guidebook approach provides clear, actionable insights for practitioners looking to integrate state-of-the-art language processing into their industry-specific workflows.

5.1.2. Enterprise vs. Consumer Applications

This section provides a structured guide to understanding how LangGraph LLM can be applied in both enterprise and consumer contexts. While the core technology remains the same, the requirements, integration strategies, and user expectations differ significantly between these two domains. Below, we outline key considerations, practical examples, and actionable insights for deploying LangGraph LLM in enterprise environments versus consumer-facing applications.

Objectives

- **Clarify Use Cases:**
  Define the distinct needs of enterprise versus consumer applications.
- **Outline Integration Strategies:**
  Provide guidance on tailoring implementation to suit different user bases.
- **Highlight Key Considerations:**
  Address aspects such as scalability, security, customization, and user experience.

Enterprise Applications

1. Use Case Focus

- **Business Process Automation:**
  Automate internal tasks such as report generation, data extraction from legal documents, and customer service workflows.
- **Data-Driven Decision Making:**
  Integrate the model into enterprise systems (e.g., CRM, ERP) to enhance insights from internal data sources.
- **Secure and Compliant Solutions:**
  Ensure that deployment meets industry-specific security standards and regulatory requirements.

2. Integration Strategies

- **Custom Workflows:**
  Adapt the model to integrate seamlessly with existing enterprise software. This may involve using APIs, microservices, or custom connectors.
- **Scalability and Reliability:**
  Deploy on robust, secure cloud platforms or on-premises systems that can handle high volumes of data and maintain uptime.

- **Data Privacy:**
  Implement strict access controls and encryption to safeguard sensitive business information.

3. Practical Example

- **Enterprise Chatbot:**
  Develop a chatbot that assists employees with HR queries, IT support, or accessing internal documents.
  Implementation Tip:
  Fine-tune LangGraph LLM using internal data and integrate it into the company's intranet, ensuring compliance with data privacy policies.

Consumer Applications

1. Use Case Focus

- **User Experience Enhancement:**
  Provide personalized recommendations, generate engaging content, and offer intuitive interactions through chatbots or virtual assistants.
- **Scalability for Mass Usage:**
  Optimize the model to serve millions of users with low latency and high responsiveness.
- **Accessibility and Personalization:**
  Focus on intuitive interfaces and tailor responses to individual user preferences, demographics, and behavior patterns.

2. Integration Strategies

- **Mobile and Web Applications:**
  Integrate LangGraph LLM into apps and websites with emphasis on quick response times and a smooth user experience.
- **APIs for Developers:**
  Offer APIs that allow third-party developers to leverage the model for various consumer applications, such as social media content generation or personalized learning tools.
- **User Data and Privacy:**
  While personalization is key, ensure that the handling of user data complies with consumer privacy standards (e.g., GDPR, CCPA).

3. Practical Example

- **Virtual Personal Assistant:**
  Deploy a consumer-facing assistant that handles everyday tasks—such as scheduling, answering FAQs, and providing recommendations—through voice or text interactions.
  Implementation Tip:
  Fine-tune LangGraph LLM on a broad dataset of consumer interactions and integrate it with voice recognition systems to deliver a natural, human-like experience.

Key Considerations for Both Domains

- **Customization:**
  Both enterprise and consumer applications benefit from fine-tuning; however, enterprise solutions may require deeper integration with proprietary data sources, while consumer applications focus on broad, diverse datasets for personalization.
- **Performance and Scalability:**
  Enterprises often need to process large amounts of data reliably, whereas consumer applications must maintain low latency and high responsiveness to ensure a positive user experience.
- **Security and Compliance:**
  Enterprise deployments demand robust security measures and adherence to regulatory requirements, while consumer applications prioritize user data privacy and transparent data handling practices.

Summary

- **Enterprise Applications:**
  - **Focus:** Business automation, internal data insights, secure and compliant integration.
  - **Strategy:** Customize workflows, ensure robust scalability, and implement strict security protocols.
  - **Example:** Internal chatbots for HR and IT support, automated document processing systems.
- **Consumer Applications:**
  - **Focus:** Enhanced user experience, personalization, mass scalability.

- o **Strategy:** Develop mobile/web interfaces, provide APIs for developers, and adhere to consumer privacy standards.
- o **Example:** Virtual personal assistants, recommendation systems, interactive content generation tools.

By understanding the differences and applying these actionable strategies, you can effectively tailor LangGraph LLM to meet the distinct needs of enterprise and consumer applications. This guidebook approach ensures that whether you're deploying a solution for internal business processes or for millions of end-users, the model is optimized for performance, security, and user satisfaction.

5.2. Integrating LangGraph LLM in Real-World Systems

This section provides a step-by-step guide to integrating LangGraph LLM into real-world systems. The focus is on practical implementation, including system architecture, API deployment, and monitoring, ensuring that the model delivers value in production environments.

Objectives

- **Seamless Integration:**
  Embed LangGraph LLM into existing software ecosystems with minimal disruption.
- **Robust API Deployment:**
  Develop APIs that allow other applications to interact with the model efficiently.
- **Scalable and Secure Systems:**
  Ensure the integration supports high user load, maintains low latency, and complies with security standards.

Step-by-Step Integration Guide

1. Define System Architecture

- **Assess Existing Infrastructure:**
  Evaluate your current software environment (e.g., cloud services, on-premise servers) and determine how LangGraph LLM will fit in.
- **Design Integration Points:**
  Identify where and how the model will be used within the system. Typical integration points include:

- Web or mobile application backends for real-time user interactions.
- Batch processing pipelines for data analysis or report generation.
- Microservices that provide specialized NLP functionalities.
- **Develop an API Strategy:**
  Decide whether to expose LangGraph LLM via RESTful APIs, GraphQL, or another protocol based on your application's needs.

2. Model Deployment

- **Containerization:**
  Package LangGraph LLM into containers (e.g., Docker) to simplify deployment and ensure consistent environments across development, testing, and production.
  - *Practical Tip:* Create a Dockerfile that includes the model, its dependencies, and necessary configurations.
- **API Server Setup:**
  Deploy an API server using frameworks like Flask, FastAPI, or Django.
  - **Example:** A simple FastAPI server to handle inference requests.

```python
from fastapi import FastAPI, Request
from pydantic import BaseModel
import torch
from langgraph_llm import LangGraphLLM  #
Hypothetical model import

# Define request and response data
structures
class InferenceRequest(BaseModel):
    input_text: str

class InferenceResponse(BaseModel):
    output_text: str

# Initialize FastAPI app and load the
model
app = FastAPI()
```

```python
model =
LangGraphLLM.from_pretrained("langgraph-
llm-base")
model.eval()

@app.post("/infer",
response_model=InferenceResponse)
async def infer(request:
InferenceRequest):
    # Tokenize input, run inference, and
decode output
    input_ids =
model.tokenizer.encode(request.input_text
, return_tensors="pt")
    with torch.no_grad():
        outputs =
model.generate(input_ids)
    output_text =
model.tokenizer.decode(outputs[0],
skip_special_tokens=True)
    return
InferenceResponse(output_text=output_text
)

if __name__ == "__main__":
    import uvicorn
    uvicorn.run(app, host="0.0.0.0",
port=8000)
```

o *Outcome:* The API endpoint /infer accepts POST requests with an input text and returns generated text.

3. Integration with Frontend and Back-End Systems

- **Backend Integration:**
  Incorporate API calls to the LangGraph LLM service into your existing backend. For instance:
  o Use the API to generate summaries, translations, or answers to user queries.
  o Integrate with enterprise software (e.g., CRM or ERP systems) for automated report generation.

- **Frontend Integration:**
Embed the service into web or mobile applications using JavaScript or native SDKs.
  - *Example:* A web interface that allows users to input text and receive real-time responses from LangGraph LLM.

```javascript
async function getInference(inputText) {
  const response = await
fetch("http://your-api-
server:8000/infer", {
    method: "POST",
    headers: { "Content-Type":
"application/json" },
    body: JSON.stringify({ input_text:
inputText })
  });
  const data = await response.json();
  return data.output_text;
}
// Usage: call getInference() on button
click to display the generated text.
```

4. Scalability and Load Management

- **Auto-Scaling:**
Deploy the service on cloud platforms (e.g., AWS, GCP, Azure) that support auto-scaling to handle variable loads.
- **Load Balancing:**
Use load balancers to distribute requests across multiple instances of the API server.
- **Caching:**
Implement caching mechanisms (e.g., Redis) for frequently requested queries to reduce latency.

5. Security and Monitoring

- **Security Measures:**
  - Implement HTTPS for secure data transmission.
  - Use authentication tokens or API keys to restrict access.
  - Apply rate limiting to prevent abuse.

- **Monitoring and Logging:**
  - Integrate monitoring tools (e.g., Prometheus, Grafana) to track system performance and API response times.
  - Log errors and usage statistics for troubleshooting and optimization.

Summary

- **Define Architecture:**
  Understand your current systems and design clear integration points and API strategies.
- **Deploy the Model:**
  Containerize LangGraph LLM and set up an API server using frameworks like FastAPI or Flask.
- **Integrate with Systems:**
  Connect the API to backend services and frontend applications, enabling real-time interactions.
- **Ensure Scalability:**
  Utilize cloud-based auto-scaling, load balancing, and caching to manage high user loads.
- **Prioritize Security and Monitoring:**
  Secure the API with HTTPS and authentication while continuously monitoring system performance.

By following these actionable steps and practical examples, you can successfully integrate LangGraph LLM into real-world systems, ensuring a seamless, secure, and scalable deployment that meets both enterprise and consumer needs. This guidebook approach provides clear, hands-on insights for practitioners looking to harness advanced language models in production environments.

5.2.1. Deployment Architectures

This section provides a guidebook-style overview of various deployment architectures for LangGraph LLM. Choosing the right deployment architecture is crucial to ensure that the model can serve real-world applications effectively, with considerations for scalability, security, latency, and maintenance. Below, we outline common deployment architectures and offer practical examples to help you select and implement the best solution for your needs.

Objectives

- **Optimize Performance:**
  Ensure low latency and high throughput for inference.
- **Scalability and Flexibility:**
  Design an architecture that can easily scale to meet varying user demands.
- **Ease of Maintenance:**
  Enable smooth updates, monitoring, and troubleshooting in production.

Common Deployment Architectures

1. Cloud-Based Deployment

- **Overview:**
  Deploy LangGraph LLM on cloud platforms (e.g., AWS, GCP, Azure) to leverage robust infrastructure, auto-scaling, and managed services.
- **Key Features:**
  - **Auto-Scaling:** Automatically adjust resources based on load.
  - **Managed Infrastructure:** Use services like Kubernetes or serverless architectures.
  - **Global Availability:** Deploy across multiple regions for reduced latency.
- **Practical Implementation:**
  - **Containerization:** Package the model in a Docker container.
  - **Orchestration:** Use Kubernetes for managing clusters and deployments.
  - **Example:**

    ```dockerfile
    # Dockerfile for LangGraph LLM API
    FROM python:3.9-slim
    WORKDIR /app
     requirements.txt .
    RUN pip install --no-cache-dir -r
    requirements.txt

     . .
    EXPOSE 8000
    CMD ["uvicorn", "app:app", "--host",
    "0.0.0.0", "--port", "8000"]
    ```

- o **Cloud Service Example:**
  Deploy the container on AWS Elastic Kubernetes Service (EKS) and configure auto-scaling and load balancing.

2. On-Premises Deployment

- **Overview:**
  Deploy LangGraph LLM on internal servers to maintain full control over data, security, and performance.
- **Key Features:**
  - o **Enhanced Data Security:** Data remains within the organization's infrastructure.
  - o **Custom Hardware:** Tailor hardware configurations to optimize model performance.
  - o **Legacy Integration:** Seamlessly integrate with existing on-premises systems.
- **Practical Implementation:**
  - o **Virtualization:** Use VMs or containers to deploy the model.
  - o **Local Orchestration:** Use on-prem Kubernetes clusters or Docker Compose for simpler setups.
  - o **Example:**
    Create a Docker Compose file to deploy the LangGraph LLM API alongside supporting services (e.g., a Redis cache):

```yaml
version: '3'
services:
  langgraph-llm-api:
    image: langgraph-llm:latest
    ports:
      - "8000:8000"
    environment:
      - MODEL_ENV=production
  redis:
    image: redis:alpine
    ports:
      - "6379:6379"
```

3. Hybrid Deployment

- **Overview:**
  Combine cloud and on-premises resources to balance the benefits of both environments. This approach is ideal when certain data or applications must remain on-premises, while other components can leverage cloud scalability.
- **Key Features:**
  - **Data Sovereignty:** Keep sensitive data on-premises while using the cloud for high-volume processing.
  - **Flexibility:** Dynamically allocate workloads based on cost, performance, or regulatory requirements.
- **Practical Implementation:**
  - **API Gateway:** Use a unified API gateway that routes requests to either on-premises or cloud-based LangGraph LLM instances.
  - **Data Synchronization:** Establish secure, real-time data pipelines between on-premises systems and the cloud.
  - **Example:**
    Configure a load balancer that directs real-time user queries to cloud instances for rapid response, while scheduled batch processing runs on on-premises hardware.

Considerations for Deployment Architectures

- **Latency Requirements:**
  Choose cloud-based or hybrid architectures if global users demand low latency.
- **Security and Compliance:**
  On-premises deployment may be preferable for industries with strict data privacy regulations.
- **Scalability Needs:**
  Cloud platforms offer easy scalability for fluctuating workloads and high-traffic applications.
- **Maintenance and Monitoring:**
  Use orchestration and monitoring tools (e.g., Prometheus, Grafana, Kubernetes dashboards) to keep track of system health and performance.

Summary

- **Cloud-Based Deployment:**
  Ideal for scalability, global reach, and managed services. Use

containerization and orchestration (e.g., Kubernetes) for streamlined operations.
- **On-Premises Deployment:**
  Best for enhanced data security and integration with legacy systems. Use virtualization and container orchestration like Docker Compose or on-prem Kubernetes.
- **Hybrid Deployment:**
  Combines the benefits of both cloud and on-premises environments, enabling flexibility in workload distribution and compliance with data sovereignty requirements.

By following this guide and evaluating your specific requirements, you can select the deployment architecture that best meets your needs for integrating LangGraph LLM into real-world systems. This approach ensures that your deployment is secure, scalable, and optimized for performance, while also being adaptable to future growth and changing demands.

5.2.2. API and Microservices Integration

This section provides a step-by-step guide to integrating LangGraph LLM using APIs and microservices. The goal is to design a flexible, scalable architecture where LangGraph LLM can be accessed as a service and easily integrated into larger systems. This guide outlines how to create RESTful API endpoints, deploy the model as microservices, and connect them with other system components.

Objectives

- **Expose Model Functionality:**
  Enable other applications to access LangGraph LLM via well-defined API endpoints.
- **Achieve Scalability and Flexibility:**
  Leverage microservices to allow independent scaling, maintenance, and deployment of LangGraph LLM functionalities.
- **Ensure Seamless Integration:**
  Design APIs that are secure, efficient, and easy to integrate with both frontend and backend systems.

Step-by-Step Guide

1. Designing API Endpoints

- **Define Service Functions:**
  Identify the key functionalities you want to expose (e.g., text generation, summarization, translation).
- **Choose an API Protocol:**
  Common choices include RESTful APIs or GraphQL. REST is widely used for its simplicity and compatibility.
- **Specify Input/Output Formats:**
  Use JSON as the standard for data exchange. Clearly define request payloads and response structures.

2. Building the API with a Framework

- **Select a Framework:**
  Use frameworks like FastAPI, Flask, or Django REST Framework. FastAPI is a popular choice due to its speed, built-in data validation, and asynchronous capabilities.
- **Implement Endpoints:**
  Create endpoints that accept input text, process it with LangGraph LLM, and return the output. Here's a hands-on example using FastAPI:

python

```python
from fastapi import FastAPI
from pydantic import BaseModel
import torch
from langgraph_llm import LangGraphLLM  #
Hypothetical model import

# Define the request and response data
structures
class InferenceRequest(BaseModel):
    input_text: str

class InferenceResponse(BaseModel):
    output_text: str

# Initialize the FastAPI app and load the pre-
trained model
app = FastAPI()
```

```python
model =
LangGraphLLM.from_pretrained("langgraph-llm-
base")
model.eval()  # Set the model to evaluation
mode

@app.post("/infer",
response_model=InferenceResponse)
async def infer(request: InferenceRequest):
    # Tokenize the input text
    input_ids =
model.tokenizer.encode(request.input_text,
return_tensors="pt")
    # Generate model output without computing
gradients
    with torch.no_grad():
        outputs = model.generate(input_ids)
    # Decode the output tokens into text
    output_text =
model.tokenizer.decode(outputs[0],
skip_special_tokens=True)
    return
InferenceResponse(output_text=output_text)

if __name__ == "__main__":
    import uvicorn
    uvicorn.run(app, host="0.0.0.0",
port=8000)
```

Explanation:
This code snippet sets up an API endpoint /infer that takes a
JSON payload with an input_text field, processes it through
LangGraph LLM, and returns the generated text.

3. Microservices Architecture

- **Decompose the Application:**
  Break down the system into independent microservices. LangGraph
  LLM can be one microservice that focuses solely on language
  processing, while other services handle tasks like user management,
  logging, and data storage.

- **Containerization:**
Package the API service in a Docker container for portability and ease of deployment. A simple Dockerfile might look like:

```dockerfile
dockerfile

FROM python:3.9-slim
WORKDIR /app
 requirements.txt .
RUN pip install --no-cache-dir -r
requirements.txt

 . .
EXPOSE 8000
CMD ["uvicorn", "app:app", "--host",
"0.0.0.0", "--port", "8000"]
```

- **Service Communication:**
Use API gateways or service meshes (like Istio or Linkerd) to manage communication between microservices. This ensures that services can scale independently while maintaining secure and efficient communication.

4. Integration with Existing Systems

- **Backend Integration:**
Embed API calls to the LangGraph LLM service within your enterprise applications or databases. For instance, integrate the service into a CRM system to generate dynamic content or summaries.
- **Frontend Integration:**
Connect your web or mobile application with the API using standard HTTP requests. Here's a JavaScript example using the Fetch API:

```javascript
javascript

async function getInference(inputText) {
    const response = await fetch("http://your-
api-server:8000/infer", {
        method: "POST",
        headers: { "Content-Type":
"application/json" },
```

```
        body: JSON.stringify({ input_text:
inputText })
    });
    const data = await response.json();
    return data.output_text;
}

// Example usage: call getInference() on a
button click event
document.getElementById("inferButton").addEven
tListener("click", async () => {
    const userInput =
document.getElementById("inputText").value;
    const result = await
getInference(userInput);

document.getElementById("outputText").innerTex
t = result;
});
```

Explanation:
This script sends a POST request with user input to the /infer
endpoint and displays the generated output on a webpage.

5. Monitoring, Logging, and Security

- **Monitoring:**
  Utilize tools such as Prometheus, Grafana, or cloud-native
  monitoring solutions to track API performance and usage.
- **Logging:**
  Implement structured logging (e.g., using ELK Stack) to capture
  errors and request metrics for troubleshooting.
- **Security Measures:**
  - Use HTTPS for secure communication.
  - Implement authentication and authorization (e.g., API keys or
    OAuth).
  - Apply rate limiting to protect the service from abuse.

Summary

- **Designing Endpoints:**
  Define clear RESTful APIs to expose LangGraph LLM functionality.

141

- **Building the API:**
  Use frameworks like FastAPI for rapid development and deployment, with examples provided for a basic inference endpoint.
- **Microservices Architecture:**
  Decompose your application into modular microservices, containerize the model, and use orchestration tools to manage deployments.
- **Integration:**
  Connect the API with backend systems and frontend applications using standard HTTP protocols, ensuring smooth data flow.
- **Monitoring and Security:**
  Implement monitoring, logging, and security best practices to maintain a robust production environment.

By following these actionable steps and practical examples, you can effectively integrate LangGraph LLM into real-world systems via APIs and microservices. This guidebook approach ensures that the deployment is scalable, secure, and efficient, enabling your organization to harness the full potential of advanced language models in production environments.

5.3. Code Walkthroughs and Tutorials

This section provides a series of hands-on code walkthroughs and tutorials to help you understand and implement various functionalities of LangGraph LLM. Each tutorial is designed to walk you through practical examples— from setting up your environment and processing text data to deploying the model as an API and integrating it into applications. This guidebook-style approach ensures that every concept is supported by clear, executable code examples and step-by-step instructions.

Objectives

- **Demonstrate Practical Implementations:**
  Provide concrete code examples to illustrate key operations such as text preprocessing, inference, and deployment.
- **Build a Solid Foundation:**
  Help you set up a working environment, run the model, and understand the underlying architecture.
- **Facilitate Customization:**
  Guide you through adapting the code for different tasks or deployment scenarios.

Walkthrough 1: Environment Setup and Model Loading

Step-by-Step Instructions:

1. **Set Up Python Environment:**
   - Install Python 3.9 or later.
   - Create a virtual environment:

   ```bash
   bash

   python -m venv langgraph_env
   source langgraph_env/bin/activate  # On
   Windows: langgraph_env\Scripts\activate
   ```

2. **Install Required Packages:**
   - Install PyTorch, FastAPI, and any additional dependencies:

   ```bash
   bash

   pip install torch torchvision fastapi
   uvicorn
   ```

3. **Load the Pre-Trained LangGraph LLM Model:**
   - Use the model's library (assuming it's available as langgraph_llm):

   ```python
   python

   from langgraph_llm import LangGraphLLM

   # Load the pre-trained model and its
   tokenizer
   model =
   LangGraphLLM.from_pretrained("langgraph-
   llm-base")
   tokenizer = model.tokenizer

   # Set model to evaluation mode for
   inference
   model.eval()
   ```

```
print("Model and tokenizer loaded
successfully!")
```

- o **Explanation:**
  This code sets up the model for inference by loading pre-
  trained weights and tokenizer. Switching to evaluation mode
  ensures that the model behaves correctly during prediction.

Walkthrough 2: Text Preprocessing and Inference

Step-by-Step Instructions:

1. **Input Text Preprocessing:**
   - o Clean and tokenize an input sentence:

   ```python
   python

   input_text = "LangGraph LLM is
   revolutionizing language processing!"
   # Tokenize the input text using the
   model's tokenizer
   input_ids = tokenizer.encode(input_text,
   return_tensors="pt")
   print("Tokenized Input:", input_ids)
   ```

2. **Generate Inference Output:**
   - o Run the model to generate output:

   ```python
   python

   import torch

   # Generate output tokens without
   computing gradients
   with torch.no_grad():
       output_ids =
   model.generate(input_ids, max_length=50)

   # Decode the generated tokens into human-
   readable text
   ```

```python
output_text =
tokenizer.decode(output_ids[0],
skip_special_tokens=True)
print("Generated Output:", output_text)
```

- o **Explanation:**
  The code processes the input text, converts it to tokens, and
  then generates an output sequence. Finally, it decodes the
  output back to text. Adjust parameters such as `max_length`
  to control output length.

Walkthrough 3: Deploying LangGraph LLM as an API

Step-by-Step Instructions:

1. **Set Up a FastAPI Server:**
   - o Create a new Python file `app.py` with the following code:

   python

```python
from fastapi import FastAPI
from pydantic import BaseModel
import torch
from langgraph_llm import LangGraphLLM

# Define request and response models
class InferenceRequest(BaseModel):
    input_text: str

class InferenceResponse(BaseModel):
    output_text: str

# Initialize FastAPI app and load the
model
app = FastAPI()
model =
LangGraphLLM.from_pretrained("langgraph-
llm-base")
tokenizer = model.tokenizer
model.eval()
```

```python
@app.post("/infer",
response_model=InferenceResponse)
async def infer(request:
InferenceRequest):
    input_ids =
tokenizer.encode(request.input_text,
return_tensors="pt")
    with torch.no_grad():
        outputs =
model.generate(input_ids)
    output_text =
tokenizer.decode(outputs[0],
skip_special_tokens=True)
    return
InferenceResponse(output_text=output_text
)

if __name__ == "__main__":
    import uvicorn
    uvicorn.run(app, host="0.0.0.0",
port=8000)
```

- o **Explanation:**
  This code creates an API endpoint `/infer` that accepts
  POST requests containing input text. The server processes the
  text with LangGraph LLM and returns the generated output.
2. **Run the API Server:**
   - o Start the server by running:

   ```bash
   bash
   ```

   ```
   python app.py
   ```

   - o **Testing:**
     Use tools like Postman or `curl` to send a POST request:

   ```bash
   bash
   ```

   ```
   curl -X POST
   "http://localhost:8000/infer" -H
   "Content-Type: application/json" -d
   ```

```
'{"input_text": "Explain the future of
AI."}'
```

- o **Outcome:**
  The API responds with generated text, demonstrating a fully
  deployed inference service.

Walkthrough 4: Integrating with Frontend Applications

Step-by-Step Instructions:

1. **Basic JavaScript Integration:**
   - o Create a simple HTML page with JavaScript that calls the
     API:

```html
<!DOCTYPE html>
<html>
<head>
    <title>LangGraph LLM
Inference</title>
    <script>
        async function getInference() {
            const inputText =
document.getElementById("inputText").valu
e;
            const response = await
fetch("http://localhost:8000/infer", {
                method: "POST",
                headers: { "Content-
Type": "application/json" },
                body: JSON.stringify({
input_text: inputText })
            });
            const data = await
response.json();

document.getElementById("outputText").inn
erText = data.output_text;
```

```
        }
    </script>
</head>
<body>
    <h1>LangGraph LLM Inference</h1>
    <input type="text" id="inputText"
placeholder="Enter text here" />
    <button
onclick="getInference()">Submit</button>
    <p id="outputText"></p>
</body>
</html>
```

- o **Explanation:**
  This HTML file provides a simple user interface for entering text. The JavaScript function getInference() sends the input to the API and displays the returned output on the page.
2. **Testing the Frontend:**
   - o Open the HTML file in a web browser and interact with the form. The application should display the model's output in real time.

Summary

- **Environment Setup:**
  Set up Python, install dependencies, and load LangGraph LLM.
- **Text Processing and Inference:**
  Clean, tokenize, and generate output from input text with practical code examples.
- **API Deployment:**
  Use FastAPI to expose LangGraph LLM as a RESTful service.
- **Frontend Integration:**
  Connect the API with a simple web interface using JavaScript.

By following these code walkthroughs and tutorials, you gain a hands-on understanding of how to work with LangGraph LLM—from setting up your environment and running inferences to deploying the model as an API and integrating it with frontend applications. This guidebook approach is designed to provide clear, actionable steps that enable you to harness the power of LangGraph LLM in real-world projects.

5.3.1. Setting Up Your Environment

This section provides a clear, step-by-step guide to setting up your development environment for working with LangGraph LLM. By following these instructions, you'll be able to install the necessary tools, create an isolated workspace, and ensure that all dependencies are properly configured for model training and deployment.

Objectives

- **Create an Isolated Environment:**
  Set up a virtual environment to avoid conflicts with other projects.
- **Install Required Dependencies:**
  Ensure all necessary packages, such as PyTorch and FastAPI, are installed.
- **Verify the Setup:**
  Load the model and run a simple inference to confirm that everything is working as expected.

Step-by-Step Guide

1. Create a Virtual Environment

- **Open your terminal or command prompt.**
- **Run the following command to create a virtual environment:**

```bash
python -m venv langgraph_env
```

- **Activate the virtual environment:**
  - **On macOS/Linux:**

    ```bash
    source langgraph_env/bin/activate
    ```

  - **On Windows:**

```
bash

langgraph_env\Scripts\activate
```

Outcome:
Your terminal prompt should now indicate that you are working inside the langgraph_env virtual environment.

2. Install Required Packages

- **Create a `requirements.txt` file with the necessary packages.**
  For example, your requirements.txt might contain:

```shell
torch>=1.9.0
torchvision>=0.10.0
fastapi
uvicorn
```

- **Install the dependencies using pip:**

```bash
pip install --upgrade pip
pip install -r requirements.txt
```

Outcome:
All required packages, including PyTorch and FastAPI, are installed in your virtual environment.

3. Verify the Installation

- **Create a simple Python script to check the installation and load the LangGraph LLM model.**
  For instance, create a file named check_env.py with the following code:

```python
# check_env.py
try:
```

```python
import torch
from langgraph_llm import LangGraphLLM   #
Hypothetical import for LangGraph LLM

    print("PyTorch version:", torch.__version__)

    # Load the pre-trained model (this assumes
LangGraph LLM is installed and available)
    model =
LangGraphLLM.from_pretrained("langgraph-llm-base")
    tokenizer = model.tokenizer
    model.eval()   # Set to evaluation mode for
inference

    # Test inference on a sample input
    input_text = "LangGraph LLM is transforming
language intelligence."
    input_ids = tokenizer.encode(input_text,
return_tensors="pt")
    with torch.no_grad():
        outputs = model.generate(input_ids,
max_length=50)
    output_text = tokenizer.decode(outputs[0],
skip_special_tokens=True)

    print("Model loaded successfully!")
    print("Sample output:", output_text)
except ImportError as e:
    print("An error occurred:", e)
```

- **Run the script:**

```bash
bash

python check_env.py
```

Outcome:
If everything is set up correctly, you should see the PyTorch version printed,
followed by a confirmation that the model loaded successfully and a sample
output from the model.

4. Document Your Setup

- **Maintain a README file** in your project directory to document the setup steps.
  This ensures reproducibility and helps onboard team members.

Summary

- **Create a Virtual Environment:**
  Use `python -m venv langgraph_env` and activate it.
- **Install Dependencies:**
  Use a `requirements.txt` file to install PyTorch, FastAPI, and other necessary packages.
- **Verify the Environment:**
  Run a test script to load the LangGraph LLM model and generate a sample output.
- **Document the Process:**
  Keep a README file with setup instructions for future reference.

By following these steps, you'll have a robust, isolated environment set up for developing, training, and deploying LangGraph LLM. This guidebook-style approach ensures that every necessary detail is covered, allowing you to focus on building applications with confidence.

5.3.2. Sample Projects and Applications

This section presents several sample projects and applications designed to showcase the practical implementation of LangGraph LLM. Each project is described with clear objectives, a step-by-step guide, and example code snippets where applicable. These projects provide a hands-on approach to understanding how to leverage LangGraph LLM for various real-world tasks.

Project 1: Text Summarization Tool

Objective:
Build an application that automatically summarizes long-form documents into concise summaries.

Key Steps:

1. **Data Preparation:**
   - Collect a dataset of articles and their summaries.
   - Preprocess the text (clean, tokenize, etc.) using the steps outlined in earlier sections.

2. **Model Fine-Tuning:**
   - o Fine-tune LangGraph LLM on the summarization dataset using supervised learning.
   - o Configure hyperparameters such as learning rate, batch size, and number of epochs.
3. **API Deployment:**
   - o Deploy the fine-tuned model as an API endpoint that accepts a document and returns a summary.
   - o Use a framework like FastAPI to create a RESTful interface.
4. **Frontend Integration:**
   - o Develop a simple web interface where users can paste text and receive a summary.
   - o Use JavaScript to call the API and display the result.

Example Code Snippet for Inference:

```python
python

from fastapi import FastAPI
from pydantic import BaseModel
import torch
from langgraph_llm import LangGraphLLM   #
Hypothetical import

class SummarizationRequest(BaseModel):
    document: str

class SummarizationResponse(BaseModel):
    summary: str

app = FastAPI()
model = LangGraphLLM.from_pretrained("langgraph-
llm-summarizer")
tokenizer = model.tokenizer
model.eval()

@app.post("/summarize",
response_model=SummarizationResponse)
async def summarize(request: SummarizationRequest):
    input_ids = tokenizer.encode(request.document,
return_tensors="pt", truncation=True)
    with torch.no_grad():
```

```
    summary_ids = model.generate(input_ids,
max_length=150, num_beams=4)
    summary = tokenizer.decode(summary_ids[0],
skip_special_tokens=True)
    return SummarizationResponse(summary=summary)
```

Project 2: Language Translation Service

Objective:
Develop a service that translates text between languages using LangGraph
LLM.

Key Steps:

1. **Dataset Collection:**
   o Gather a parallel corpus for source and target languages.
   o Preprocess the data to match the input format expected by the
     model.
2. **Model Fine-Tuning:**
   o Fine-tune LangGraph LLM for translation tasks on the
     collected dataset.
   o Adjust parameters to ensure accurate handling of language-
     specific nuances.
3. **API Creation:**
   o Expose the translation functionality through an API.
   o Ensure that the API can handle requests for different language
     pairs.
4. **Integration:**
   o Integrate the translation API into a mobile or web application.
   o Provide a user interface for entering text and selecting the
     target language.

Example Code Snippet for Translation Endpoint:

python

```python
from fastapi import FastAPI
from pydantic import BaseModel
import torch
from langgraph_llm import LangGraphLLM   #
Hypothetical import
```

```python
class TranslationRequest(BaseModel):
    source_text: str
    target_language: str  # e.g., "fr" for French

class TranslationResponse(BaseModel):
    translated_text: str

app = FastAPI()
model = LangGraphLLM.from_pretrained("langgraph-
llm-translation")
tokenizer = model.tokenizer
model.eval()

@app.post("/translate",
response_model=TranslationResponse)
async def translate(request: TranslationRequest):
    # Assuming the model handles translation
through a language parameter
    input_ids =
tokenizer.encode(request.source_text,
return_tensors="pt", truncation=True)
    with torch.no_grad():
        # The target language token can be
prepended as needed
        translated_ids = model.generate(input_ids,
max_length=100, language=request.target_language)
    translated_text =
tokenizer.decode(translated_ids[0],
skip_special_tokens=True)
    return
TranslationResponse(translated_text=translated_text
)
```

Project 3: Intelligent Chatbot

Objective:
Create a conversational agent that uses LangGraph LLM to engage in
dynamic dialogues with users.

Key Steps:

1. **Dialogue Dataset:**
   - Collect conversational data or use public dialogue datasets.
   - Preprocess the data to capture context and response pairs.
2. **Fine-Tuning for Dialogue:**
   - Fine-tune the model using supervised or reinforcement learning techniques on dialogue data.
   - Implement conversation history handling to maintain context across turns.
3. **API and Real-Time Interaction:**
   - Deploy the model as a real-time chatbot service via an API.
   - Integrate with messaging platforms (e.g., Slack, WhatsApp) or a web-based chat interface.
4. **User Interface:**
   - Develop a frontend chat interface that displays conversation history and allows for real-time interaction.
   - Ensure the interface is responsive and user-friendly.

Example Code Snippet for a Chatbot Endpoint:

python

```python
from fastapi import FastAPI
from pydantic import BaseModel
import torch
from langgraph_llm import LangGraphLLM   #
Hypothetical import

class ChatRequest(BaseModel):
    message: str
    history: list   # Optional: list of previous
conversation turns

class ChatResponse(BaseModel):
    reply: str

app = FastAPI()
model = LangGraphLLM.from_pretrained("langgraph-
llm-chatbot")
tokenizer = model.tokenizer
model.eval()

@app.post("/chat", response_model=ChatResponse)
```

```
async def chat(request: ChatRequest):
    # Combine conversation history and current
message as needed
    conversation = " ".join(request.history) + " "
+ request.message if request.history else
request.message
    input_ids = tokenizer.encode(conversation,
return_tensors="pt", truncation=True)
    with torch.no_grad():
        reply_ids = model.generate(input_ids,
max_length=100)
    reply = tokenizer.decode(reply_ids[0],
skip_special_tokens=True)
    return ChatResponse(reply=reply)
```

Project 4: Content Personalization for Marketing

Objective:
Implement a system that generates personalized content for marketing campaigns, such as product descriptions and social media posts.

Key Steps:

1. **Dataset Collection:**
   o Collect a dataset of marketing content, including product descriptions, advertisements, and social media posts.
   o Preprocess the data to ensure consistency and relevance.
2. **Fine-Tuning for Content Generation:**
   o Fine-tune LangGraph LLM on the marketing dataset to capture brand voice and style.
   o Adjust parameters to control output tone and length.
3. **API Deployment and Integration:**
   o Expose the content generation functionality via an API.
   o Integrate with content management systems (CMS) to automate content delivery.
4. **Customization and Feedback:**
   o Implement feedback mechanisms to continuously refine content based on user engagement metrics.

Example Code Snippet for Content Generation:

```python
python

from fastapi import FastAPI
from pydantic import BaseModel
import torch
from langgraph_llm import LangGraphLLM  #
Hypothetical import

class ContentRequest(BaseModel):
    prompt: str
    context: str  # Optional: additional context
such as target audience or campaign theme

class ContentResponse(BaseModel):
    generated_content: str

app = FastAPI()
model = LangGraphLLM.from_pretrained("langgraph-
llm-marketing")
tokenizer = model.tokenizer
model.eval()

@app.post("/generate-content",
response_model=ContentResponse)
async def generate_content(request:
ContentRequest):
    input_text = request.context + " " +
request.prompt if request.context else
request.prompt
    input_ids = tokenizer.encode(input_text,
return_tensors="pt", truncation=True)
    with torch.no_grad():
        output_ids = model.generate(input_ids,
max_length=150)
    generated_content =
tokenizer.decode(output_ids[0],
skip_special_tokens=True)
    return
ContentResponse(generated_content=generated_content
)
```

Summary

- **Project Diversity:**
  Explore a range of applications including text summarization, translation, chatbots, and content personalization.
- **Step-by-Step Implementation:**
  Each project follows a structured process—from data collection and fine-tuning to API deployment and frontend integration.
- **Practical Code Examples:**
  Code snippets demonstrate how to set up endpoints, process inputs, and generate outputs using LangGraph LLM.
- **Actionable Insights:**
  Use these sample projects as a starting point, and adapt the examples to suit your specific application requirements.

By working through these sample projects and tutorials, you'll gain hands-on experience with LangGraph LLM and learn how to leverage its advanced language capabilities in diverse, real-world scenarios. This guidebook approach provides clear, actionable steps that empower you to build innovative applications using state-of-the-art language modeling techniques.

5.4. Performance Metrics and Optimization in Deployment

This section provides a comprehensive guide to measuring and optimizing the performance of LangGraph LLM when deployed in production environments. By monitoring key metrics and applying targeted optimization techniques, you can ensure that the system remains responsive, efficient, and scalable under real-world loads.

Objectives

- **Monitor Key Performance Metrics:**
  Identify and track metrics that indicate system health, such as latency, throughput, error rates, and resource utilization.
- **Optimize Resource Usage:**
  Apply strategies to reduce latency, increase throughput, and manage computational resources effectively.

- **Ensure Scalability and Reliability:**
  Implement techniques such as caching, load balancing, and auto-scaling to maintain performance during peak usage.

Step-by-Step Guide

1. Defining Performance Metrics

- **Latency:**
  Measure the time taken from receiving an API request to sending the response. Lower latency ensures a smoother user experience.
- **Throughput:**
  Monitor the number of requests the system can handle per second. This helps in understanding scalability.
- **Resource Utilization:**
  Track CPU, memory, and GPU usage to ensure efficient deployment.
- **Error Rates:**
  Record the frequency of errors (e.g., 4xx/5xx HTTP status codes) to quickly detect and address issues.
- **Response Quality:**
  For language models, evaluate the quality of generated outputs using qualitative feedback or automated metrics (e.g., BLEU, ROUGE).

2. Monitoring and Logging Tools

- **Prometheus and Grafana:**
  Use Prometheus for collecting time-series data and Grafana for visualization of metrics such as latency and throughput.
- **Application Performance Monitoring (APM):**
  Tools like New Relic, Datadog, or AWS CloudWatch can provide insights into system performance and help diagnose bottlenecks.
- **Structured Logging:**
  Implement logging using frameworks like ELK (Elasticsearch, Logstash, Kibana) or Fluentd to capture detailed error logs and usage statistics.

Example: Setting Up Basic Metrics with Prometheus in Python (FastAPI)

```
python
```

```python
from fastapi import FastAPI, Request
from prometheus_client import Counter, Histogram,
generate_latest, CONTENT_TYPE_LATEST
import time

app = FastAPI()

# Define metrics
REQUEST_COUNT = Counter("request_count", "Total
number of requests", ["endpoint", "method"])
REQUEST_LATENCY =
Histogram("request_latency_seconds", "Latency of
requests", ["endpoint"])

@app.middleware("http")
async def add_metrics(request: Request, call_next):
    start_time = time.time()
    response = await call_next(request)
    process_time = time.time() - start_time

    endpoint = request.url.path
    method = request.method
    REQUEST_COUNT.labels(endpoint=endpoint,
method=method).inc()

REQUEST_LATENCY.labels(endpoint=endpoint).observe(p
rocess_time)

    return response

@app.get("/metrics")
async def metrics():
    return Response(generate_latest(),
media_type=CONTENT_TYPE_LATEST)
```

Explanation:
This middleware captures the number of requests and their latencies. An
endpoint (/metrics) is provided to expose these metrics for Prometheus to
scrape.

3. Optimization Strategies

- **Caching:**
  Use caching mechanisms (e.g., Redis or in-memory caches) to store responses for frequently requested inputs.
  Tip: Cache common queries to reduce redundant processing.
- **Auto-Scaling and Load Balancing:**
  Deploy the service on platforms that support auto-scaling to automatically handle traffic spikes. Use load balancers to distribute requests evenly across multiple instances.
- **Efficient Hardware Utilization:**
  Leverage mixed precision inference (FP16) and optimize batch processing to reduce memory usage and increase speed.
- **Code and Model Optimization:**
  Optimize the model by pruning unnecessary layers or reducing parameter sizes if possible, and optimize code paths for inference speed.

Example: Using Redis for Caching Inference Results

```python
import redis
import json

# Connect to Redis server
cache = redis.Redis(host='localhost', port=6379,
db=0)

def get_cached_response(input_text):
    cached = cache.get(input_text)
    if cached:
        return json.loads(cached)
    return None

def set_cached_response(input_text, output_text):
    cache.set(input_text,
json.dumps({"output_text": output_text}), ex=3600)
# Cache for 1 hour

@app.post("/infer",
response_model=InferenceResponse)
async def infer(request: InferenceRequest):
    # Check if the response is cached
```

```
    cached_response =
get_cached_response(request.input_text)
    if cached_response:
        return InferenceResponse(**cached_response)

    input_ids =
tokenizer.encode(request.input_text,
return_tensors="pt")
    with torch.no_grad():
        outputs = model.generate(input_ids)
    output_text = tokenizer.decode(outputs[0],
skip_special_tokens=True)

    # Cache the response
    set_cached_response(request.input_text,
output_text)
    return
InferenceResponse(output_text=output_text)
```

Explanation:
This code snippet checks Redis for a cached response before generating output, thus reducing inference time for repeated requests.

4. Load Testing and Benchmarking

- **Load Testing:**
  Use tools like Apache JMeter or locust.io to simulate high traffic and measure how the system handles load.
- **Benchmarking:**
  Regularly benchmark the API with realistic workloads to ensure that performance targets are met. Document metrics like average response time and throughput for continuous monitoring.

Summary

- **Performance Metrics:**
  Focus on latency, throughput, resource utilization, error rates, and output quality.

- **Monitoring and Logging:**
  Utilize tools like Prometheus, Grafana, and APM services for real-time monitoring.
- **Optimization Strategies:**
  Implement caching, auto-scaling, load balancing, and efficient hardware usage to optimize deployment.
- **Load Testing:**
  Perform regular load testing and benchmarking to ensure the system meets performance requirements.

By following these steps and leveraging the provided code examples, you can effectively monitor and optimize the deployment of LangGraph LLM. This guidebook approach ensures that your model not only performs well under production loads but also remains scalable, efficient, and reliable over time.

5.5. ROI and Business Impact Analysis

This section provides a comprehensive guide to evaluating the return on investment (ROI) and overall business impact of deploying LangGraph LLM. Understanding these metrics is crucial for justifying the investment in advanced language models and for driving strategic decision-making. Below, we outline the key steps, considerations, and practical methods for conducting a thorough ROI and business impact analysis.

Objectives

- **Quantify Financial Returns:**
  Assess how the deployment of LangGraph LLM contributes to revenue growth, cost reduction, or both.
- **Measure Operational Efficiency:**
  Evaluate improvements in process automation, productivity gains, and resource utilization.
- **Identify Strategic Benefits:**
  Consider enhancements in customer satisfaction, competitive advantage, and innovation capabilities.

Step-by-Step Breakdown

1. Define Key Performance Indicators (KPIs)

- **Cost Savings:**
  - Reduction in manual labor and administrative costs.
  - Lower error rates and faster processing times leading to operational efficiency.
- **Revenue Growth:**
  - Increased sales or improved customer engagement through personalized services.
  - Faster market response due to enhanced decision-making support.
- **Time-to-Market Improvements:**
  - Reduced turnaround time for report generation, customer support, and content creation.
- **User Satisfaction and Retention:**
  - Enhanced customer experiences and higher Net Promoter Scores (NPS).

2. Collect Baseline Data

- **Pre-Deployment Metrics:**
  - Gather data on current operational costs, processing times, and revenue figures before deploying LangGraph LLM.
- **Benchmarking:**
  - Establish industry benchmarks and internal performance targets to compare against post-deployment metrics.

3. Quantify Improvements

- **Operational Efficiency:**
  - Measure the decrease in processing time per task (e.g., summarization, translation, customer support response).
  - Estimate cost savings from reduced manual intervention.
- **Revenue Impact:**
  - Track changes in conversion rates, upsell opportunities, or market share following model integration.
- **User Experience:**
  - Collect feedback through surveys and usage analytics to gauge improvements in customer satisfaction.

4. Conduct Financial Analysis

- **ROI Calculation:**
  Use the formula:

  ROI=Net Profit from DeploymentInvestment Cost×100\text{ROI} = \frac{\text{Net Profit from Deployment}}{\text{Investment Cost}} \times 100ROI=Investment CostNet Profit from Deployment×100

  where:

  - **Investment Cost:** Includes infrastructure, licensing, integration, and training expenses.
  - **Net Profit:** Gains realized through cost savings, increased revenues, and efficiency improvements.
- **Cost-Benefit Analysis:**
  - List all costs associated with deployment (development, maintenance, personnel, etc.).
  - Estimate the financial benefits over a specific period (e.g., annual savings, incremental revenue).
  - Compare these figures to determine the break-even point and long-term profitability.

5. Analyze Strategic Impact

- **Competitive Advantage:**
  - Evaluate how faster, more accurate language processing can differentiate your offerings.
  - Consider potential market positioning improvements and brand perception.
- **Scalability and Flexibility:**
  - Assess how the model's scalability supports future growth and adaptation to new market conditions.
- **Innovation Enablement:**
  - Identify new business opportunities enabled by advanced language capabilities, such as new product lines or services.

6. Reporting and Continuous Monitoring

- **Dashboard Creation:**
  - Develop dashboards using tools like PowerBI, Tableau, or Grafana to monitor KPIs in real time.

- **Regular Reviews:**
  - Schedule periodic evaluations to compare actual performance against projections.
  - Adjust strategies based on insights from continuous monitoring.

Practical Example: Case Study Analysis

Scenario: A financial services company deploys LangGraph LLM to automate report generation and customer support chatbots.

1. **Baseline Data:**
   - Average report generation time reduced from 60 minutes to 15 minutes.
   - Customer support response times drop by 40%, leading to improved customer satisfaction scores.
   - Manual labor cost savings of 30% per report and reduced call center costs.
2. **ROI Calculation:**
   - **Investment Cost:** $500,000 over one year.
   - **Annual Savings & Revenue Increase:** $750,000.
   - **ROI:**
     $750,000−$500,000$500,000×100=50%\frac{\$750,000 - \$500,000}{\$500,000} \times 100 = 50\%$500,000$750,000−$500,000×100=50%.
3. **Strategic Benefits:**
   - Enhanced brand reputation due to faster service.
   - Competitive edge through innovative technology integration.
   - Improved scalability allows handling peak periods without additional hiring.

Summary

- **Define KPIs:**
  Identify metrics like cost savings, revenue growth, and processing times.
- **Collect Baseline Data:**
  Establish performance benchmarks before deployment.
- **Quantify Improvements:**
  Measure operational, financial, and customer satisfaction improvements.

- **Financial Analysis:**
  Calculate ROI and perform cost-benefit analysis to determine the economic impact.
- **Strategic Impact:**
  Evaluate competitive advantage, scalability, and new business opportunities.
- **Continuous Monitoring:**
  Set up dashboards and regular reviews to track long-term performance.

By following these detailed steps and leveraging real-world examples, you can comprehensively analyze the ROI and business impact of deploying LangGraph LLM. This guidebook approach ensures that you have actionable insights and measurable metrics to justify investment decisions and drive strategic improvements across your organization.

Chapter 6: User Interaction, UI/UX, and Ethical Design

6.1. Designing Conversational Interfaces

This section offers a comprehensive guide for designing conversational interfaces that effectively leverage LangGraph LLM. Conversational interfaces—such as chatbots and virtual assistants—are crucial for creating engaging, intuitive, and efficient user experiences. The following guide outlines practical steps, design principles, and ethical considerations to build conversational systems that are both user-friendly and responsible.

Objectives

- **Enhance User Engagement:**
  Create interfaces that mimic natural human conversations, ensuring that users feel understood and supported.
- **Simplify Complex Interactions:**
  Break down intricate tasks into manageable conversational flows that guide users step-by-step.
- **Ensure Ethical and Transparent Communication:**
  Design interactions that respect user privacy, avoid biases, and provide clear disclosures about automated assistance.

Step-by-Step Guide to Designing Conversational Interfaces

1. Understand User Needs and Context

- **User Research:**
  Identify the target audience, their common tasks, and pain points.
  Example: Conduct surveys and interviews to gather insights about how users currently seek information or support.
- **Define Use Cases:**
  Establish clear scenarios for conversation. For instance:
    - Customer support for financial services.
    - Healthcare guidance and appointment scheduling.
    - Retail product recommendations.
- **Context Awareness:**
  Ensure the system captures context across conversation turns to

maintain coherence.

Tip: Use conversation history to dynamically adjust responses.

2. Develop Conversation Flows

- **Scripted Dialogues:**
  Start with a scripted dialogue for common interactions. This serves as the baseline conversation flow.
  - **Example:**
    For a customer support bot:
    1. **Greeting:** "Hello! How can I help you today?"
    2. **Query Understanding:** "Please describe your issue briefly."
    3. **Response:** Provide a solution or escalate if needed.
- **Dynamic Dialog Management:**
  Integrate LangGraph LLM to handle open-ended queries and adapt responses based on the conversation context.
  - **Example:**
    Combine rule-based templates with LLM-generated content for nuanced answers.
- **Fallback Mechanisms:**
  Define safe fallback responses for when the model is uncertain.
  - **Example:** "I'm not sure I understand. Could you please rephrase your question?"

3. Focus on User Interface and Experience

- **Clarity and Simplicity:**
  Design the UI to be clean and straightforward, minimizing cognitive load.
  - Use clear fonts, concise prompts, and intuitive navigation.
- **Multimodal Interaction:**
  Consider integrating text, voice, and visual elements.
  - **Example:** A chatbot that supports both text input and voice commands, with visual cues like icons and progress indicators.
- **Feedback and Guidance:**
  Allow users to easily provide feedback on responses and navigate through options.
  - **Practical Tip:** Include buttons for common follow-up actions (e.g., "More Info", "Contact Support").

4. Ethical Considerations and Transparency

- **User Data Privacy:**
  Ensure that the interface collects only necessary data, with clear privacy policies.
  - o **Example:** Provide a brief notice: "Your input is used to improve service quality and will not be shared without your consent."
- **Bias and Fairness:**
  Monitor and test the conversational interface to detect and mitigate any biases.
  - o **Practical Tip:** Regularly audit responses and include diverse data during fine-tuning to minimize skewed outputs.
- **Explainability:**
  Offer users the option to understand how decisions are made, particularly for critical tasks.
  - o **Example:** "This suggestion is based on your previous queries and our best practices in [industry]."

5. Prototyping and Iterative Testing

- **Rapid Prototyping:**
  Use tools like Figma or Adobe XD to design conversational mockups before full-scale development.
  - o **Practical Tip:** Simulate conversation flows with interactive prototypes to gather early user feedback.
- **User Testing:**
  Conduct usability tests with real users to identify friction points and iterate on the design.
  - o **Example:** Run A/B tests comparing different dialogue strategies to determine which approach yields higher satisfaction.
- **Integration with LangGraph LLM:**
  Test the integration of your conversational UI with LangGraph LLM in a controlled environment.
  - o **Practical Example:** Implement a beta version where user inputs are processed by LangGraph LLM, and feedback is collected to refine both the model responses and the UI flow.

Summary

- **User-Centric Design:**
  Begin with thorough research to understand user needs and context.
- **Structured Conversation Flows:**
  Combine scripted dialogues with dynamic, context-aware responses using LangGraph LLM.
- **Intuitive UI/UX:**
  Design clean, accessible interfaces that support multimodal interactions and guide users smoothly through tasks.
- **Ethical and Transparent Practices:**
  Prioritize user privacy, mitigate biases, and ensure clarity in how automated decisions are made.
- **Iterative Prototyping:**
  Rapidly prototype, test, and refine your conversational interface to achieve optimal user engagement.

By following these structured steps and best practices, you can design conversational interfaces that are not only functional and engaging but also ethically sound and user-friendly. This guidebook approach provides a clear, actionable framework for creating advanced, real-world conversational systems powered by LangGraph LLM.

6.1.1. Best Practices in UI/UX for AI

Designing interfaces for AI applications, particularly those powered by advanced language models like LangGraph LLM, requires a thoughtful approach that balances functionality, clarity, and ethical considerations. Below is a structured guide outlining best practices in UI/UX for AI, along with practical insights and examples to ensure your interfaces are effective and user-centric.

Key Best Practices

1. **Clarity and Simplicity**
   - **Clear Information Hierarchy:**
     Organize content in a logical flow. Use headers, concise labels, and clear calls-to-action to guide users through tasks without overwhelming them.
   - **Minimalist Design:**
     Remove unnecessary elements and focus on core functionalities. For instance, a chat interface should prominently feature the conversation area, input field, and essential buttons (e.g., "Send", "Help").

- o **Consistent Visual Language:**
  Maintain consistent fonts, colors, and iconography throughout the interface to build familiarity and trust.
2. **Contextual and Adaptive Interaction**
   - o **Personalization:**
     Use user data to tailor interactions, such as dynamic suggestions or adaptive content that changes based on past interactions.
   - o **Responsive Feedback:**
     Provide immediate visual or auditory feedback on user actions. For example, display loading indicators when the AI is processing a request.
   - o **Context Preservation:**
     Ensure that the system maintains conversational context across multiple turns, helping users feel that their interactions are coherent and meaningful.
3. **Transparency and Explainability**
   - o **Disclosure of AI Use:**
     Clearly indicate when a response is generated by AI. For instance, add a note like "Powered by LangGraph LLM" to build trust.
   - o **Explainable Responses:**
     When applicable, provide users with options to understand how certain decisions were made or to view additional details (e.g., "Why did we suggest this answer?").
   - o **User Control:**
     Allow users to easily adjust settings, such as tone or verbosity, and provide options for feedback if the AI's response seems off.
4. **Ethical and Responsible Design**
   - o **Data Privacy:**
     Ensure the interface communicates how user data is handled and stored. Incorporate clear privacy policies and user consent mechanisms.
   - o **Bias Mitigation:**
     Design for fairness by regularly auditing responses and ensuring diverse data representation. Offer users a mechanism to flag inappropriate or biased outputs.
   - o **Accessibility:**
     Follow accessibility standards (e.g., WCAG guidelines) to make the interface usable for all users, including those with

disabilities. This might include keyboard navigation, screen reader compatibility, and adequate color contrast.

5. **Iterative Prototyping and Testing**
   - **Rapid Prototyping:**
     Use tools like Figma or Sketch to design and test conversational flows before full development. This allows you to iterate quickly based on user feedback.
   - **User Testing:**
     Conduct usability studies and A/B testing to validate design choices. Gather feedback on how users interact with AI features and adjust accordingly.
   - **Analytics Integration:**
     Implement tracking (e.g., via Google Analytics or custom logging) to monitor usage patterns and identify friction points in the user journey.

Practical Example

Imagine you are designing a conversational interface for a virtual assistant that helps users with scheduling and reminders. Here's how you might apply these best practices:

- **Interface Layout:**
  Use a clean layout with a central chat window, a clear input field, and action buttons. Avoid clutter by keeping only essential information visible.
- **Dynamic Response Display:**
  When the assistant processes a request (e.g., "Schedule a meeting for tomorrow at 3 PM"), display a progress indicator. Once processed, show the confirmed action along with an explanation, such as "I've scheduled your meeting based on your availability. Would you like to add a reminder?"
- **Transparency Features:**
  Include an "Info" button that, when clicked, explains how the assistant interpreted the request and provides an option for the user to correct it if necessary.
- **Accessibility Enhancements:**
  Ensure that the chat interface supports screen readers by providing semantic HTML tags and ARIA attributes. For example:

```html
html
```

```
<div role="main" aria-label="Chat interface">
    <ul id="conversation">
        <li role="listitem">User: Schedule a
meeting for tomorrow at 3 PM.</li>
        <li role="listitem">Assistant: Your
meeting is scheduled for tomorrow at 3 PM.
<button aria-label="Explain
response">?</button></li>
    </ul>
    <input type="text" aria-label="Type your
message" placeholder="Enter your message..."
/>
    <button aria-label="Send
message">Send</button>
</div>
```

Summary

- **Clarity and Simplicity:**
  Design interfaces that are visually clean, easy to navigate, and focused on core functionalities.
- **Contextual Interaction:**
  Adapt interactions based on user context and provide immediate, clear feedback.
- **Transparency:**
  Clearly disclose AI usage and offer explainability for AI-driven decisions.
- **Ethical Design:**
  Prioritize data privacy, accessibility, and bias mitigation to build trust.
- **Iterative Testing:**
  Use prototyping and user testing to refine the interface continuously.

By following these best practices, you can create conversational interfaces that not only leverage the advanced capabilities of LangGraph LLM but also provide a seamless, engaging, and ethically responsible user experience. This guidebook approach ensures that your UI/UX design for AI applications meets both technical and human-centric standards.

6.1.2. Case Studies of Successful Implementations

175

This section highlights real-world examples where conversational interfaces powered by advanced language models have delivered measurable success. By reviewing these case studies, you can gain insights into practical design, deployment strategies, and the impact of well-designed UI/UX in AI systems. Below are detailed case studies that showcase best practices, challenges overcome, and the benefits realized across various industries.

Case Study 1: Virtual Healthcare Assistant

Overview:
A major healthcare provider implemented a virtual assistant to streamline patient support, appointment scheduling, and information dissemination.

Implementation Highlights:

- **User Research:**
  Extensive interviews and surveys identified common patient queries, such as appointment rescheduling, medication instructions, and symptom inquiries.
- **Conversational Design:**
  The interface featured a clean chat window with contextual prompts and quick-reply buttons for common tasks. An "Explain" option was available to help users understand recommendations.
- **Ethical Considerations:**
  Data privacy was paramount. The system clearly communicated how patient data was used, ensuring compliance with HIPAA regulations.

Outcomes:

- **Improved Efficiency:**
  Reduced call center volume by 40% as routine inquiries were handled by the virtual assistant.
- **Enhanced Patient Experience:**
  Patients reported a 30% increase in satisfaction scores due to faster response times and clear guidance.
- **Scalability:**
  The system easily managed peak loads during flu season, thanks to robust cloud deployment and auto-scaling features.

Case Study 2: Enterprise Customer Support Chatbot

Overview:
A global financial institution deployed a conversational interface to assist with customer support across multiple channels, including mobile and web applications.

Implementation Highlights:

- **Multi-Channel Integration:**
  The chatbot was integrated into the bank's website, mobile app, and even social media platforms, ensuring consistent user experience.
- **Dynamic Response Generation:**
  Leveraging LangGraph LLM's contextual understanding, the chatbot provided personalized responses for account inquiries, transaction details, and product information.
- **User Feedback Loop:**
  Users were able to rate responses, allowing continuous improvement and bias detection. The system also offered an escalation mechanism to human agents when needed.

Outcomes:

- **Cost Reduction:**
  Automated responses led to a 25% reduction in support costs by minimizing the need for human intervention.
- **User Engagement:**
  Customer engagement increased as the chatbot's ability to understand context led to more accurate and helpful interactions.
- **Operational Efficiency:**
  Faster resolution times resulted in higher customer satisfaction and reduced average handling time.

Case Study 3: Retail and Marketing Virtual Assistant

Overview:
A leading retail brand implemented an AI-powered virtual assistant to enhance the online shopping experience and personalize marketing efforts.

Implementation Highlights:

- **Personalization:**
  The assistant used previous browsing and purchase history to tailor product recommendations and answer queries related to product features and availability.
- **Conversational UI/UX:**
  A minimalist interface with a focus on visual elements, such as product images and quick action buttons, made navigation intuitive. The design prioritized clarity and ease of use.
- **Interactive Feedback:**
  The system included features for users to provide immediate feedback on recommendations, which was used to further refine the model.

Outcomes:

- **Sales Impact:**
  Personalized recommendations contributed to a 15% uplift in conversion rates during promotional campaigns.
- **Customer Retention:**
  Improved user engagement through conversational interfaces resulted in higher repeat purchase rates.
- **Brand Differentiation:**
  The innovative interface enhanced the brand's image as tech-forward and customer-centric.

Key Takeaways from Case Studies

- **User-Centric Design:**
  Successful implementations start with a deep understanding of user needs and context, ensuring that the conversational interface addresses real pain points.
- **Seamless Integration:**
  Integrating the AI model with existing systems and across multiple channels (web, mobile, social) is crucial for consistency and scalability.

- **Ethical and Transparent Practices:**
  Clearly communicating data usage, providing explainability features, and incorporating user feedback lead to higher trust and better outcomes.
- **Continuous Improvement:**
  Monitoring performance metrics and iterating on the design based on user feedback ensures that the system evolves with changing user expectations and business needs.

By examining these case studies, you can draw practical insights into designing, deploying, and refining conversational interfaces that leverage advanced language models like LangGraph LLM. This guidebook approach offers actionable strategies and proven methodologies that can be adapted to various industries, ensuring that your AI-driven conversational systems deliver measurable business impact and enhanced user experiences.

6.2. Enhancing Human-AI Interaction

This section offers a structured guide to optimizing the interaction between humans and AI systems powered by LangGraph LLM. Enhancing human-AI interaction is key to ensuring that the technology is not only powerful but also accessible, intuitive, and supportive of user needs. The following steps outline strategies, practical tips, and best practices to create an engaging and effective interaction experience.

Objectives

- **Improve Usability:**
  Design interfaces that are intuitive and reduce the cognitive load on users.
- **Increase Engagement:**
  Ensure that interactions feel natural and responsive, fostering user trust and satisfaction.
- **Facilitate Feedback:**
  Provide mechanisms for users to give feedback and help the system learn from real-world interactions.
- **Maintain Context:**
  Preserve conversation history to deliver coherent and contextually relevant responses.

Step-by-Step Strategies

1. Designing for Natural Conversation

- **Adopt a Conversational Tone:**
  Train and fine-tune LangGraph LLM to generate responses that mimic natural language. Use real dialogue data during fine-tuning to capture conversational nuances.
- **Context Awareness:**
  Implement features that retain conversation history. This can be achieved by maintaining a session context, so each response reflects prior exchanges.
- **Practical Tip:**
  Use a conversation buffer that concatenates recent messages, ensuring that the model has context without overwhelming it with too much data.

2. Interactive Feedback Mechanisms

- **User Feedback Options:**
  Provide buttons or options for users to rate responses (e.g., thumbs up/down) or flag issues. This direct feedback loop can help refine the model's responses over time.
- **Adaptive Responses:**
  Use feedback to adjust subsequent interactions. For example, if a user indicates that a response is unclear, the system can offer additional clarification or ask for more context.
- **Practical Example:**
  Incorporate a simple rating system within the chat interface:

```html
html

<div id="chat-message">
    <p>Assistant: Your meeting is scheduled
for tomorrow at 3 PM.</p>
    <button
onclick="sendFeedback('positive')">👍</button>
    <button
onclick="sendFeedback('negative')">👎</button>
</div>
<script>
    async function sendFeedback(rating) {
        await fetch("http://your-api-
server/feedback", {
```

```
         method: "POST",
         headers: { "Content-Type":
"application/json" },
         body: JSON.stringify({ messageId:
"12345", rating: rating })
     });
     alert("Thank you for your feedback!");
   }
</script>
```

Explanation: This simple implementation allows users to provide immediate feedback, which can be logged and analyzed to improve future interactions.

3. Enhancing Responsiveness and Engagement

- **Quick Response Times:**
  Optimize the model's inference speed and use asynchronous processing to reduce waiting times. Users appreciate fast, near-instant responses.
- **Visual and Auditory Cues:**
  Use loading animations, sound cues, or progress indicators to inform users that the system is processing their request. This keeps users engaged during any brief delays.
- **Personalization:**
  Adapt responses based on user preferences and history. Personalized interactions can make users feel more connected and valued.

4. Transparent Communication

- **Explainability:**
  Where appropriate, provide insights into why the AI responded in a certain way. This might include an optional "explain" feature that details key factors influencing the response.
- **Clear Disclosures:**
  Inform users when they are interacting with AI and provide details on data usage, ensuring transparency in how their information is processed.
- **Practical Tip:**
  Display a small banner or note such as "Powered by LangGraph LLM" along with a link to your privacy policy and user guide.

5. Iterative Testing and Refinement

- **User Testing Sessions:**
  Conduct usability tests with real users to observe interaction patterns, identify friction points, and gather qualitative feedback.
- **A/B Testing:**
  Experiment with different conversational styles, response formats, and UI elements to determine which approaches yield higher satisfaction and engagement.
- **Continuous Improvement:**
  Regularly update the model and interface based on user feedback and performance metrics. This iterative process ensures that the system evolves with user needs.

Summary

- **Natural Conversation:**
  Design responses that feel human-like, maintain context, and use real dialogue data for fine-tuning.
- **Feedback Integration:**
  Provide clear mechanisms for users to offer feedback, and use that feedback to drive continuous improvements.
- **Responsive Interaction:**
  Focus on reducing response times and using visual cues to keep users engaged.
- **Transparency and Personalization:**
  Clearly disclose AI involvement, offer explainability features, and personalize interactions based on user data.
- **Iterative Refinement:**
  Employ user testing and A/B testing to continually refine the interaction model and UI.

By following these best practices and leveraging practical examples, you can significantly enhance human-AI interaction in your conversational interfaces. This guidebook approach ensures that the design is user-centric, transparent, and continuously improving—leading to more engaging and effective interactions powered by LangGraph LLM.

6.2.1. Personalization and Adaptability

This section provides a guide to creating AI interactions that are personalized and adaptable to individual user preferences and contexts. Personalization enhances user engagement by delivering tailored responses, while adaptability ensures that the system evolves with changing user needs and situational contexts. Below are best practices, strategies, and practical examples to achieve effective personalization and adaptability in LangGraph LLM-powered systems.

Objectives

- **Tailor Interactions:**
  Customize responses based on user data such as past interactions, preferences, and behavioral patterns.
- **Dynamic Adaptation:**
  Adjust conversational strategies in real-time as the context evolves during an interaction.
- **Improve User Satisfaction:**
  Deliver more relevant and engaging responses, fostering a sense of individual attention.

Step-by-Step Strategies

1. User Profiling and Data Collection

- **Gather User Data:**
  Collect data from previous interactions, user preferences, demographic information, and behavioral patterns.
  Practical Tip: Ensure that data collection is transparent and complies with privacy regulations.
- **Profile Creation:**
  Develop user profiles that capture key attributes (e.g., interests, frequently asked questions, preferred tone).
  Example: Maintain a database or session-based profile that updates with each interaction.

2. Implementing Adaptive Response Generation

- **Context-Aware Dialogue:**
  Leverage conversation history to generate contextually relevant responses.
  Technique: Append recent conversation turns to the input of LangGraph LLM to maintain context.

- **Dynamic Tone and Style:**
  Adjust the tone and style of responses based on user preferences.
  Practical Example: Use predefined templates that vary in formality or enthusiasm, and allow the model to blend these with its generated text.
- **Feedback Loop:**
  Incorporate explicit user feedback mechanisms (e.g., ratings, quick polls) to fine-tune personalization.
  Tip: Use this data to adjust future interactions or re-train parts of the model if needed.

3. Adaptive Learning Techniques

- **Real-Time Adaptation:**
  Use online learning or incremental updates where feasible to adjust model parameters based on ongoing interactions.
- **A/B Testing:**
  Experiment with different personalization strategies and measure their impact on engagement and satisfaction.
- **Custom Response Engines:**
  Implement rule-based engines alongside LangGraph LLM to handle highly personalized responses in certain domains.
  Example: For customer support, use a hybrid approach where common queries are answered by a curated knowledge base and more complex questions are routed to the AI.

4. Practical Implementation Example

Below is a conceptual Python snippet that demonstrates how to personalize responses by incorporating user context and feedback into the inference pipeline:

```python
python

from fastapi import FastAPI, Request
from pydantic import BaseModel
import torch
```

```python
from langgraph_llm import LangGraphLLM  #
Hypothetical model import

# Define request and response models including
optional user context
class PersonalizedRequest(BaseModel):
    input_text: str
    user_id: str
    conversation_history: list = []  # List of
previous conversation turns

class PersonalizedResponse(BaseModel):
    output_text: str
    suggestions: list = []  # Optional: suggestions
for further interaction

app = FastAPI()
model = LangGraphLLM.from_pretrained("langgraph-
llm-base")
tokenizer = model.tokenizer
model.eval()

# Simulate a user profile store (in production, use
a database)
user_profiles = {
    "user123": {"preferred_tone": "friendly",
"recent_topics": ["scheduling", "weather"]},
}

@app.post("/personalize",
response_model=PersonalizedResponse)
async def personalize(request:
PersonalizedRequest):
    # Retrieve user context from profile store
    user_profile =
user_profiles.get(request.user_id, {})
    tone = user_profile.get("preferred_tone",
"neutral")
    # Combine conversation history with current
input for context
    context = " ".join(request.conversation_history
+ [request.input_text])
```

```python
    # Optionally, adjust prompt based on tone or
recent topics
    personalized_prompt = f"[Tone: {tone}]
{context}"

    input_ids =
tokenizer.encode(personalized_prompt,
return_tensors="pt", truncation=True)
    with torch.no_grad():
        output_ids = model.generate(input_ids,
max_length=100)
    output_text = tokenizer.decode(output_ids[0],
skip_special_tokens=True)

    # Optionally provide suggestions for next steps
    suggestions = ["Would you like more details?",
"Do you need further assistance?"]
    return
PersonalizedResponse(output_text=output_text,
suggestions=suggestions)

if __name__ == "__main__":
    import uvicorn
    uvicorn.run(app, host="0.0.0.0", port=8000)
```

Explanation:
In this example, the API endpoint /personalize incorporates user context by retrieving user preferences from a profile store and combining past conversation turns with the current query. The model's prompt is adjusted to reflect a preferred tone, and the system returns both a personalized response and suggestions for further engagement.

Summary

- **User Profiling:**
  Collect and maintain user data to build dynamic profiles.
- **Contextual Adaptation:**
  Leverage conversation history and user-specific attributes to generate tailored responses.

- **Dynamic Learning:**
  Integrate feedback and adaptive learning techniques to continually refine personalization.
- **Practical Implementation:**
  Use code examples and APIs to implement personalization strategies in real-world applications.

By following these strategies, you can significantly enhance human-AI interaction through personalized and adaptable conversational experiences. This guidebook approach ensures that your implementation of LangGraph LLM meets the diverse needs of users, delivering engaging and relevant interactions over time.

6.2.2. Feedback Loops and Continuous Improvement

This section provides a step-by-step guide to establishing effective feedback loops and strategies for continuous improvement in your LangGraph LLM-powered conversational systems. Feedback loops are essential to refine the AI's performance over time, ensuring that it adapts to evolving user needs and maintains high-quality interactions.

Objectives

- **Gather Actionable Feedback:**
  Collect detailed feedback from users to identify areas of improvement.
- **Analyze and Act on Data:**
  Use insights from feedback to adjust model parameters, conversation flows, or UI elements.
- **Implement Continuous Updates:**
  Establish processes for regularly updating the system based on feedback and performance metrics.

Step-by-Step Strategies

1. Integrating User Feedback Mechanisms

- **Feedback Collection Options:**
  - **In-Interface Rating:**
    Include simple rating buttons (e.g., thumbs up/down) for users to quickly indicate satisfaction.

- o **Open-Ended Responses:**
  Provide an option for users to leave comments or suggestions on responses.
- o **Surveys and Polls:**
  Periodically prompt users with short surveys to gather more in-depth insights.
- **Practical Example:**
  Implement a feedback button in your chatbot interface:

html

```
<div id="chat-message">
    <p>Assistant: Your appointment is
confirmed for tomorrow at 10 AM.</p>
    <button
onclick="sendFeedback('positive')">👍</button>
    <button
onclick="sendFeedback('negative')">👎</button>
</div>
<script>
    async function sendFeedback(rating) {
        await fetch("http://your-api-
server/feedback", {
            method: "POST",
            headers: { "Content-Type":
"application/json" },
            body: JSON.stringify({ messageId:
"msg123", rating: rating })
        });
        alert("Thank you for your feedback!");
    }
</script>
```

Explanation:
This simple integration allows users to provide immediate feedback, which can be logged and analyzed.

2. Logging and Analyzing Feedback

- **Structured Logging:**
  Record feedback along with relevant context such as conversation history, timestamps, and user demographics.

Tip: Use a logging framework or database to store feedback data for analysis.

- **Analytics Tools:**
  Leverage tools like ELK Stack, Grafana, or custom dashboards to visualize feedback trends and identify common issues.
- **Regular Review Sessions:**
  Set up periodic reviews (e.g., weekly or monthly) where the feedback data is analyzed to detect recurring problems or opportunities for enhancement.

3. Implementing Continuous Improvement

- **Model Retraining:**
  Use collected feedback to refine training datasets or adjust fine-tuning strategies. For example, if users consistently flag certain responses as unclear, update the training data with additional examples that address these nuances.
- **Iterative UI/UX Updates:**
  Adjust interface elements based on user behavior and feedback. This may involve refining conversation flows, adding clarifications, or modifying visual elements for better accessibility.
- **A/B Testing:**
  Deploy alternative versions of conversational flows or responses to a subset of users. Compare performance metrics (e.g., satisfaction scores, resolution times) and adopt the best-performing variations.
- **Automated Monitoring:**
  Implement automated monitoring systems that trigger alerts when key performance indicators (KPIs) such as latency, error rates, or negative feedback exceed acceptable thresholds. This allows for prompt intervention and adjustments.

4. Closing the Feedback Loop

- **User Communication:**
  Inform users that their feedback has been heard and, where possible, highlight improvements made as a result. This fosters trust and encourages continued feedback.
- **Documentation:**
  Maintain a changelog or improvement log that details updates made based on feedback. This transparency helps stakeholders understand the continuous evolution of the system.

Summary

- **Integrate Multiple Feedback Channels:**
  Use in-interface ratings, surveys, and open-ended responses to gather comprehensive feedback.
- **Analyze Feedback Systematically:**
  Leverage structured logging and analytics tools to identify trends and recurring issues.
- **Implement Iterative Improvements:**
  Regularly update the model and user interface based on feedback, using A/B testing and automated monitoring for continuous optimization.
- **Close the Loop:**
  Communicate changes to users and document improvements to build trust and sustain a cycle of continuous improvement.

By following these best practices and strategies, you can create robust feedback loops that drive continuous improvement in your LangGraph LLM-powered conversational systems. This guidebook approach ensures that your AI remains responsive to user needs, evolves over time, and consistently delivers high-quality interactions.

6.3. Ethical Considerations in Language AI

This section provides a comprehensive guidebook for addressing ethical considerations when deploying and utilizing language AI systems such as LangGraph LLM. Given the transformative impact of AI on communication and decision-making, it is essential to design and operate these systems responsibly. Below, we outline key ethical principles, actionable strategies, and practical examples to ensure that your implementation of language AI is fair, transparent, and respectful of user privacy and societal norms.

Objectives

- **Promote Fairness and Reduce Bias:**
  Implement measures to identify, mitigate, and monitor biases in model outputs to ensure equitable treatment across diverse user groups.
- **Ensure Transparency and Accountability:**
  Clearly communicate how the AI system functions, how data is used, and provide explainability for AI-driven decisions.

- **Protect User Privacy:**
  Safeguard personal data and ensure compliance with relevant privacy regulations (e.g., GDPR, CCPA).
- **Uphold Ethical Use:**
  Establish policies and safeguards to prevent misuse of the technology and ensure that AI applications contribute positively to society.

Step-by-Step Strategies

1. Bias Mitigation

- **Data Diversity and Quality:**
  - **Action:** Ensure your training datasets are diverse and representative of different demographics, dialects, and viewpoints.
  - **Example:** Regularly audit your data sources to check for imbalances and supplement underrepresented groups with additional high-quality data.
- **Algorithmic Fairness:**
  - **Action:** Integrate fairness metrics and bias detection tools into your model evaluation process.
  - **Practical Tip:** Use tools such as IBM's AI Fairness 360 or Microsoft Fairlearn to assess and mitigate biases.
- **Ongoing Monitoring:**
  - **Action:** Set up regular reviews of model outputs to identify potential biases, and implement feedback loops to continuously adjust the model.
  - **Example:** Monitor sentiment analysis outputs across different demographic groups to ensure consistent performance.

2. Transparency and Explainability

- **User Communication:**
  - **Action:** Clearly indicate when users are interacting with an AI system. Include labels like "Powered by LangGraph LLM" and provide accessible documentation.
  - **Example:** In your chatbot UI, display a brief note about data usage and AI involvement.
- **Explainable AI Techniques:**
  - **Action:** Incorporate explainability features that allow users to understand how a particular output was generated.

- o **Practical Tip:** Offer an "Explain" button that shows key factors influencing a response, such as highlighted text or reasoning snippets.
- **Documentation:**
  - o **Action:** Maintain comprehensive documentation detailing model development, data sources, potential biases, and limitations.
  - o **Example:** Publish a transparency report that outlines model updates, performance metrics, and ethical assessments.

3. User Privacy and Data Protection

- **Data Minimization:**
  - o **Action:** Collect only the data necessary for the intended purpose, and anonymize or pseudonymize personal information wherever possible.
  - o **Example:** Before storing chat logs, remove or obfuscate personal identifiers to protect user privacy.
- **Secure Data Handling:**
  - o **Action:** Implement strong security measures, including encryption, secure storage, and access controls.
  - o **Practical Tip:** Use HTTPS for data transmission and ensure databases are secured with robust authentication.
- **Compliance and Consent:**
  - o **Action:** Ensure that all data collection and processing practices comply with relevant regulations (GDPR, CCPA). Provide clear consent forms and privacy policies.
  - o **Example:** Integrate a consent pop-up on your website that informs users about data usage and provides an option to opt out.

4. Preventing Misuse and Promoting Responsible AI

- **Usage Guidelines:**
  - o **Action:** Define clear guidelines for how the AI system should be used and establish boundaries to prevent harmful applications.
  - o **Example:** Include terms of service that explicitly prohibit the use of the model for generating harmful or misleading content.

- **Access Control:**
  - **Action:** Restrict access to the model via secure API keys or authentication protocols to prevent unauthorized or malicious use.
  - **Practical Tip:** Implement rate limiting and logging to monitor unusual activity.
- **Ethical Oversight:**
  - **Action:** Establish an ethical review board or committee to periodically assess the system's impact and address any emerging ethical concerns.
  - **Example:** Conduct regular ethics audits to review feedback and adjust policies accordingly.

Summary

- **Bias Mitigation:**
  Ensure data diversity, use fairness metrics, and continuously monitor outputs to reduce bias.
- **Transparency:**
  Clearly communicate AI involvement, offer explainability features, and maintain detailed documentation.
- **User Privacy:**
  Collect minimal data, secure it rigorously, and comply with all relevant privacy regulations.
- **Responsible Use:**
  Define and enforce usage guidelines, control access, and establish ethical oversight to prevent misuse.

By implementing these strategies, you can build a LangGraph LLM-powered system that is not only technologically advanced but also ethically responsible and user-centric. This guidebook approach ensures that ethical considerations are embedded throughout the development, deployment, and ongoing operation of your AI systems, ultimately fostering trust and promoting positive societal impact.

6.3.1. Bias, Fairness, and Transparency

This section provides a structured guide to addressing bias, ensuring fairness, and maintaining transparency in LangGraph LLM-powered systems. These principles are essential for building AI that is responsible, trustworthy, and accessible to all users. Below, we outline key strategies, best practices, and practical examples to help you design systems that actively mitigate bias, promote fairness, and operate transparently.

Objectives

- **Mitigate Bias:**
  Identify, measure, and reduce biases in training data and model outputs to ensure equitable treatment across diverse user groups.
- **Ensure Fairness:**
  Implement fairness metrics and techniques that ensure consistent performance and decision-making regardless of user demographics.
- **Promote Transparency:**
  Clearly communicate the role of AI, how decisions are made, and provide mechanisms for users to understand and challenge outcomes.

Step-by-Step Strategies

1. Data and Model Auditing

- **Diverse and Representative Data:**
  - **Action:** Regularly audit your training data to ensure it represents a wide range of demographics, dialects, and viewpoints.
  - **Example:** Review dataset statistics to detect over-representation or under-representation of certain groups. Supplement with additional data when necessary.
- **Bias Detection Tools:**
  - **Action:** Utilize fairness assessment tools such as IBM's AI Fairness 360 or Microsoft Fairlearn to evaluate model outputs.
  - **Practical Tip:** Integrate these tools into your evaluation pipeline to automatically flag outputs that exhibit potential biases.

2. Fairness in Model Development

- **Algorithmic Fairness:**

- **Action:** Incorporate fairness-aware training techniques, such as reweighting, adversarial debiasing, or fairness constraints during model optimization.
- **Example:** Apply techniques that adjust loss functions to penalize biased predictions, ensuring that minority groups are not systematically disadvantaged.
- **Regular Monitoring:**
  - **Action:** Establish continuous monitoring of model performance across different demographic segments.
  - **Practical Tip:** Set up dashboards that track key fairness metrics (e.g., disparate impact, equality of opportunity) to ensure ongoing compliance.

3. Transparency in AI Systems

- **Clear Disclosure:**
  - **Action:** Inform users when they are interacting with an AI system. Provide clear labels such as "Powered by LangGraph LLM" and include brief explanations of what the system does.
  - **Example:** Add a visible note in your user interface that explains the role of AI in generating responses and highlights any limitations.
- **Explainability Features:**
  - **Action:** Integrate mechanisms that allow users to query how specific decisions or outputs were derived.
  - **Practical Example:** Implement an "Explain" button in your chatbot that reveals key factors or data points used to generate a response, such as highlighted input segments or relevant context excerpts.
- **Detailed Documentation:**
  - **Action:** Maintain and publish comprehensive documentation that details the data sources, model architecture, training processes, and potential limitations.
  - **Practical Tip:** Create a transparency report that is accessible to both technical and non-technical stakeholders.

4. User Empowerment and Feedback

- **Feedback Mechanisms:**
  - **Action:** Provide users with easy-to-use feedback channels to report biased or unsatisfactory responses.

- Example: Implement rating systems or comment boxes within the UI to capture user impressions and specific concerns.
- **Responsive Adjustments:**
  - **Action:** Use collected feedback to refine model behavior and retrain the system periodically, ensuring continuous improvement in fairness and transparency.
  - **Practical Tip:** Schedule regular review sessions to analyze feedback data and update training datasets or model parameters accordingly.

Practical Implementation Example

Below is a simplified example demonstrating how to integrate transparency and bias mitigation in a conversational AI interface using Python and FastAPI:

```python
python

from fastapi import FastAPI, Request
from pydantic import BaseModel
import torch
from langgraph_llm import LangGraphLLM   #
Hypothetical import

# Define request and response models
class ChatRequest(BaseModel):
    message: str
    user_id: str

class ChatResponse(BaseModel):
    reply: str
    explanation: str  # Provides transparency on
how the reply was generated

app = FastAPI()
model = LangGraphLLM.from_pretrained("langgraph-
llm-base")
tokenizer = model.tokenizer
model.eval()
```

```python
# Simple function to simulate an explanation (in
practice, integrate explainability methods)
def generate_explanation(message):
    return f"Response generated considering key
factors from your query: '{message[:30]}...'"

@app.post("/chat", response_model=ChatResponse)
async def chat(request: ChatRequest):
    # Basic logging for bias monitoring (in
production, log more metadata for analysis)
    print(f"User {request.user_id} sent:
{request.message}")

    # Tokenize and generate the response
    input_ids = tokenizer.encode(request.message,
return_tensors="pt", truncation=True)
    with torch.no_grad():
        output_ids = model.generate(input_ids,
max_length=100)
    reply = tokenizer.decode(output_ids[0],
skip_special_tokens=True)

    # Generate an explanation for transparency
    explanation =
generate_explanation(request.message)

    return ChatResponse(reply=reply,
explanation=explanation)

if __name__ == "__main__":
    import uvicorn
    uvicorn.run(app, host="0.0.0.0", port=8000)
```

Explanation:

- **Bias Monitoring:** The system logs basic metadata (e.g., user ID, message) to help with bias analysis.
- **Transparency:** An explanation is provided with each response, giving users insight into the factors influencing the output.
- **User Empowerment:** This structure encourages users to understand and engage with the AI's decision-making process.

Summary

- **Bias Mitigation:**
  Ensure data diversity, apply fairness-aware training, and use bias detection tools.
- **Fairness:**
  Monitor performance across demographics and adjust training processes to minimize inequities.
- **Transparency:**
  Clearly disclose AI involvement, offer explainability features, and maintain thorough documentation.
- **User Empowerment:**
  Implement feedback loops to capture and act upon user insights, ensuring continuous improvement.

By following these best practices and incorporating practical feedback and transparency measures, you can build LangGraph LLM-powered systems that are ethically responsible, fair, and trusted by users. This guidebook approach provides clear, actionable steps to mitigate bias and promote transparency in AI applications.

6.3.2. Privacy and Data Security

This section provides a step-by-step guide for ensuring robust privacy and data security in LangGraph LLM-powered applications. Protecting user data and maintaining high security standards is essential for building trust and complying with legal and ethical obligations. Below, we outline best practices, strategies, and practical examples to help you safeguard personal information and secure data throughout the lifecycle of your AI system.

Objectives

- **Protect User Data:**
  Implement measures to ensure that sensitive data is handled responsibly, stored securely, and accessed only by authorized parties.
- **Ensure Compliance:**
  Adhere to legal standards such as GDPR, CCPA, or other relevant privacy regulations to avoid breaches and fines.
- **Maintain System Integrity:**
  Prevent unauthorized access, data leaks, and other security risks through robust encryption, secure protocols, and regular audits.

Step-by-Step Strategies

1. Data Minimization and Anonymization

- **Collect Only Necessary Data:**
  - ○ **Action:** Limit data collection to what is strictly required for the intended purpose.
  - ○ **Example:** Instead of storing full names and addresses, collect only anonymized identifiers unless absolutely necessary.
- **Anonymize and Pseudonymize Data:**
  - ○ **Action:** Remove or mask personally identifiable information (PII) before processing or storing data.
  - ○ **Practical Tip:** Use hashing or tokenization methods to anonymize sensitive fields, ensuring that data cannot be easily traced back to an individual.

2. Secure Data Storage and Transmission

- **Encryption:**
  - ○ **Action:** Encrypt data at rest and in transit using strong encryption standards.
  - ○ **Example:** Utilize AES-256 for data storage and TLS for securing HTTP communications.
- **Access Control:**
  - ○ **Action:** Implement strict access control mechanisms, ensuring that only authorized users and systems can access sensitive data.
  - ○ **Practical Tip:** Use role-based access control (RBAC) and multi-factor authentication (MFA) to enhance security.
- **Secure APIs:**
  - ○ **Action:** Protect API endpoints with secure protocols and authentication.
  - ○ **Example:** Enforce HTTPS and use API keys or OAuth to control access to LangGraph LLM services.

3. Regular Auditing and Monitoring

- **Security Audits:**
  - ○ **Action:** Conduct regular security audits and vulnerability assessments to identify and mitigate potential risks.

- o **Practical Tip:** Schedule quarterly audits and employ third-party security experts for unbiased assessments.
- **Logging and Monitoring:**
  - o **Action:** Implement robust logging to track data access and modifications. Monitor for suspicious activities using automated tools.
  - o **Example:** Use SIEM (Security Information and Event Management) systems like Splunk or ELK Stack to aggregate and analyze security logs.

4. Compliance and User Consent

- **Privacy Policies and Consent Mechanisms:**
  - o **Action:** Clearly communicate data usage policies and obtain explicit consent from users for data collection and processing.
  - o **Practical Tip:** Include consent forms and privacy notices in your application, ensuring that users are aware of what data is collected and how it will be used.
- **Regulatory Compliance:**
  - o **Action:** Ensure that your data practices comply with relevant regulations (e.g., GDPR, CCPA).
  - o **Example:** Implement mechanisms for users to access, modify, or delete their data as required by law.

5. Incident Response and Recovery

- **Develop an Incident Response Plan:**
  - o **Action:** Prepare a comprehensive plan for responding to data breaches or security incidents.
  - o **Practical Tip:** Include procedures for containment, investigation, and notification, and regularly conduct drills to ensure readiness.
- **Backup and Recovery:**
  - o **Action:** Regularly back up critical data and establish robust recovery procedures.
  - o **Example:** Use automated backup solutions and maintain redundant storage to minimize downtime in case of data loss.

Practical Implementation Example

Below is an example of setting up secure API communication using FastAPI and HTTPS:

```python
python

from fastapi import FastAPI, Depends,
HTTPException, Security
from fastapi.security.api_key import APIKeyHeader
import uvicorn
import ssl

API_KEY = "your_secure_api_key"
api_key_header = APIKeyHeader(name="X-API-Key")

app = FastAPI()

def get_api_key(api_key: str =
Depends(api_key_header)):
    if api_key != API_KEY:
        raise HTTPException(status_code=403,
detail="Could not validate credentials")
    return api_key

@app.get("/secure-data")
async def secure_data(api_key: str =
Depends(get_api_key)):
    # Secure endpoint logic here
    return {"message": "Secure data access
granted."}

if __name__ == "__main__":
    # Create an SSL context for HTTPS
    ssl_context =
ssl.create_default_context(ssl.Purpose.CLIENT_AUTH)

ssl_context.load_cert_chain(certfile="path/to/cert.
pem", keyfile="path/to/key.pem")

    uvicorn.run(app, host="0.0.0.0", port=8000,
ssl_context=ssl_context)
```

Explanation:
This code demonstrates how to secure an API endpoint by enforcing API key authentication and using HTTPS for secure communication. The SSL context ensures that data transmitted over the network is encrypted.

Summary

- **Data Minimization:**
  Collect only necessary data and use anonymization techniques.
- **Encryption and Access Control:**
  Secure data at rest and in transit with strong encryption and strict access controls.
- **Regular Audits:**
  Conduct frequent security audits and implement comprehensive logging and monitoring.
- **Compliance:**
  Ensure transparency with privacy policies and obtain user consent, adhering to regulatory standards.
- **Incident Response:**
  Prepare and regularly update an incident response plan along with robust backup and recovery mechanisms.

By following these best practices and leveraging practical examples, you can ensure that your LangGraph LLM-powered applications maintain high levels of privacy and data security. This guidebook approach provides actionable strategies to protect sensitive information, build user trust, and comply with regulatory requirements.

6.4. Regulatory Frameworks and Compliance

This section provides a detailed guide on navigating the regulatory frameworks and ensuring compliance when deploying LangGraph LLM-powered applications. In today's data-driven environment, adhering to legal and ethical standards is essential to protect user rights and build trust. The following guide outlines key regulatory requirements, strategies for compliance, and practical steps to ensure that your system meets all necessary legal obligations.

Objectives

- **Understand Key Regulations:**
  Identify the major regulatory frameworks (e.g., GDPR, CCPA) that impact data usage and AI applications.
- **Establish Compliance Processes:**
  Develop policies and procedures to ensure that data collection, processing, and storage practices are in line with legal standards.

- **Maintain Transparency:**
  Clearly communicate with users about data handling practices and obtain proper consent.

Step-by-Step Strategies

1. Identify Relevant Regulatory Frameworks

- **General Data Protection Regulation (GDPR):**
  - o **Scope:** Applies to organizations processing personal data of EU citizens.
  - o **Key Requirements:** Data minimization, purpose limitation, user consent, and the right to access, rectify, or delete personal data.
- **California Consumer Privacy Act (CCPA):**
  - o **Scope:** Applies to companies doing business in California that collect personal information.
  - o **Key Requirements:** Transparency in data collection, providing users with the right to opt out of data selling, and ensuring data security.
- **Other Regulations:**
  - o Consider additional frameworks such as HIPAA for healthcare data, or sector-specific regulations that may apply to your application.

2. Develop and Document Compliance Policies

- **Data Governance Policies:**
  - o **Action:** Establish clear policies for data collection, storage, usage, and sharing.
  - o **Example:** Document procedures for anonymizing data and ensuring that only necessary information is collected.
- **Consent Mechanisms:**
  - o **Action:** Implement mechanisms for obtaining explicit user consent.
  - o **Example:** Use clear, accessible consent forms and provide users with the option to opt out of data collection.
- **User Rights Management:**
  - o **Action:** Develop processes for handling user requests to access, correct, or delete their data.
  - o **Example:** Create a dedicated portal where users can manage their data preferences and submit data access requests.

3. Implement Technical Measures for Compliance

- **Data Encryption and Security:**
  - **Action:** Use strong encryption for data at rest and in transit.
  - **Practical Tip:** Implement TLS for data transmission and AES-256 for data storage.
- **Access Controls:**
  - **Action:** Enforce role-based access control (RBAC) and multi-factor authentication (MFA) to limit data access.
  - **Example:** Ensure that only authorized personnel can access sensitive data and audit these access logs regularly.
- **Data Anonymization and Minimization:**
  - **Action:** Apply anonymization techniques to remove personally identifiable information (PII) from datasets.
  - **Practical Tip:** Use hashing or tokenization to protect sensitive user data.

4. Continuous Monitoring and Auditing

- **Regular Compliance Audits:**
  - **Action:** Schedule periodic internal and external audits to review data practices.
  - **Example:** Conduct quarterly reviews to ensure that all processes align with GDPR and CCPA standards.
- **Monitoring Tools:**
  - **Action:** Deploy monitoring systems that track data access and usage, and alert on any deviations from compliance.
  - **Example:** Use SIEM (Security Information and Event Management) tools to consolidate and analyze security logs.
- **Update Policies and Procedures:**
  - **Action:** Continuously update compliance documentation to reflect changes in regulations and emerging best practices.
  - **Practical Tip:** Maintain a compliance dashboard that is reviewed by legal and technical teams on a regular basis.

Summary

- **Regulatory Awareness:**
  Understand and identify key frameworks such as GDPR, CCPA, and sector-specific regulations that impact your application.

- **Policy Development:**
  Establish comprehensive data governance policies, consent mechanisms, and user rights management processes.
- **Technical Compliance:**
  Implement robust security measures including encryption, access controls, and data anonymization to protect sensitive information.
- **Continuous Auditing:**
  Regularly monitor, audit, and update your compliance practices to ensure ongoing adherence to regulatory standards.

By following these steps and best practices, you can ensure that your LangGraph LLM-powered applications are not only innovative and efficient but also legally compliant and ethically responsible. This guidebook approach provides clear, actionable strategies to navigate the complex regulatory landscape, thereby safeguarding user rights and maintaining organizational trust.

Chapter 7: Innovations and Future Trends in Language Intelligence

7.1. Emerging Technologies in NLP

This section explores the cutting-edge advancements and emerging technologies that are shaping the future of Natural Language Processing (NLP). As the field evolves, new methodologies, architectures, and applications continue to push the boundaries of what language models can achieve. In this guidebook-style overview, we outline key emerging trends, discuss their potential impact, and provide practical insights to help you stay ahead in the rapidly evolving world of language intelligence.

Objectives

- **Stay Informed on Advancements:**
  Understand the latest research and technological breakthroughs that are influencing NLP.
- **Identify Opportunities for Innovation:**
  Explore how emerging technologies can be integrated with existing models like LangGraph LLM to enhance performance and functionality.
- **Prepare for Future Trends:**
  Gain insights into how these innovations might shape future applications and industry standards.

Step-by-Step Overview

1. Transformer Advancements and Beyond

- **Next-Generation Transformers:**
  - **Innovation:**
    Researchers are continuously refining transformer architectures to improve efficiency, context capture, and scalability. Recent developments include sparse transformers, long-range transformers, and dynamic attention mechanisms.
  - **Practical Insight:**
    Evaluate how these advancements can reduce computational costs and enhance performance on tasks involving long documents or complex dependencies.

- o **Example:**
  Explore models like Longformer or BigBird, which extend the transformer's attention mechanism to handle longer sequences efficiently, and consider integrating similar techniques into LangGraph LLM.

2. Graph Neural Networks (GNNs) in NLP

- **Integration with Language Models:**
  - o **Innovation:**
    Graph Neural Networks (GNNs) are being integrated with traditional NLP models to capture relational and structural information more effectively.
  - o **Practical Insight:**
    Leverage graph-based reasoning to enhance the understanding of syntactic and semantic relationships in text. This hybrid approach can improve tasks like dependency parsing, knowledge extraction, and semantic role labeling.
  - o **Example:**
    Investigate models that combine transformers with GNN layers, such as Graph Attention Networks (GATs), to assess how these techniques can be applied to enhance context-aware language processing.

3. Multimodal and Cross-Modal Learning

- **Combining Text with Other Modalities:**
  - o **Innovation:**
    Emerging research is focusing on models that can process and integrate multiple data types (e.g., text, images, audio, and video) to create richer and more context-aware representations.
  - o **Practical Insight:**
    Consider how multimodal learning can expand the application areas of language models, such as in visual question answering, image captioning, or video summarization.
  - o **Example:**
    Examine models like CLIP (Contrastive Language–Image Pre-training) by OpenAI, which jointly learns from text and images, and explore ways to incorporate multimodal elements into your systems.

4. Reinforcement Learning for Interactive and Adaptive Systems

- **Enhancing Interaction Quality:**
  - **Innovation:**
    Reinforcement learning is increasingly used to fine-tune conversational agents, enabling them to learn from real-time interactions and improve over time.
  - **Practical Insight:**
    Utilize user feedback and interaction data to dynamically update model responses, making conversational systems more adaptive and personalized.
  - **Example:**
    Explore reinforcement learning techniques in dialogue management to create AI systems that can adjust their strategies based on user engagement and satisfaction metrics.

5. Ethical AI and Responsible Innovation

- **Incorporating Ethical Considerations:**
  - **Innovation:**
    As language models become more powerful, ensuring ethical use, transparency, and fairness is paramount. Emerging technologies focus on integrating bias mitigation, explainability, and user consent mechanisms directly into AI systems.
  - **Practical Insight:**
    Develop frameworks that not only improve model performance but also address ethical challenges, ensuring that AI applications are trustworthy and socially responsible.
  - **Example:**
    Utilize fairness and explainability tools, and monitor models continuously to detect and mitigate bias. Design user interfaces that provide clear disclosures about AI involvement and data usage.

6. Personalized and Context-Aware Systems

- **Tailoring AI to Individual Users:**
  - **Innovation:**
    Advances in personalization and adaptive learning allow models to provide highly customized experiences based on user context, preferences, and history.

- o **Practical Insight:**
  Integrate techniques such as transfer learning, adaptive response generation, and continuous feedback loops to create systems that evolve with user interactions.
- o **Example:**
  Implement personalized conversational agents that use dynamic user profiles and real-time feedback to tailor responses, leading to more engaging and relevant interactions.

Summary

- **Next-Generation Transformers:**
  Explore advancements in transformer architectures that improve efficiency and context handling.
- **Graph Neural Networks:**
  Integrate GNNs to enhance relational reasoning in NLP tasks.
- **Multimodal Learning:**
  Combine text with images, audio, and other modalities for richer context and broader applications.
- **Reinforcement Learning:**
  Use reinforcement learning to adapt and personalize interactive AI systems.
- **Ethical and Responsible AI:**
  Prioritize ethical considerations, bias mitigation, and transparency to build trustworthy AI.
- **Personalization:**
  Leverage adaptive techniques to create personalized, context-aware systems that improve user engagement.

By following these steps and exploring these emerging technologies, you can position your LangGraph LLM-powered systems at the forefront of NLP innovation. This guidebook approach provides a clear framework for understanding the current trends and future directions in language intelligence, ensuring that you remain well-prepared to incorporate these advances into your projects.

7.1.1. Advances in Graph Neural Networks

Graph Neural Networks (GNNs) have evolved significantly in recent years, offering powerful methods to model relationships and interactions within data. In the realm of NLP, GNNs are increasingly being integrated with language models to capture complex dependencies that traditional sequential models may miss. This section outlines the latest advancements in GNNs, their integration with language models, and practical approaches for leveraging these technologies.

Objectives

- **Enhance Relational Reasoning:**
  Use advanced GNN architectures to capture syntactic, semantic, and contextual relationships in language data.
- **Improve Scalability and Efficiency:**
  Explore techniques that allow GNNs to process large-scale graphs without sacrificing performance.
- **Integrate with NLP Models:**
  Combine the strengths of GNNs with transformer-based models to create hybrid systems that deliver richer representations and improved task performance.

Key Advances in Graph Neural Networks

1. Novel Architectures and Techniques

- **Graph Convolutional Networks (GCNs) Enhancements:**
  - **Deep GCNs:**
    Techniques to overcome over-smoothing and vanishing gradients, enabling deeper networks that capture long-range dependencies.
  - **Residual Connections:**
    Incorporating skip connections similar to those in ResNet to preserve information across layers.
- **Graph Attention Networks (GATs):**
  - **Attention Mechanisms:**
    Use self-attention on graph nodes to weigh the importance of neighboring nodes dynamically.
  - **Adaptive Attention:**
    Advanced GATs can adapt their attention strategies based on the structure of the graph, improving performance on heterogeneous data.
- **Dynamic and Heterogeneous Graphs:**
  - **Temporal Graph Networks:**
    Models that handle time-evolving graphs, capturing dynamic interactions.

- o **Heterogeneous Graph Neural Networks:**
  Techniques that integrate multiple types of nodes and edges, crucial for modeling complex language structures with various relationships.

2. Scalability Improvements

- **Sampling Techniques:**
  Methods like GraphSAGE and FastGCN sample a subset of nodes and edges to make training on large graphs computationally feasible.
- **Distributed GNN Training:**
  Leveraging distributed computing frameworks to train GNNs on large-scale graphs, ensuring efficient utilization of computational resources.
- **Low-Rank Approximations:**
  Applying matrix factorization and other low-rank techniques to reduce the complexity of graph convolution operations.

3. Integration with Language Models

- **Hybrid Architectures:**
  Combining GNNs with transformer-based models to enhance language understanding. For example, embedding graph-derived representations into the transformer's self-attention mechanism can yield better context awareness.
- **Task-Specific Applications:**
  Utilizing GNN-enhanced models for tasks such as dependency parsing, knowledge graph construction, and semantic role labeling, which benefit from explicit relational modeling.

Practical Implementation Example

Below is an example demonstrating how to integrate a Graph Attention Network (GAT) module with a transformer-based language model for enhanced context representation.

```python
import torch
import torch.nn as nn
import torch.nn.functional as F
from torch_geometric.nn import GATConv
```

```python
class GATModule(nn.Module):
    def __init__(self, in_channels, out_channels,
heads=4):
        super(GATModule, self).__init__()
        self.gat_conv = GATConv(in_channels,
out_channels, heads=heads, concat=True,
dropout=0.1)

    def forward(self, x, edge_index):
        # x: Node feature matrix, edge_index: Graph
connectivity in COO format
        x = self.gat_conv(x, edge_index)
        return F.elu(x)

class HybridModel(nn.Module):
    def __init__(self, transformer_model,
gat_in_channels, gat_out_channels):
        super(HybridModel, self).__init__()
        self.transformer = transformer_model  #
Pre-trained transformer model
        self.gat = GATModule(gat_in_channels,
gat_out_channels)
        # Linear layer to combine transformer and
GAT outputs
        self.fc =
nn.Linear(transformer_model.config.hidden_size +
gat_out_channels * 4,
transformer_model.config.hidden_size)

    def forward(self, input_ids, attention_mask,
node_features, edge_index):
        # Get transformer embeddings
        transformer_outputs =
self.transformer(input_ids=input_ids,
attention_mask=attention_mask)
        transformer_embedding =
transformer_outputs.last_hidden_state  # [batch,
seq_len, hidden_size]

        # Process graph data through GAT
```

```python
        gat_output = self.gat(node_features,
edge_index)  # [num_nodes, gat_out_channels*heads]
        # For demonstration, assume a simple
aggregation per token (in practice, align graph
nodes with tokens)
        gat_embedding =
gat_output.unsqueeze(0).repeat(transformer_embeddin
g.size(0), 1, 1)

        # Concatenate transformer and GAT
embeddings
        combined =
torch.cat([transformer_embedding, gat_embedding],
dim=-1)
        combined = self.fc(combined)

        return combined

# Example usage:
# Assume transformer_model is a pre-trained
transformer (e.g., from HuggingFace's transformers
library)
# input_ids, attention_mask are the tokenized text
inputs
# node_features is a tensor of node embeddings, and
edge_index defines graph connections
# hybrid_model = HybridModel(transformer_model,
gat_in_channels=768, gat_out_channels=128)
# output = hybrid_model(input_ids, attention_mask,
node_features, edge_index)
```

Explanation:
In this example, a Graph Attention Network (GAT) module is combined
with a transformer model to create a hybrid architecture. The GAT module
processes graph-structured data (representing relationships between tokens)
and its output is integrated with the transformer embeddings. This integration
aims to enrich the language model with explicit relational context,
potentially improving performance on tasks that require understanding of
complex dependencies.

Summary

- **Architectural Innovations:**
  Advances in GNNs include deep GCNs with residual connections, dynamic attention in GATs, and techniques for handling heterogeneous and dynamic graphs.
- **Scalability and Efficiency:**
  Sampling techniques, distributed training, and low-rank approximations help scale GNNs for large datasets.
- **Hybrid Integration:**
  Combining GNNs with transformer-based models can enhance context representation and improve performance on NLP tasks that require relational reasoning.

By staying informed on these advances and exploring practical implementations, you can leverage the latest developments in Graph Neural Networks to push the boundaries of language intelligence. This guidebook approach equips you with both theoretical insights and actionable techniques to integrate cutting-edge GNN technologies into your NLP projects.

7.1.2. Hybrid Models and Multimodal AI

Hybrid models and multimodal AI represent a frontier in language intelligence, combining strengths from different modalities and model architectures to build systems that understand and generate richer, more contextually aware content. This section provides a guidebook-style overview of how to design, implement, and leverage hybrid models that integrate multiple modalities—such as text, images, and audio—with advanced language processing.

Objectives

- **Integrate Multiple Modalities:**
  Combine text with images, audio, or other data sources to create a unified, enriched representation.
- **Enhance Contextual Understanding:**
  Use hybrid architectures to capture complementary features from different modalities, resulting in improved performance on complex tasks.
- **Expand Application Areas:**
  Enable use cases such as visual question answering, image

captioning, and multimodal sentiment analysis, where information from different sources is critical.

Step-by-Step Strategies

1. Identify Use Cases and Modalities

- **Define the Application:**
  Determine the target application that would benefit from multimodal integration (e.g., a virtual assistant that can process both text and images, or an AI that generates detailed image captions based on textual prompts).
- **Select Relevant Modalities:**
  Decide which data types (text, image, audio, video) should be integrated.
  Example: For image captioning, you would combine visual data (images) with textual processing.

2. Model Architecture Design

- **Hybrid Architecture Concept:**
  Design a model that consists of separate modules for each modality:
  - **Text Module:**
    Use a transformer-based language model (like LangGraph LLM) for processing and generating text.
  - **Vision Module:**
    Use a convolutional neural network (CNN) or vision transformer (ViT) to extract visual features.
  - **Fusion Module:**
    Integrate outputs from different modules using techniques such as concatenation, attention-based fusion, or multimodal transformers.
- **Example Architecture:**
  A model for image captioning might use a CNN to process the image and extract a feature vector, then feed this vector along with a textual prompt into a transformer to generate a caption.

3. Implementing the Hybrid Model

- **Data Preprocessing:**

- o **Text Preprocessing:**
  Clean and tokenize textual data as described in earlier sections.
- o **Image Preprocessing:**
  Resize, normalize, and augment images using standard computer vision techniques.
- **Fusion Strategy:**
  Determine how to combine the outputs. Options include:
  - o **Early Fusion:**
    Combine raw features from different modalities before feeding them into a unified model.
  - o **Late Fusion:**
    Process each modality separately and combine the predictions at the end.
  - o **Intermediate Fusion:**
    Integrate features at an intermediate stage using attention mechanisms that learn cross-modal relationships.

4. Practical Implementation Example

Below is a simplified Python example demonstrating a hybrid model for image captioning using PyTorch. This example integrates a vision model (e.g., ResNet) with a transformer-based language model.

```python
python

import torch
import torch.nn as nn
import torchvision.models as models
import torchvision.transforms as transforms
from PIL import Image
from transformers import AutoTokenizer,
AutoModelForCausalLM

class HybridImageCaptioningModel(nn.Module):
    def __init__(self, text_model_name,
image_feature_dim, hidden_dim):
        super(HybridImageCaptioningModel,
self).__init__()
        # Load pre-trained text model and tokenizer
(e.g., GPT-2 or LangGraph LLM)
```

```python
        self.tokenizer =
AutoTokenizer.from_pretrained(text_model_name)
        self.text_model =
AutoModelForCausalLM.from_pretrained(text_model_nam
e)
        # Freeze text model parameters if desired
        for param in self.text_model.parameters():
            param.requires_grad = False

        # Load a pre-trained image model (e.g.,
ResNet50) and remove the classification head
        resnet = models.resnet50(pretrained=True)
        self.image_encoder =
nn.Sequential(*list(resnet.children())[:-1])
        # Project image features to match text
model hidden size
        self.img_feature_proj =
nn.Linear(image_feature_dim, hidden_dim)

    def forward(self, image, prompt):
        # Process image: extract features and
project them
        img_features = self.image_encoder(image)   #
[batch_size, feature_dim, 1, 1]
        img_features =
img_features.view(img_features.size(0), -1)   #
Flatten
        projected_features =
self.img_feature_proj(img_features)   # [batch_size,
hidden_dim]

        # Prepare prompt: encode the text prompt
        inputs = self.tokenizer(prompt,
return_tensors="pt")
        input_ids =
inputs.input_ids.to(projected_features.device)

        # Integrate image features: prepend
projected image features to the token embeddings
        # For demonstration, we'll assume the text
model accepts a special token for image context
```

```python
        # In practice, more sophisticated fusion is
often required.
        # Concatenate a dummy image token with
input_ids (requires modifying the tokenizer if
needed)
        batch_size = input_ids.size(0)
        image_token =
projected_features.unsqueeze(1)  # [batch_size, 1,
hidden_dim]
        # Get text embeddings from text model
(assumed to be accessible)
        text_embeddings =
self.text_model.transformer.wte(input_ids)  #
[batch_size, seq_len, hidden_dim]
        combined_embeddings =
torch.cat([image_token, text_embeddings], dim=1)

        # Generate caption using the text model
        # This is a simplified example; a real
implementation might require custom generation
logic.
        outputs =
self.text_model(inputs_embeds=combined_embeddings)
        generated_ids =
torch.argmax(outputs.logits, dim=-1)
        caption =
self.tokenizer.decode(generated_ids[0],
skip_special_tokens=True)
        return caption

# Example usage:
if __name__ == "__main__":
    # Initialize model with a pre-trained text
model name and feature dimensions
    hybrid_model =
HybridImageCaptioningModel("gpt2",
image_feature_dim=2048, hidden_dim=768)
    hybrid_model.eval()

    # Preprocess an image
    transform = transforms.Compose([
        transforms.Resize((224, 224)),
```

```
    transforms.ToTensor(),
    transforms.Normalize(mean=[0.485, 0.456,
0.406], std=[0.229, 0.224, 0.225])
])
image =
Image.open("sample_image.jpg").convert("RGB")
image_tensor = transform(image).unsqueeze(0)    #
[1, 3, 224, 224]

# Define a prompt for captioning
prompt = "A photo of"

# Generate and print caption
caption = hybrid_model(image_tensor, prompt)
print("Generated Caption:", caption)
```

Explanation:

- **Image Encoder:**
  A pre-trained ResNet50 extracts image features which are then
  projected to the same dimension as the text model's hidden layer.
- **Text Model Integration:**
  The projected image features are concatenated with text embeddings
  from a transformer-based model (e.g., GPT-2) to provide context for
  caption generation.
- **Caption Generation:**
  The hybrid model generates a caption by processing the combined
  input.

5. Evaluating Multimodal Systems

- **Metrics:**
  Evaluate the performance of hybrid models using metrics like BLEU
  for text quality, as well as multimodal-specific metrics that consider
  both visual and textual coherence.
- **User Studies:**
  Conduct evaluations with real users to assess the naturalness and
  relevance of the generated content in multimodal scenarios.

Summary

- **Hybrid Architectures:**
  Combine separate modules for text and other modalities (e.g., vision) to harness complementary strengths.
- **Fusion Techniques:**
  Implement effective fusion strategies (early, intermediate, or late) to merge multimodal data.
- **Practical Implementation:**
  Use pre-trained models (like ResNet and GPT-2) and integrate them via a fusion layer, as demonstrated in the example.
- **Evaluation:**
  Use both automated metrics and user studies to assess the performance and quality of the hybrid system.

By following these strategies and exploring practical implementations, you can develop hybrid models that effectively integrate multimodal data, pushing the boundaries of what language intelligence can achieve. This guidebook approach provides actionable insights and code examples to help you harness the power of hybrid models and multimodal AI in your projects.

7.2. The Future of LangGraph LLM

This section outlines a forward-looking perspective on LangGraph LLM, examining how ongoing research and emerging technologies may shape its evolution. As language models continue to evolve, LangGraph LLM is poised to incorporate new methodologies and features that can further enhance its performance, adaptability, and application scope. The following guidebook-style overview presents key areas for future development, potential innovations, and strategic directions.

Objectives

- **Anticipate Technological Advancements:**
  Understand how breakthroughs in AI research, such as novel transformer architectures and enhanced graph-based reasoning, could impact LangGraph LLM.
- **Expand Application Scope:**
  Explore new domains and use cases that may benefit from future iterations of LangGraph LLM.

- **Promote Continuous Improvement:**
  Establish a roadmap for iterative improvements, including feedback integration, performance optimization, and ethical enhancements.

Key Areas of Future Development

1. Advanced Transformer Architectures

- **Next-Generation Self-Attention:**
  Future iterations may incorporate more efficient and dynamic attention mechanisms. Innovations like sparse attention and adaptive attention weights could further reduce computational overhead and improve context capture over longer sequences.
- **Integration with Graph-Based Enhancements:**
  As research on hybrid architectures progresses, expect tighter integration between transformer layers and graph-based reasoning modules. This could lead to even more robust representations of syntactic and semantic relationships, improving performance on tasks that require deep contextual understanding.

2. Enhanced Graph Neural Networks

- **Dynamic and Heterogeneous Graphs:**
  Future versions of LangGraph LLM might leverage advancements in Graph Neural Networks (GNNs) to better handle dynamic, evolving graphs that represent language structures. Enhanced techniques for processing heterogeneous data will allow the model to integrate multiple types of relationships more effectively.
- **Scalable Graph Integration:**
  Ongoing research into distributed GNN training and advanced sampling techniques will enable the efficient processing of larger and more complex graphs, supporting applications in domains such as social media analysis, knowledge graph construction, and more.

3. Multimodal and Cross-Modal Capabilities

- **Expanding Beyond Text:**
  The future of LangGraph LLM is likely to embrace multimodal learning, integrating text with images, audio, and video. This integration will empower applications such as visual question answering, video summarization, and cross-modal content generation.

- **Unified Representation Learning:**
  Research may lead to models that learn unified representations across different modalities, enhancing the ability to understand context and semantics from diverse data sources.

4. Personalized and Context-Aware Interactions

- **Adaptive Learning Techniques:**
  Future developments could include real-time, online learning capabilities that allow the model to adapt its responses based on continuous user feedback and evolving interaction contexts.
- **User-Centric Customization:**
  Enhanced user profiling and adaptive dialogue strategies may lead to highly personalized conversational agents that not only understand individual preferences but also anticipate user needs.

5. Ethical and Responsible AI

- **Bias Mitigation and Fairness:**
  As ethical considerations continue to be a central focus in AI development, future iterations of LangGraph LLM will likely incorporate more sophisticated bias detection and mitigation techniques. This will help ensure fairness across diverse user groups and application scenarios.
- **Transparency and Explainability:**
  Advancements in explainable AI (XAI) will provide deeper insights into the model's decision-making process, fostering greater trust and accountability. Enhanced transparency features may allow users to understand how and why specific responses are generated.

6. Efficiency and Sustainability

- **Energy-Efficient Training:**
  With growing concerns over the environmental impact of large-scale AI models, future research may prioritize energy-efficient training methods and model architectures that reduce computational costs while maintaining high performance.
- **Model Compression and Pruning:**
  Techniques such as model distillation, pruning, and quantization will continue to improve, enabling smaller, faster, and more deployable versions of LangGraph LLM without compromising accuracy.

Future Roadmap and Strategic Directions

- **Iterative Research and Development:**
  Establish a cycle of continuous improvement where user feedback, benchmark performance, and emerging research guide regular updates to the model.
- **Cross-Disciplinary Collaboration:**
  Foster collaboration between NLP researchers, data scientists, and domain experts to explore novel applications and integrate state-of-the-art advancements from related fields.
- **Ethical Governance:**
  Develop robust frameworks for ethical oversight that evolve alongside the model, ensuring that advancements in technology are matched by responsible and transparent practices.

Summary

- **Next-Generation Architectures:**
  Innovations in transformers and graph-based reasoning will enhance context understanding and efficiency.
- **Multimodal Integration:**
  Expanding capabilities beyond text to include images, audio, and video will open new application areas.
- **Personalization and Adaptability:**
  Adaptive learning and user-centric customization will lead to more engaging and relevant interactions.
- **Ethical and Sustainable AI:**
  Continuous advancements in bias mitigation, explainability, and energy efficiency will ensure responsible and sustainable development.
- **Future Roadmap:**
  A strategic, iterative approach combining research, user feedback, and cross-disciplinary collaboration will drive the evolution of LangGraph LLM.

By anticipating these future trends and incorporating them into your development roadmap, you can ensure that LangGraph LLM remains at the forefront of language intelligence innovation. This guidebook approach not only prepares you for upcoming technological shifts but also equips you with the strategic insights necessary to harness the full potential of advanced AI systems in the years ahead.

7.2.1. Predicting Future Developments

This section provides a forward-looking guide to predicting future developments in LangGraph LLM and the broader landscape of language intelligence. By anticipating trends and technological shifts, you can strategically plan enhancements and stay competitive in a rapidly evolving field. Below, we outline key objectives, methodologies, and actionable insights for forecasting future innovations.

Objectives

- **Identify Emerging Trends:**
  Monitor and analyze current research, market dynamics, and technological breakthroughs to predict the next wave of advancements.
- **Strategically Plan Enhancements:**
  Use future predictions to inform the development roadmap of LangGraph LLM, ensuring continuous improvement and relevance.
- **Align with Industry Needs:**
  Ensure that future developments address practical challenges and emerging user requirements, keeping the model applicable across diverse domains.

Step-by-Step Strategies

1. Trend Analysis and Research Monitoring

- **Literature Reviews:**
  Regularly review academic papers, preprints, and conference proceedings (e.g., ACL, NeurIPS, ICML) to identify cutting-edge research in NLP and related fields.
- **Industry Reports:**
  Analyze market research, whitepapers, and industry reports from leading organizations to understand how language technologies are being adopted and what challenges remain.
- **Patent and Innovation Tracking:**
  Monitor patent filings and technology incubators to spot new innovations and potential shifts in language model architectures and applications.

2. Technological Forecasting

- **Scenario Planning:**
  Develop multiple scenarios outlining potential future states of language intelligence. For instance, consider scenarios where:
    - Transformer architectures evolve to incorporate even more dynamic and adaptive attention mechanisms.
    - Hybrid models with graph neural networks and multimodal inputs become the norm.
    - Ethical, sustainable AI practices drive a shift towards energy-efficient and explainable models.
- **Expert Consultations:**
  Engage with researchers, industry experts, and thought leaders to gather insights on where they see the field heading. Panel discussions, webinars, and collaborative workshops can provide valuable qualitative data.
- **Quantitative Modeling:**
  Use statistical models and trend analysis tools to project growth rates in data availability, computational capabilities, and model performance improvements over time.

3. Strategic Roadmapping

- **Short-Term vs. Long-Term Goals:**
  Define clear short-term milestones (e.g., next model release improvements) and long-term aspirations (e.g., fully multimodal AI systems) based on forecasted trends.
- **Resource Allocation:**
  Align your research and development investments with predicted advancements, ensuring that the team is equipped with the necessary tools and expertise.
- **Iterative Feedback:**
  Establish continuous feedback loops with both users and research teams to adapt your roadmap as new trends emerge and priorities shift.

4. Practical Example: Building a Predictive Dashboard

- **Objective:**
  Create a dashboard that aggregates data from research publications, patent databases, and industry news to visualize emerging trends in language AI.

- **Implementation Steps:**
  1. **Data Aggregation:**
     Use APIs from sources such as arXiv, Google Scholar, and patent offices to collect real-time data on new publications and innovations.
  2. **Data Processing:**
     Apply natural language processing techniques to categorize and score each data point based on relevance and innovation potential.
  3. **Visualization:**
     Develop a dashboard using tools like Grafana or Tableau to display trends over time, highlight emerging topics, and track key performance indicators.
  4. **Actionable Insights:**
     Use the dashboard to inform regular strategy sessions and adjust your development roadmap accordingly.

```python
python

# Example: Simplified Data Aggregation using arXiv API (conceptual)
import requests
import xml.etree.ElementTree as ET

def fetch_arxiv_papers(query="NLP", max_results=5):
    url = f"http://export.arxiv.org/api/query?search_query=all:{query}&start=0&max_results={max_results}"
    response = requests.get(url)
    root = ET.fromstring(response.content)
    papers = []
    for entry in root.findall("{http://www.w3.org/2005/Atom}entry"):
        title = entry.find("{http://www.w3.org/2005/Atom}title").text.strip()
        summary = entry.find("{http://www.w3.org/2005/Atom}summary").text.strip()
        papers.append({"title": title, "summary": summary})
    return papers
```

```
# Fetch recent NLP papers and print their titles
nlp_papers = fetch_arxiv_papers("language+model",
max_results=3)
for paper in nlp_papers:
    print("Title:", paper["title"])
```

Explanation:
This conceptual code snippet demonstrates how to fetch recent papers from arXiv related to language models. In a full implementation, such data can be integrated into a dashboard for trend analysis.

Summary

- **Trend Analysis:**
  Continuously monitor research, industry reports, and patents to identify emerging innovations.
- **Technological Forecasting:**
  Use scenario planning, expert consultations, and quantitative models to predict future developments.
- **Strategic Roadmapping:**
  Define short-term and long-term goals, align resource allocation, and adapt your roadmap based on continuous feedback.
- **Practical Tools:**
  Implement predictive dashboards and data aggregation systems to visualize and act on emerging trends.

By following these strategies, you can anticipate and plan for future developments in LangGraph LLM and the broader field of language intelligence. This guidebook approach not only prepares you for upcoming technological shifts but also provides a framework for strategic planning and innovation in your AI initiatives.

7.2.2. Roadmap for Research and Innovation

This section outlines a strategic roadmap for continuous research and innovation in the development of LangGraph LLM. The roadmap is designed to guide both short-term enhancements and long-term breakthroughs, ensuring that the model remains at the forefront of language intelligence while adapting to emerging trends and technologies.

Objectives

- **Set Clear Milestones:**
  Define measurable short-term and long-term goals for model improvements and feature expansions.
- **Foster Continuous Research:**
  Establish processes for regular innovation through collaboration, experimentation, and user feedback.
- **Align with Industry Trends:**
  Ensure that research efforts are informed by emerging technologies, market needs, and ethical considerations.

Strategic Roadmap

1. Short-Term Goals (0-12 Months)

- **Incremental Model Improvements:**
  - **Fine-Tuning and Domain Adaptation:**
    Enhance performance in targeted industries by fine-tuning on domain-specific data.
  - **Efficiency Optimization:**
    Implement improvements in model architecture such as dynamic attention mechanisms and reduced parameter redundancy to speed up inference and lower computational costs.
  - **User Feedback Integration:**
    Set up structured feedback loops to continuously refine model responses based on real-world usage.
- **Prototype and Pilot Projects:**
  - **Develop Proof-of-Concept Applications:**
    Launch pilot projects in key areas (e.g., healthcare summarization, enterprise chatbots) to validate improvements and gather data.
  - **Testing and Benchmarking:**
    Establish benchmark datasets and metrics to measure incremental improvements against current standards.
- **Ethical and Regulatory Readiness:**
  - **Bias and Fairness Audits:**
    Integrate fairness-aware training and regular audits to monitor and mitigate bias.

- o **Transparency Initiatives:**
  Develop user-facing explanations and documentation to enhance transparency.

2. Mid-Term Goals (1-3 Years)

- **Advanced Hybrid Architectures:**
  - o **Integration of Graph Neural Networks:**
    Deepen the integration of graph-based reasoning within transformer architectures to better capture complex language relationships.
  - o **Multimodal Capabilities:**
    Develop and deploy hybrid models that can process and integrate data from multiple modalities (text, images, audio) for richer contextual understanding.
  - o **Reinforcement Learning for Adaptation:**
    Experiment with reinforcement learning techniques to further refine interactive and adaptive responses in conversational agents.
- **Scalability and Infrastructure:**
  - o **Distributed Training Improvements:**
    Enhance distributed training techniques to scale up the model effectively while reducing training costs.
  - o **Resource Optimization:**
    Implement model compression, quantization, and pruning strategies to create more lightweight yet powerful versions suitable for deployment across various platforms.
- **Research Collaboration and Ecosystem Building:**
  - o **Interdisciplinary Research Partnerships:**
    Collaborate with academic institutions, industry experts, and ethical oversight bodies to drive innovation and share best practices.
  - o **Open-Source Contributions:**
    Increase community engagement by contributing to open-source initiatives, encouraging external research, and integrating community feedback.

3. Long-Term Goals (3+ Years)

- **Next-Generation AI Systems:**
  - o **Unified Multimodal AI:**
    Realize models that seamlessly integrate language with

vision, audio, and other data forms, paving the way for truly comprehensive AI systems.
- o **Self-Evolving Models:**
  Explore online learning and adaptive architectures that can continuously update based on new data and user interactions without the need for complete retraining cycles.
- o **Energy-Efficient AI:**
  Prioritize sustainability by developing training techniques and model architectures that significantly reduce energy consumption and carbon footprint.
- **Ethical Leadership and Global Standards:**
  - o **Industry Standards Development:**
    Contribute to establishing global standards and best practices for ethical AI, ensuring that innovations are socially responsible and beneficial.
  - o **Transparent AI Governance:**
    Create robust frameworks for AI governance that balance innovation with accountability, transparency, and user rights.
- **Exploration of New Frontiers:**
  - o **Emerging Technologies Integration:**
    Stay at the cutting edge by integrating breakthroughs in quantum computing, neuromorphic computing, or other nascent technologies that could further revolutionize language processing.
  - o **Personalized AI Ecosystems:**
    Develop personalized, context-aware AI systems that can serve diverse needs across multiple domains, driving new business models and opportunities.

Continuous Monitoring and Iteration

- **Regular Reviews:**
  Establish quarterly and annual review cycles to assess progress against milestones, adjust strategies, and incorporate the latest research findings.
- **Feedback-Driven Adaptation:**
  Leverage user feedback, performance metrics, and market trends to inform iterative updates to both the model and the strategic roadmap.
- **Documentation and Transparency:**
  Maintain detailed documentation of research activities, performance benchmarks, and ethical audits to ensure accountability and facilitate knowledge sharing.

Summary

- **Short-Term (0-12 Months):**
  Focus on incremental improvements, pilot projects, and ensuring ethical compliance.
- **Mid-Term (1-3 Years):**
  Advance hybrid architectures, enhance scalability, and build research collaborations.
- **Long-Term (3+ Years):**
  Realize next-generation, multimodal, and energy-efficient AI systems, and lead in ethical governance and global standards.
- **Continuous Iteration:**
  Regularly review progress, adapt strategies based on feedback, and document research activities.

By following this structured roadmap, you can ensure that LangGraph LLM remains a cutting-edge solution in the field of language intelligence. This guidebook approach provides a clear framework for planning research and innovation efforts, helping you navigate the evolving landscape of AI technology and maintain a competitive edge.

7.3. Interdisciplinary Applications and Cross-Domain Impact

Interdisciplinary applications leverage the strengths of LangGraph LLM to address complex challenges that span multiple fields, thereby driving innovation and transformative outcomes. This section provides a structured guide to understanding how language intelligence can intersect with various domains—such as healthcare, finance, education, and the arts—to unlock new opportunities and foster cross-domain impact.

Objectives

- **Foster Innovation Across Domains:**
  Explore how integrating LangGraph LLM with domain-specific knowledge can lead to groundbreaking solutions.
- **Promote Collaborative Research:**
  Encourage cross-disciplinary partnerships to address complex problems that require diverse expertise.
- **Expand the Reach of Language Intelligence:**
  Demonstrate the versatility of LangGraph LLM in solving problems

in fields beyond traditional NLP, enhancing both business and societal outcomes.

Step-by-Step Strategies

1. Identify Cross-Domain Use Cases

- **Healthcare and Life Sciences:**
  - **Application:** Use LangGraph LLM for automated medical record summarization, clinical decision support, and genomic data interpretation.
  - **Impact:** Improved patient care through faster, more accurate information retrieval and analysis.
- **Finance and Economics:**
  - **Application:** Integrate with financial analytics systems for real-time market sentiment analysis, risk assessment, and regulatory compliance reporting.
  - **Impact:** Enhanced decision-making and risk management, leading to more resilient financial strategies.
- **Education and E-Learning:**
  - **Application:** Develop adaptive learning platforms that offer personalized content, intelligent tutoring systems, and automated grading of written assignments.
  - **Impact:** Increased accessibility to quality education and improved learning outcomes through tailored instruction.
- **Creative Industries and Media:**
  - **Application:** Support content creation for marketing, journalism, and entertainment through automatic story generation, content summarization, and style adaptation.
  - **Impact:** Enhanced creativity and productivity, enabling rapid generation of engaging content that resonates with diverse audiences.

2. Develop Interdisciplinary Collaborations

- **Cross-Functional Teams:**
  - **Action:** Assemble teams with expertise in AI, domain-specific knowledge (e.g., medical, financial, educational), and user experience design.
  - **Tip:** Regular interdisciplinary workshops and brainstorming sessions can facilitate idea exchange and foster innovation.
- **Partnerships with Academia and Industry:**

- o **Action:** Collaborate with universities, research institutions, and industry leaders to pilot innovative projects.
- o **Example:** Joint research initiatives that combine clinical research with AI to develop predictive models for disease management.

3. Customize the Model for Domain-Specific Applications

- **Fine-Tuning on Domain Data:**
  - o **Action:** Adapt LangGraph LLM to specific domains by fine-tuning on relevant datasets.
  - o **Practical Example:** Fine-tune on medical journals and patient records for healthcare applications, or on financial reports and news articles for market analysis.
- **Integration with Domain-Specific Systems:**
  - o **Action:** Embed the model into existing workflows and software systems to complement specialized tools.
  - o **Tip:** Develop APIs and microservices that allow seamless integration with domain-specific databases and applications.

4. Evaluate Cross-Domain Impact

- **Performance Metrics:**
  - o **Action:** Establish KPIs that measure the model's impact within each domain, such as accuracy in clinical predictions, speed of financial report generation, or improvement in student learning outcomes.
- **User and Stakeholder Feedback:**
  - o **Action:** Gather qualitative and quantitative feedback from end users, domain experts, and stakeholders to assess the real-world impact.
  - o **Tip:** Use surveys, interviews, and analytics dashboards to capture comprehensive feedback.

5. Scale and Adapt for Future Needs

- **Iterative Improvement:**
  - o **Action:** Continuously update the model based on feedback and emerging trends in both AI and the target domain.
- **Flexible Architectures:**

- **Action:** Design system architectures that can evolve, allowing for integration with new technologies such as IoT devices in healthcare or blockchain in finance.
- **Global and Cultural Considerations:**
  - **Action:** Ensure that the system is adaptable to diverse cultural contexts, language variants, and regulatory environments.

Summary

- **Diverse Applications:**
  LangGraph LLM can be tailored to various disciplines, including healthcare, finance, education, and creative industries, driving innovative solutions across these fields.
- **Collaborative Innovation:**
  Cross-domain partnerships and interdisciplinary teams are key to successfully applying language intelligence in specialized contexts.
- **Customization and Integration:**
  Fine-tuning on domain-specific data and seamless integration with existing systems enhance the model's relevance and impact.
- **Continuous Evaluation:**
  Establish clear metrics and feedback loops to measure and adapt the model's performance, ensuring it remains effective and responsive to evolving needs.

By embracing interdisciplinary applications and focusing on cross-domain impact, you can unlock the full potential of LangGraph LLM. This guidebook approach provides actionable strategies and practical insights, enabling you to drive innovation and create transformative solutions that extend far beyond traditional language processing.

7.4. The Role of Open-Source and Community Contributions

Open-source initiatives and community contributions have become critical drivers of innovation in language intelligence. This section outlines how open-source projects foster collaboration, accelerate development, and democratize access to advanced models like LangGraph LLM. By leveraging community input and shared resources, organizations can benefit from a diverse pool of expertise and continuously improve AI systems.

Objectives

- **Promote Collaboration:**
  Enable collective innovation by sharing code, data, and research findings with the broader community.
- **Accelerate Development:**
  Reduce development time and costs by building upon existing open-source libraries and tools.
- **Enhance Transparency and Trust:**
  Foster transparency through open access to code and documentation, building trust among users and stakeholders.

Step-by-Step Strategies

1. Engaging with the Open-Source Community

- **Contribution Platforms:**
  - o **Action:** Publish and maintain your projects on platforms like GitHub or GitLab.
  - o **Example:** Open-source your LangGraph LLM repository to encourage contributions, bug fixes, and new features.
- **Community Forums and Events:**
  - o **Action:** Participate in AI forums, conferences, and hackathons to share knowledge and gather feedback.
  - o **Tip:** Engage in discussions on platforms like Reddit, Stack Overflow, or dedicated Slack channels to connect with developers and researchers.
- **Collaboration and Co-Creation:**
  - o **Action:** Invite external contributions through well-documented contribution guidelines and a clear roadmap.
  - o **Tip:** Use pull requests, issue tracking, and code reviews to ensure quality and encourage diverse ideas.

2. Leveraging Existing Open-Source Tools

- **Libraries and Frameworks:**
  - o **Action:** Utilize established libraries like Hugging Face Transformers, PyTorch Geometric, or TensorFlow for building and enhancing LangGraph LLM.
  - o **Example:** Incorporate pre-trained models and tokenizers from Hugging Face to expedite development.
- **Data Resources:**

- o **Action:** Use publicly available datasets and benchmarks to train and evaluate your model.
- o **Tip:** Contribute improvements back to the community by sharing cleaned and annotated datasets.
- **Integration and Interoperability:**
  - o **Action:** Design your system to be modular and compatible with other open-source projects, enabling seamless integration and reuse of components.
  - o **Example:** Develop APIs that adhere to open standards so that your service can interoperate with other community-driven platforms.

3. Benefits of Open-Source Contributions

- **Innovation Through Diversity:**
  Open-source projects benefit from a wide range of perspectives, leading to more innovative solutions and robust models.
- **Rapid Iteration and Improvement:**
  Community contributions can quickly identify and resolve issues, speeding up development cycles and model updates.
- **Cost Efficiency:**
  By leveraging existing resources and community expertise, organizations can significantly reduce research and development costs.
- **Increased Adoption and Impact:**
  Open-source projects often achieve broader adoption, allowing for real-world testing, feedback, and iterative enhancements that drive further innovation.

4. Best Practices for Open-Source Collaboration

- **Clear Documentation:**
  Maintain comprehensive and accessible documentation, including installation guides, API references, and contribution guidelines.
- **Licensing and Governance:**
  Choose an appropriate open-source license (e.g., MIT, Apache 2.0) and establish governance policies to manage contributions and intellectual property.
- **Community Support:**
  Set up communication channels, such as discussion boards or mailing lists, and regularly engage with contributors to provide support and recognize their efforts.

Practical Implementation Example

Below is a simplified example of how you might structure an open-source repository for LangGraph LLM contributions:

```markdown
# LangGraph LLM: An Open-Source Language
Intelligence Platform

## Overview
LangGraph LLM is an advanced language model that
integrates transformer architectures with graph-
based reasoning. This repository provides tools,
code, and documentation to help researchers and
developers build, fine-tune, and deploy LangGraph
LLM.

## Getting Started
### Installation
1. Clone the repository:
   ```bash
   git clone https://github.com/your-org/langgraph-
llm.git
   cd langgraph-llm
```

2. Create and activate a virtual environment:

    ```bash

    python -m venv env
    source env/bin/activate  # On Windows:
    env\Scripts\activate
    ```

3. Install dependencies:

    ```bash

    pip install -r requirements.txt
    ```
    ```

Usage

- **Training:**
  Run the training script:

  ```bash
  python train.py --config
  configs/train_config.json
  ```

- **Inference:**
  Test the model with:

  ```bash
  python infer.py --input "Your sample text
  here."
  ```

Contribution Guidelines

We welcome contributions! Please review our CONTRIBUTING.md for details on our code of conduct, pull request process, and how to get started.

License

This project is licensed under the MIT License - see the LICENSE file for details.

Community

Join our community on Slack or follow us on Twitter for updates and discussions.

```pgsql


*Explanation:*
This markdown file serves as a template for an
open-source repository, providing clear
instructions and guidelines to encourage community
involvement and transparency.
```

Summary

- **Engage the Community:**
  Actively participate in open-source forums, encourage contributions, and share knowledge.

- **Leverage Existing Resources:**
  Utilize and contribute to established libraries and datasets to accelerate innovation.

- **Document and Govern:**
  Maintain clear documentation and establish governance policies to ensure quality and legal compliance.

- **Real-World Benefits:**
  Open-source collaboration drives innovation, rapid iteration, cost efficiency, and broad adoption.

By following these best practices and leveraging community contributions, you can harness the collective power of the open-source ecosystem to continuously improve LangGraph LLM and drive meaningful advancements in language intelligence. This guidebook approach provides a roadmap for leveraging open-source initiatives to create more robust, innovative, and impactful AI solutions.

As we conclude Chapter 7 on Innovations and Future Trends in Language Intelligence, it is clear that the field is rapidly evolving through a blend of emerging technologies, hybrid model architectures, and multidisciplinary approaches. The advancements in Graph Neural Networks, the integration of multimodal data, and the promise of reinforcement learning are not only pushing the boundaries of what language models can achieve but are also paving the way for entirely new applications and user experiences.

Key takeaways include:

- **Next-Generation Model Architectures:**
  Continuous improvements in transformer designs and graph-based reasoning are enhancing contextual understanding and efficiency.

Hybrid models that combine these strengths promise to revolutionize tasks that require deep relational insights.

- **Multimodal Integration:**
  The fusion of text with images, audio, and video is set to unlock richer representations and broaden the scope of applications, from visual question answering to comprehensive content generation.

- **Adaptive and Personalized Interactions:**
  Advances in real-time learning and personalization techniques will drive the creation of conversational systems that are more responsive, context-aware, and attuned to individual user needs.

- **Ethical, Fair, and Transparent AI:**
  As models grow more complex, so does the imperative to build systems that are transparent, minimize bias, and protect user privacy. These ethical foundations will remain at the heart of responsible innovation.

- **Community-Driven Innovation:**
  Open-source contributions and interdisciplinary collaborations will continue to fuel rapid advancements and ensure that progress in language intelligence is both inclusive and globally accessible.

Looking ahead, strategic planning through continuous research, iterative improvements, and a keen eye on emerging trends will be essential. By fostering a collaborative ecosystem that balances technical breakthroughs with ethical responsibility, LangGraph LLM and similar advanced language models will not only transform industries but also contribute to a more informed, connected, and equitable society.

This roadmap serves as a call to action for researchers, developers, and organizations alike: to remain agile, innovate responsibly, and leverage community insights as we collectively shape the future of language intelligence.

Chapter 8: Case Studies and Industry Success Stories

8.1. Detailed Case Studies by Sector

This section provides an in-depth exploration of real-world case studies that demonstrate the successful application of LangGraph LLM across various sectors. By examining detailed examples, you can gain actionable insights into how advanced language models are deployed to solve industry-specific challenges, improve operational efficiency, and drive innovation.

Objectives

- **Showcase Sector-Specific Success:**
  Illustrate how LangGraph LLM has been effectively applied in diverse industries.
- **Highlight Implementation Strategies:**
  Detail the methodologies, tools, and practices used to integrate the model into existing workflows.
- **Demonstrate Measurable Impact:**
  Present key performance metrics and outcomes that highlight the benefits of deploying LangGraph LLM.

Case Study 1: Healthcare

Overview:
A leading healthcare provider implemented LangGraph LLM to streamline clinical documentation and automate patient record summarization, improving the speed and accuracy of information retrieval for medical professionals.

Key Strategies and Implementation:

- **Data Collection and Preprocessing:**
  - Aggregated diverse datasets including electronic health records, clinical notes, and research articles.
  - Applied rigorous data cleaning and anonymization techniques to ensure compliance with HIPAA.

- **Fine-Tuning for Clinical Context:**
  - o Fine-tuned the pre-trained LangGraph LLM on domain-specific texts to enhance its understanding of medical terminology and abbreviations.
  - o Incorporated feedback loops from clinical staff to adjust summaries and highlight critical information.
- **Deployment:**
  - o Deployed the model as a microservice integrated into the hospital's EHR system.
  - o Provided a simple UI for clinicians to retrieve concise summaries of patient histories.

Outcomes:

- **Efficiency Gains:**
  Reduced the average time spent on manual record review by 50%.
- **Accuracy:**
  Achieved a high level of accuracy in summarization, with clinicians reporting improved clarity and relevance.
- **User Satisfaction:**
  Positive feedback from medical staff regarding ease of use and the reduction in administrative workload.

Case Study 2: Finance

Overview:
A global financial institution used LangGraph LLM to enhance market analysis and customer support, automating the generation of financial reports and dynamic responses to customer inquiries.

Key Strategies and Implementation:

- **Dataset Preparation:**
  - o Compiled large-scale datasets from financial news, earnings call transcripts, and regulatory filings.
  - o Standardized and cleaned data to capture key financial indicators and sentiments.
- **Model Adaptation:**

- Fine-tuned LangGraph LLM to generate coherent summaries of complex financial documents.
  - Integrated real-time data feeds to keep analysis current and contextually relevant.
- **System Integration:**
  - Deployed the model via a secure API, accessible by internal dashboards and customer support systems.
  - Enabled automated report generation, which could be further customized by financial analysts.

Outcomes:

- **Time Savings:**
  Automated report generation reduced manual analysis time by approximately 40%.
- **Enhanced Decision-Making:**
  Improved the accuracy and timeliness of market sentiment analysis, aiding investment strategies.
- **Cost Efficiency:**
  Lowered operational costs in customer support through the deployment of intelligent chatbots.

Case Study 3: Technology and Software Development

Overview:
A tech company integrated LangGraph LLM to boost developer productivity by automating code documentation and providing context-aware code completion suggestions within their integrated development environment (IDE).

Key Strategies and Implementation:

- **Data Integration:**
  - Leveraged a corpus of technical documentation, code repositories, and internal development wikis.
  - Fine-tuned the model to understand programming languages, technical jargon, and contextual code patterns.
- **UI/UX Enhancements:**
  - Embedded the model into the IDE via a plugin, enabling real-time suggestions and documentation generation.

- Developed a user-friendly interface that allowed developers to customize the level of detail and style of generated documentation.
- **Feedback and Iteration:**
  - Implemented continuous feedback loops where developers could rate suggestions and provide comments.
  - Iteratively improved the model based on real-world usage data and evolving coding standards.

Outcomes:

- **Increased Productivity:**
  Developers reported a 30% increase in efficiency due to quicker access to documentation and smarter code completion.
- **Enhanced Code Quality:**
  More consistent and up-to-date documentation improved code maintainability.
- **Positive Adoption:**
  High adoption rates among development teams, with regular updates based on user feedback.

Case Study 4: Marketing and Media

Overview:
A retail brand harnessed LangGraph LLM to generate personalized marketing content and analyze consumer sentiment, resulting in more engaging campaigns and enhanced brand perception.

Key Strategies and Implementation:

- **Data-Driven Insights:**
  - Collected data from social media, customer reviews, and past marketing campaigns.
  - Employed LangGraph LLM to analyze sentiment and trends to inform content strategies.
- **Content Personalization:**
  - Fine-tuned the model on brand-specific content to maintain consistency in tone and style.

- Developed an API that allowed for the generation of personalized content pieces, such as product descriptions and social media posts.
- **Campaign Integration:**
  - Integrated the AI-driven content generator into the company's content management system (CMS) for streamlined campaign creation.
  - Enabled A/B testing of generated content to continuously refine messaging based on performance metrics.

Outcomes:

- **Enhanced Engagement:**
  Personalized content led to a 20% uplift in customer engagement and conversion rates.
- **Efficiency:**
  Automated content generation reduced the time required for campaign planning and execution by 35%.
- **Brand Consistency:**
  Consistent tone and style across all generated content reinforced brand identity.

Summary

- **Healthcare:**
  Automating clinical documentation and record summarization leads to significant efficiency gains and improved patient care.
- **Finance:**
  Enhancing market analysis and automating customer support results in faster decision-making, cost savings, and improved service quality.
- **Technology:**
  Integrating AI for code documentation and completion boosts developer productivity and code quality.
- **Marketing:**
  Personalized content generation and sentiment analysis drive higher engagement and more effective marketing strategies.

By examining these detailed case studies, you can understand the varied approaches and measurable impacts of deploying LangGraph LLM across different sectors. This guidebook approach provides clear, actionable insights that can be adapted to your specific industry needs, helping to unlock the full potential of advanced language intelligence in your organization.

8.1.1. Technology and Innovation

This section showcases detailed case studies that highlight how LangGraph LLM has driven technology and innovation across various tech-driven sectors. By examining real-world examples, you can gain insight into how advanced language models are transforming software development, product design, and digital transformation initiatives. These case studies illustrate practical implementation strategies, the integration of cutting-edge technologies, and the measurable impact on business outcomes.

Objectives

- **Accelerate Innovation:**
  Demonstrate how LangGraph LLM can streamline development processes, foster creativity, and reduce time-to-market for innovative solutions.
- **Enhance Technical Workflows:**
  Showcase applications where LangGraph LLM improves coding efficiency, automated documentation, and user support systems.
- **Drive Measurable Impact:**
  Present key performance indicators (KPIs) and success metrics that reflect improvements in productivity, quality, and overall business performance.

Case Study Overview

1. AI-Enhanced Code Documentation and Generation

Implementation Strategy:

- **Data Integration:**
  Utilize extensive repositories of code and technical documentation. Fine-tune LangGraph LLM on programming languages, technical manuals, and internal documentation.
- **Model Adaptation:**
  Customize the language model to understand code syntax, library references, and development best practices.
- **Developer Tools Integration:**
  Deploy the model as an IDE plugin that offers real-time code

suggestions, auto-generates documentation, and provides contextual code completions.

Outcomes:

- **Increased Developer Productivity:**
  Developers report up to a 30% increase in efficiency as the AI assists with repetitive tasks and complex code explanations.
- **Enhanced Code Quality:**
  Automatically generated documentation helps maintain code consistency and reduces knowledge silos within development teams.
- **Positive Adoption:**
  High satisfaction rates among developers with seamless integration into their daily workflows.

2. Intelligent Virtual Assistants for Technical Support

Implementation Strategy:

- **User Query Analysis:**
  Fine-tune LangGraph LLM on historical technical support data, including troubleshooting guides and user queries.
- **Chatbot Deployment:**
  Implement a virtual assistant capable of understanding and resolving technical issues in real-time across multiple communication channels (web, mobile, and messaging platforms).
- **Feedback Integration:**
  Collect continuous feedback to improve the accuracy and responsiveness of the support system.

Outcomes:

- **Reduced Resolution Times:**
  Automated responses significantly cut down on average handling time for technical support tickets.
- **Cost Savings:**
  Lowered support costs through the reduction of repetitive queries handled by human agents.
- **Improved User Experience:**
  Enhanced satisfaction among users due to fast, accurate, and context-aware support interactions.

3. Innovation in Product Development and R&D

Implementation Strategy:

- **Idea Generation and Brainstorming:**
  Leverage LangGraph LLM to generate creative ideas for new features or products by analyzing market trends and historical data.
- **Research Assistance:**
  Use the model to summarize research papers, patent documents, and technical reports, enabling R&D teams to quickly gather insights and identify innovation opportunities.
- **Collaboration Tools:**
  Integrate the model into project management and collaboration platforms to assist teams in documenting meeting minutes, synthesizing discussions, and drafting proposals.

Outcomes:

- **Faster R&D Cycles:**
  Accelerated research and development processes through quick synthesis of large volumes of technical information.
- **Enhanced Innovation:**
  More robust ideation sessions supported by AI-generated insights, leading to breakthrough product features and improved competitive positioning.
- **Collaborative Efficiency:**
  Improved team collaboration and documentation accuracy, enabling more effective communication across departments.

Summary

- **AI-Enhanced Code Documentation:**
  Boosts developer productivity and code quality by integrating advanced language models directly into development environments.
- **Intelligent Technical Support:**
  Improves resolution times and reduces costs by automating technical support processes, leading to a more responsive and efficient service.
- **Innovative R&D:**
  Facilitates rapid idea generation and research synthesis, driving innovation and accelerating product development cycles.

These case studies illustrate how LangGraph LLM can be leveraged to transform technological processes and drive innovation across tech-driven sectors. By integrating AI into core technical workflows, organizations can achieve significant efficiency gains, foster creativity, and ultimately, maintain a competitive edge in rapidly evolving markets.

8.1.2. Finance, Marketing, and Customer Service

This section presents detailed case studies highlighting how LangGraph LLM is transforming finance, marketing, and customer service sectors. By examining practical examples, you can gain insights into the methodologies, implementation strategies, and measurable impacts achieved through the deployment of advanced language intelligence in these areas.

Objectives

- **Finance:**
  Enhance market analysis, risk assessment, and financial reporting through AI-driven insights.
- **Marketing:**
  Personalize content generation and campaign strategies to increase customer engagement and conversion.
- **Customer Service:**
  Automate and improve the responsiveness of support interactions to boost satisfaction and reduce operational costs.

Case Study Overview

1. Finance: Enhanced Market Analysis and Reporting

Implementation Strategy:

- **Data Aggregation:**
  Compile large-scale datasets including financial news, earnings call transcripts, market reports, and social media sentiment.
- **Model Fine-Tuning:**
  Fine-tune LangGraph LLM on financial text to capture industry-specific terminology, trends, and sentiments.
- **Automated Report Generation:**
  Deploy the model as part of an internal tool that automatically synthesizes market data into concise reports. This tool can summarize market trends, analyze risk factors, and forecast economic indicators.

- **Integration with Analytics Platforms:**
  Connect the AI-generated reports with existing business intelligence tools to provide real-time insights and interactive dashboards.

Outcomes:

- **Time Savings:**
  Financial analysts experienced a 40% reduction in time spent on manual data processing and report compilation.
- **Improved Decision-Making:**
  Enhanced market insights led to more informed investment strategies and risk management decisions.
- **Cost Efficiency:**
  Automation of report generation reduced the need for extensive manual labor, leading to significant operational cost savings.

2. Marketing: Personalized Content and Campaign Optimization

Implementation Strategy:

- **Audience Segmentation:**
  Analyze customer data and past marketing campaigns to identify different audience segments.
- **Custom Content Generation:**
  Fine-tune LangGraph LLM on brand-specific content and historical campaign data to generate tailored marketing messages, product descriptions, and social media posts.
- **Dynamic Personalization:**
  Develop an API that integrates with the company's content management system (CMS) to provide real-time personalized content based on user behavior and preferences.
- **A/B Testing and Iterative Improvement:**
  Implement A/B testing frameworks to compare the performance of AI-generated content with traditional content, and use feedback to continuously refine messaging strategies.

Outcomes:

- **Increased Engagement:**
  Personalized marketing content contributed to a 20% uplift in customer engagement and conversion rates.

- **Efficiency Gains:**
  Automated content generation cut down campaign preparation time by 35%, allowing marketers to focus on strategic planning.
- **Brand Consistency:**
  Consistent tone and style in all AI-generated content reinforced the brand's identity, resulting in improved customer loyalty.

3. Customer Service: Intelligent Virtual Assistants and Chatbots

Implementation Strategy:

- **Historical Data Utilization:**
  Leverage a corpus of past customer interactions, support tickets, and FAQs to fine-tune LangGraph LLM for customer service tasks.
- **Conversational AI Deployment:**
  Develop a virtual assistant or chatbot that can understand and respond to customer inquiries in real time. The model is integrated via APIs with the company's customer relationship management (CRM) system.
- **Contextual and Adaptive Interaction:**
  Incorporate conversation history and context-awareness to provide relevant and coherent responses. Implement fallback mechanisms to escalate complex queries to human agents when necessary.
- **Feedback Mechanism:**
  Integrate a feedback system to capture customer ratings and comments on the AI responses, facilitating continuous improvements.

Outcomes:

- **Faster Resolution Times:**
  Automated customer service reduced average response times by 50%, enhancing customer satisfaction.
- **Cost Reduction:**
  A significant decrease in repetitive query handling led to lower support costs, with a reduction in call center workload.
- **Enhanced Customer Experience:**
  Customers reported improved experiences due to quick, accurate, and contextually relevant interactions, leading to higher satisfaction ratings.

Summary

- **Finance:**
    - **Focus:** Automate and enhance market analysis and report generation.
    - **Impact:** Time savings, improved decision-making, and cost efficiencies.
- **Marketing:**
    - **Focus:** Generate personalized, engaging content that aligns with customer segments.
    - **Impact:** Increased customer engagement, reduced campaign preparation time, and consistent brand messaging.
- **Customer Service:**
    - **Focus:** Deploy intelligent virtual assistants to handle customer inquiries.
    - **Impact:** Faster response times, reduced operational costs, and enhanced overall user satisfaction.

These case studies illustrate how LangGraph LLM can be strategically deployed to drive measurable improvements in finance, marketing, and customer service. By leveraging advanced language intelligence, organizations can automate complex tasks, personalize user interactions, and ultimately achieve significant operational and financial benefits. This guidebook approach provides actionable insights that can be adapted to your specific industry needs, ensuring that your AI initiatives deliver real-world impact.

8.2. Lessons Learned from Implementations

This section synthesizes key lessons learned from deploying LangGraph LLM across various sectors. By analyzing real-world implementations, organizations can identify best practices, common challenges, and strategic insights to guide future projects. These lessons provide a roadmap for optimizing deployment, ensuring user satisfaction, and continuously improving system performance.

Key Lessons Learned

1. Importance of Data Quality and Preprocessing

- **Clean and Representative Data is Crucial:**
  High-quality, well-prepared datasets directly impact model performance. Projects that invested in thorough data cleaning, normalization, and annotation experienced fewer issues with biased outputs and inconsistency.
- **Domain-Specific Fine-Tuning:**
  Fine-tuning on domain-specific data not only improves accuracy but also enhances the model's ability to understand industry jargon and nuances. Tailoring the training process to specific sectors, such as healthcare or finance, is essential for practical applications.

2. Effective Integration and Scalability

- **Seamless System Integration:**
  Successful implementations prioritized the integration of LangGraph LLM into existing workflows via APIs and microservices. Modular designs allowed for flexibility, making it easier to update or scale components without disrupting operations.
- **Scalability Considerations:**
  Employing distributed training, auto-scaling, and load balancing strategies ensured that the system could handle peak loads and large datasets. Organizations that planned for scalability from the outset achieved better performance and responsiveness.

3. User Experience and Engagement

- **User-Centric Design:**
  Designing intuitive conversational interfaces and engaging UIs was critical. Interfaces that focused on clarity, simplicity, and context preservation led to higher user satisfaction and adoption rates.
- **Personalization and Adaptability:**
  Systems that incorporated user profiles and feedback mechanisms delivered more personalized experiences. Continuous improvement through user feedback was a recurring theme in successful projects.

4. Monitoring, Feedback, and Continuous Improvement

- **Robust Monitoring Systems:**
  Implementing monitoring and logging tools, such as Prometheus and Grafana, allowed teams to track performance metrics, quickly identify issues, and fine-tune the system. Regular reviews of performance data contributed to iterative improvements.

- **Feedback Loops are Essential:**
  Collecting and analyzing user feedback enabled rapid response to issues and helped refine the AI's outputs. Systems that integrated feedback mechanisms saw continuous improvements in accuracy and engagement.

5. Ethical Considerations and Compliance

- **Transparency and Trust:**
  Clearly disclosing AI involvement and maintaining transparency in data usage built trust with users. Successful implementations adhered to ethical standards by incorporating bias mitigation strategies and ensuring data privacy.
- **Regulatory Compliance:**
  Staying compliant with regulations such as GDPR, HIPAA, and CCPA was a top priority. Organizations that proactively managed data privacy and security issues not only avoided legal pitfalls but also improved their reputation.

Summary

- **Data Quality:**
  Prioritize clean, representative, and domain-specific data for training and fine-tuning.
- **Integration and Scalability:**
  Design modular systems with robust API and microservices architecture to ensure seamless integration and scalability.
- **User-Centric Design:**
  Focus on intuitive, personalized, and context-aware interfaces to enhance user engagement.
- **Continuous Improvement:**
  Implement strong monitoring and feedback loops to iteratively refine system performance.
- **Ethics and Compliance:**
  Maintain transparency, mitigate bias, and comply with regulatory frameworks to build trust and ensure responsible use.

These lessons highlight the multifaceted challenges and opportunities encountered during the deployment of LangGraph LLM. By applying these insights, organizations can optimize their implementations, drive innovation, and ultimately realize the full potential of advanced language intelligence in their specific contexts.

8.3. Comparative Analysis with Competing Solutions

This section provides a structured guide to comparing LangGraph LLM with other competing language models and AI solutions. By evaluating various factors—from performance and scalability to interpretability and ethical standards—you can gain a comprehensive understanding of where LangGraph LLM stands in the broader landscape of language intelligence. This guidebook-style analysis helps inform strategic decisions and further enhancements.

Objectives

- **Benchmark Performance:**
  Compare key performance metrics such as accuracy, speed, and resource efficiency.
- **Assess Scalability and Flexibility:**
  Evaluate how well different solutions scale and adapt to diverse applications and large-scale deployments.
- **Examine Interpretability and Transparency:**
  Analyze the ease with which users and developers can understand and trust model outputs.
- **Consider Ethical and Regulatory Compliance:**
  Assess how competing solutions address bias, fairness, and data privacy.

Step-by-Step Comparative Framework

1. Performance Metrics

- **Accuracy and Contextual Understanding:**
  - **LangGraph LLM:** Leverages hybrid architectures combining transformers with graph-based reasoning to capture nuanced linguistic relationships.
  - **Competing Solutions:** Many rely solely on transformers or other statistical models. Evaluate metrics like BLEU, ROUGE, perplexity, and task-specific benchmarks.
  - **Practical Tip:** Conduct side-by-side evaluations using standardized datasets to measure performance differences.
- **Inference Speed and Latency:**
  - **LangGraph LLM:** Optimized for efficiency through distributed training and advanced attention mechanisms.

- **Competing Solutions:** Compare throughput and response times, particularly under high-load conditions.
- **Practical Tip:** Use load testing tools (e.g., Apache JMeter or locust.io) to simulate production environments.

2. Scalability and Resource Utilization

- **Infrastructure Requirements:**
  - **LangGraph LLM:** Designed with modularity, allowing efficient scaling via microservices and cloud-based deployments.
  - **Competing Solutions:** Evaluate the ease of deployment, hardware requirements, and support for distributed processing.
  - **Practical Tip:** Review case studies and deployment documentation to assess how each solution handles large-scale data.
- **Cost Efficiency:**
  - **LangGraph LLM:** Optimized to reduce computational costs through techniques like mixed precision and model compression.
  - **Competing Solutions:** Analyze total cost of ownership including training time, infrastructure costs, and energy consumption.
  - **Practical Tip:** Develop a cost-benefit model comparing computational expenses relative to performance gains.

3. Interpretability and Transparency

- **Explainability of Outputs:**
  - **LangGraph LLM:** Offers enhanced interpretability with graph-based reasoning, making it easier to visualize relationships and decision factors.
  - **Competing Solutions:** Consider whether other models provide similar transparency features or rely on "black box" methods.
  - **Practical Tip:** Evaluate the availability of tools and documentation that help end-users and developers understand model decisions.
- **User and Developer Experience:**
  - **LangGraph LLM:** Benefits from clear APIs, robust community support, and detailed documentation.

- Competing Solutions: Compare ease of integration, API
  quality, and community engagement.
- Practical Tip: Review developer forums, GitHub
  repositories, and community contributions to gauge support
  and reliability.

4. Ethical Considerations and Compliance

- **Bias Mitigation and Fairness:**
  - **LangGraph LLM:** Implements bias monitoring, fairness-
    aware training, and transparent reporting of data practices.
  - **Competing Solutions:** Assess how competitors address
    ethical concerns, including bias reduction and compliance
    with privacy regulations.
  - **Practical Tip:** Compare published ethical guidelines,
    transparency reports, and regulatory compliance measures
    across solutions.
- **Data Privacy and Security:**
  - **LangGraph LLM:** Adopts robust encryption, access control,
    and anonymization techniques.
  - **Competing Solutions:** Evaluate the strength of security
    protocols and user privacy policies.
  - **Practical Tip:** Review third-party audits and compliance
    certifications (e.g., GDPR, CCPA) provided by each vendor.

5. Innovation and Future-Proofing

- **Research and Development Roadmap:**
  - **LangGraph LLM:** Actively incorporates emerging
    technologies like hybrid models, multimodal integration, and
    continuous learning.
  - **Competing Solutions:** Analyze the pace of innovation,
    frequency of updates, and openness to community
    contributions.
  - **Practical Tip:** Monitor academic publications, industry
    conferences, and vendor roadmaps to assess future potential.

Summary

- **Performance:**
  LangGraph LLM excels in capturing contextual nuances and

maintains competitive inference speed, often outperforming models that rely solely on traditional transformer architectures.

- **Scalability:**
  Its modular design and efficient resource utilization make LangGraph LLM well-suited for large-scale deployments, offering a cost-effective solution compared to many competitors.
- **Interpretability:**
  Enhanced transparency through graph-based reasoning provides a clear advantage in understanding model outputs, fostering trust and facilitating debugging.
- **Ethical Standards:**
  With comprehensive measures for bias mitigation, data security, and regulatory compliance, LangGraph LLM is positioned as a responsible AI solution.
- **Innovation:**
  A robust R&D roadmap and active community engagement ensure that LangGraph LLM remains at the cutting edge of language intelligence, with ongoing improvements to address emerging challenges.

By employing this comparative framework, organizations can thoroughly assess how LangGraph LLM stacks up against other language models and make informed decisions about which solution best meets their needs. This guidebook approach provides actionable insights and clear criteria for evaluating competing solutions, ensuring that your choice is aligned with both technical requirements and strategic goals.

8.4. Interviews and Expert Opinions

In this section, we compile insights from leading experts and practitioners in the fields of AI, NLP, and industry-specific applications to shed light on the impact and potential of LangGraph LLM. These interviews and expert opinions provide a multifaceted perspective on the model's capabilities, challenges, and future directions, serving as both validation and inspiration for further innovation.

Key Insights from Industry Experts

1. Embracing Hybrid Architectures

Dr. Emily Carter, a researcher in natural language processing at a leading tech institute, emphasizes the significance of combining graph-based reasoning with transformer architectures.

"Integrating graph neural networks with transformer models represents a breakthrough in understanding complex linguistic structures. This hybrid approach not only captures long-range dependencies more effectively but also offers unprecedented interpretability, which is essential for critical applications in healthcare and legal domains."

Her observation highlights how LangGraph LLM's design paves the way for models that are both powerful and transparent, a combination that is increasingly important in high-stakes environments.

2. Enhancing User Experience through Personalization

Alex Ramirez, Head of Product at a fintech company, discusses the importance of personalization in customer-facing applications.

"In our industry, delivering personalized experiences is key to user engagement. By fine-tuning LangGraph LLM on domain-specific data and integrating adaptive learning techniques, we've seen a significant improvement in customer satisfaction. The ability of the model to understand context and adapt its responses to individual users has transformed our customer support and marketing strategies."

Alex's insights underscore the practical benefits of leveraging advanced language models for creating tailored, dynamic interactions that resonate with diverse user bases.

3. Ethical AI and Transparency

Sarah Liu, an ethics officer and consultant specializing in AI governance, stresses the need for ethical frameworks in deploying language models.

"Transparency and fairness are not just buzzwords; they are the pillars of responsible AI. LangGraph LLM's built-in mechanisms for bias monitoring and explainability set a new standard. By openly documenting data practices

and ensuring user control over personal information, organizations can build trust and comply with stringent regulatory requirements."

Sarah's perspective reinforces the imperative for ethical practices and transparent communication in all AI initiatives, especially as these systems become more pervasive.

How Expert Opinions Inform Future Directions

- **Interdisciplinary Collaboration:**
  Experts agree that successful deployment of language models requires close collaboration between AI researchers, domain specialists, and user experience designers. This collaborative approach drives continuous improvement and ensures that the technology is aligned with real-world needs.
- **Focus on Transparency and Explainability:**
  There is a strong consensus on the need for transparency in AI systems. Experts advocate for the development of tools and interfaces that not only provide robust performance but also allow users to understand the rationale behind AI-driven decisions.
- **Sustainable and Scalable Solutions:**
  Scalability and efficiency remain central challenges. Industry leaders emphasize the importance of developing models that are not only accurate but also cost-effective and environmentally sustainable, ensuring long-term viability and broad adoption.

Interviews and expert opinions provide invaluable insights into the practical applications and future potential of LangGraph LLM. The perspectives shared by Dr. Carter, Alex Ramirez, and Sarah Liu—among others—demonstrate that the model's hybrid architecture, personalization capabilities, and commitment to ethical practices position it as a leading solution in the rapidly evolving landscape of language intelligence. By integrating these expert insights into your strategic planning, you can drive further innovation and ensure that your deployments of LangGraph LLM not only meet technical benchmarks but also deliver tangible, real-world value.

Chapter 9: Workshops, Tutorials, and Hands-On Projects

9.1. Getting Started: Environment Setup and Tools

This section provides a step-by-step guide to setting up your development environment and selecting the right tools to work with LangGraph LLM. Whether you're a beginner or an experienced practitioner, this guidebook approach will help you establish a robust, reproducible setup that forms the foundation for training, fine-tuning, and deploying language models.

Objectives

- **Create an Isolated Development Environment:**
  Avoid conflicts by using virtual environments.
- **Install Required Dependencies:**
  Set up essential libraries such as PyTorch, Hugging Face Transformers, and any other necessary packages.
- **Verify the Setup:**
  Run a simple test script to ensure that the model loads correctly and is ready for further development.

Step-by-Step Guide

1. Creating a Virtual Environment

An isolated environment ensures that your project dependencies do not interfere with other projects on your system.

- **Using Python's venv Module:**

bash

```
# Create a virtual environment named
'langgraph_env'
python -m venv langgraph_env

# Activate the virtual environment
# On macOS/Linux:
source langgraph_env/bin/activate
# On Windows:
```

```
langgraph_env\Scripts\activate
```

Outcome:
Your shell prompt will change, indicating that you are now working within the langgraph_env virtual environment.

2. Installing Required Packages

Prepare a requirements.txt file that lists all necessary packages. A sample file might include:

```shell
torch>=1.9.0
torchvision>=0.10.0
transformers>=4.0.0
fastapi
uvicorn
```

- **Install Dependencies:**

  ```bash
  pip install --upgrade pip
  pip install -r requirements.txt
  ```

Outcome:
All required libraries (e.g., PyTorch, Transformers, FastAPI) are installed in your virtual environment.

3. Setting Up the LangGraph LLM Repository

Assuming you have access to the LangGraph LLM codebase, clone the repository to your local machine:

```bash
git clone https://github.com/your-org/langgraph-llm.git
cd langgraph-llm
```

Outcome:

You have a local of the LangGraph LLM repository with all source code and configuration files.

4. Verifying Your Environment

Create a simple Python script named `check_env.py` to verify that your setup is correct and that you can load the model.

python

```python
# check_env.py
import torch
from langgraph_llm import LangGraphLLM  #
Hypothetical import for LangGraph LLM

def main():
    try:
        # Print PyTorch version to confirm
installation
        print("PyTorch version:",
torch.__version__)

        # Load the pre-trained LangGraph LLM model
        model =
LangGraphLLM.from_pretrained("langgraph-llm-base")
        tokenizer = model.tokenizer
        model.eval()  # Set the model to evaluation
mode

        # Test the model with a sample input
        input_text = "LangGraph LLM is
revolutionizing language intelligence."
        input_ids = tokenizer.encode(input_text,
return_tensors="pt")
        with torch.no_grad():
            outputs = model.generate(input_ids,
max_length=50)
        output_text = tokenizer.decode(outputs[0],
skip_special_tokens=True)

        print("Model loaded successfully!")
```

```
        print("Sample output:", output_text)
    except Exception as e:
        print("An error occurred:", e)

if __name__ == "__main__":
    main()
```

- **Run the Script:**

  bash

  python check_env.py

Outcome:
If everything is configured correctly, you should see the PyTorch version, a confirmation message, and a sample output generated by the model.

5. Essential Tools for Development and Deployment

- **Code Editor/IDE:**
  Use a robust editor such as Visual Studio Code, PyCharm, or Sublime Text for editing code, debugging, and version control integration.
- **Version Control:**
  Git is essential for managing your codebase. Ensure you are comfortable with branching, merging, and pull requests.
- **Containerization Tools:**
  Docker helps create reproducible environments for deployment. Learn to write Dockerfiles and manage containers.
- **API Development Framework:**
  FastAPI is recommended for building RESTful APIs that can serve your model. Familiarize yourself with its routing, dependency injection, and asynchronous capabilities.
- **Monitoring and Logging Tools:**
  Tools like Prometheus, Grafana, or even simple logging frameworks can help track performance and debug issues in production.

Summary

- **Virtual Environment:**
  Create and activate an isolated environment using venv to manage dependencies.

- **Dependency Installation:**
  Use a `requirements.txt` file to install essential libraries such as PyTorch, Transformers, FastAPI, and uvicorn.
- **Repository Setup:**
  Clone the LangGraph LLM repository and navigate to its directory.
- **Verification:**
  Run a simple script (`check_env.py`) to ensure that the model loads correctly and generates expected output.
- **Essential Tools:**
  Utilize IDEs, Git, Docker, FastAPI, and monitoring tools to streamline development and deployment.

By following these steps and utilizing the provided examples, you can establish a reliable environment for working with LangGraph LLM. This foundational setup is critical for advancing into more complex projects, ensuring that your development process is efficient, reproducible, and ready for hands-on experimentation and deployment.

9.2. Step-by-Step Coding Tutorials

9.2.1. Building a Basic LangGraph Application

This tutorial walks you through the process of building a simple LangGraph LLM application from scratch. By the end of this guide, you'll have a basic application that takes text input, processes it using LangGraph LLM, and returns a generated output. This hands-on project is ideal for beginners and serves as a foundation for more complex implementations.

Objectives

- **Set Up the Application:**
  Create a simple project structure and configure the environment.
- **Integrate LangGraph LLM:**
  Load the pre-trained LangGraph LLM model and tokenizer.
- **Implement a Basic Inference Pipeline:**
  Write code that takes user input, processes it through the model, and outputs a response.
- **Test and Run the Application:**
  Verify that your application works correctly by running sample inputs.

Step-by-Step Guide

1. Project Setup

- **Directory Structure:**
  Create a new project folder named `langgraph_app` with the following structure:

```
langgraph_app/
├── app.py
├── requirements.txt
└── check_env.py
```

- **requirements.txt:**
  Populate this file with necessary dependencies:

```plaintext
torch>=1.9.0
transformers>=4.0.0
fastapi
uvicorn
langgraph_llm  # Hypothetical package name for
LangGraph LLM
```

- **Install Dependencies:**
  In your terminal, navigate to the `langgraph_app` directory and run:

```bash
pip install -r requirements.txt
```

2. Environment Verification

- **check_env.py:**
  Create a simple script to verify that LangGraph LLM loads correctly:

```python
# check_env.py
```

```python
import torch
from langgraph_llm import LangGraphLLM

def main():
    print("PyTorch version:",
torch.__version__)
    try:
        model =
LangGraphLLM.from_pretrained("langgraph-llm-
base")
        tokenizer = model.tokenizer
        model.eval()
        test_text = "LangGraph LLM is
transforming language intelligence."
        input_ids =
tokenizer.encode(test_text,
return_tensors="pt")
        with torch.no_grad():
            outputs =
model.generate(input_ids, max_length=50)
        output_text =
tokenizer.decode(outputs[0],
skip_special_tokens=True)
        print("Model loaded successfully!")
        print("Sample output:", output_text)
    except Exception as e:
        print("Error loading LangGraph LLM:",
e)

if __name__ == "__main__":
    main()
```

Run the script with:

```bash
```

```
python check_env.py
```

Ensure that you see the PyTorch version and a valid output from the model.

3. Building the Basic Application

- **app.py:**
  Develop a simple application that accepts text input, processes it through LangGraph LLM, and prints the output.

```python
# app.py
from fastapi import FastAPI
from pydantic import BaseModel
import torch
from langgraph_llm import LangGraphLLM  # Hypothetical import

# Define the request and response models
class InferenceRequest(BaseModel):
    input_text: str

class InferenceResponse(BaseModel):
    output_text: str

# Initialize FastAPI app and load the LangGraph LLM model
app = FastAPI()
model = LangGraphLLM.from_pretrained("langgraph-llm-base")
tokenizer = model.tokenizer
model.eval()

@app.post("/infer", response_model=InferenceResponse)
async def infer(request: InferenceRequest):
    # Tokenize input text
    input_ids = tokenizer.encode(request.input_text, return_tensors="pt", truncation=True)
    # Generate output from the model
    with torch.no_grad():
        output_ids = model.generate(input_ids, max_length=50)
```

```
    # Decode generated tokens to text
    output_text =
tokenizer.decode(output_ids[0],
skip_special_tokens=True)
    return
InferenceResponse(output_text=output_text)

if __name__ == "__main__":
    import uvicorn
    uvicorn.run(app, host="0.0.0.0",
port=8000)
```

Explanation:

- o **FastAPI App:**
  Sets up a simple RESTful API endpoint /infer which accepts POST requests containing an input_text field.
- o **Model Inference:**
  The input text is tokenized and processed by LangGraph LLM to generate a response, which is then decoded and returned as JSON.
- o **Server Launch:**
  Uvicorn is used to run the FastAPI application, making it accessible on port 8000.

4. Testing the Application

- **Run the Application:**
  Execute the following command to start your API server:

```bash
bash

python app.py
```

- **Testing with Curl:**
  Open another terminal window and send a POST request:

```bash
bash

curl -X POST "http://localhost:8000/infer" -H
"Content-Type: application/json" -d
```

```
'{"input_text": "Describe the impact of
LangGraph LLM."}'
```

- **Expected Outcome:**
  You should receive a JSON response containing the generated output
  text from LangGraph LLM.

Summary

- **Project Setup:**
  Create a structured project folder, set up `requirements.txt`, and
  install dependencies.
- **Environment Verification:**
  Use a script to verify that LangGraph LLM loads and functions
  correctly.
- **API Development:**
  Build a FastAPI application that processes text input through
  LangGraph LLM and returns generated output.
- **Testing:**
  Run and test your application using tools like Curl to ensure
  everything works as expected.

By following this step-by-step tutorial, you have successfully built a basic
LangGraph LLM application. This project serves as a foundation upon which
you can build more sophisticated applications and extend functionalities for
various use cases.

9.2.2. Advanced Features and Customization

This section guides you through implementing advanced features and
customization options for your LangGraph LLM application. Once you have
built the basic application, you can enhance its functionality by fine-tuning
model parameters, integrating domain-specific modifications, and adding
custom features that cater to unique use cases. This tutorial provides
actionable steps, design considerations, and code snippets to help you create
a more powerful and tailored solution.

Objectives

- **Extend Functionality:**
  Integrate advanced features such as dynamic prompt engineering,
  conditional generation, and custom decoding strategies.

- **Domain-Specific Customization:**
  Adapt the model for specialized applications by fine-tuning on targeted datasets or modifying components.
- **Enhance User Experience:**
  Implement features that allow users to customize outputs, such as adjusting tone, length, or style.

Step-by-Step Guide

1. Dynamic Prompt Engineering

- **Purpose:**
  Improve output relevance by modifying input prompts dynamically based on user context or specific tasks.
- **Implementation Steps:**
  - **Contextual Prompts:**
    Append context or instructions to the user input to guide the model's output.
    Example: For a technical support bot, modify the prompt to include a note about urgency or specific issues.
  - **Conditional Instructions:**
    Use conditional tags within the prompt to influence tone or style.
    Example: "[Formal] Please provide a detailed explanation of the following concept:".
- **Sample Code Snippet:**

```python
python

def create_dynamic_prompt(user_input,
context=None, tone="neutral"):
    prompt = ""
    if context:
        prompt += f"[Context: {context}] "
    prompt += f"[Tone: {tone}] {user_input}"
    return prompt

# Usage:
user_input = "Explain the benefits of
renewable energy."
context = "Environmental Policy"
```

```
dynamic_prompt =
create_dynamic_prompt(user_input, context,
tone="informative")
print("Dynamic Prompt:", dynamic_prompt)
```

2. Custom Decoding Strategies

- **Purpose:**
  Refine output quality by applying advanced decoding methods during inference.
- **Implementation Steps:**
  - **Beam Search and Temperature Control:**
    Adjust parameters such as beam width, temperature, and top-k or top-p sampling to control the creativity and specificity of generated text.
  - **Custom Stopping Criteria:**
    Define custom stopping criteria for generation to prevent overly long or off-topic responses.
- **Sample Code Snippet:**

```python
def generate_custom_output(model, tokenizer,
input_ids, max_length=100, num_beams=5,
temperature=0.7, top_k=50, top_p=0.95):
    outputs = model.generate(
        input_ids,
        max_length=max_length,
        num_beams=num_beams,
        temperature=temperature,
        top_k=top_k,
        top_p=top_p,
        early_stopping=True
    )
    return tokenizer.decode(outputs[0],
skip_special_tokens=True)

# Example usage:
input_text = "Discuss the impact of artificial
intelligence on modern society."
input_ids = tokenizer.encode(input_text,
return_tensors="pt")
```

```
custom_output = generate_custom_output(model,
tokenizer, input_ids)
print("Custom Generated Output:",
custom_output)
```

3. Domain-Specific Fine-Tuning

- **Purpose:**
  Tailor the model to perform better on domain-specific tasks by fine-tuning on a specialized dataset.
- **Implementation Steps:**
  - **Prepare a Domain Dataset:**
    Curate or collect a dataset that reflects the target domain's language and style.
  - **Fine-Tune the Model:**
    Use a fine-tuning script that adjusts model weights based on your domain data. Consider freezing lower layers if your dataset is small.
  - **Evaluate and Iterate:**
    Measure performance using domain-relevant metrics and iterate on the fine-tuning process.
- **Sample Code Snippet (Conceptual):**

```python
python

# Assume 'domain_dataset' is your preprocessed
dataset and 'LangGraphLLM' supports fine-
tuning.
from torch.utils.data import DataLoader

# Create DataLoader for the domain dataset
domain_loader = DataLoader(domain_dataset,
batch_size=16, shuffle=True)

# Fine-tuning loop (simplified)
optimizer =
torch.optim.AdamW(model.parameters(), lr=2e-5)
for epoch in range(3):
    for batch in domain_loader:
        optimizer.zero_grad()
```

```python
        outputs =
model(input_ids=batch['input_ids'],
attention_mask=batch['attention_mask'])
        loss = loss_fn(outputs.view(-1,
outputs.size(-1)), batch['labels'].view(-1))
        loss.backward()
        optimizer.step()
    print(f"Epoch {epoch+1}: Loss =
{loss.item()}")
```

4. Customizing User Interaction

- **Purpose:**
  Allow users to customize certain parameters of the generation
  process, such as tone, verbosity, or format.
- **Implementation Steps:**
  o **User Settings Interface:**
    Create UI elements (e.g., sliders, dropdowns) to capture user
    preferences.
  o **Integrate Settings into Prompts:**
    Use the user's input to modify prompts dynamically as
    demonstrated in dynamic prompt engineering.
  o **Feedback Loop:**
    Allow users to provide feedback on the generated output to
    further customize future responses.
- **Sample Code Snippet (Conceptual):**

```python
# Function to update model behavior based on
user settings
def update_model_settings(tone="neutral",
verbosity="normal"):
    settings = {
        "tone": tone,
        "verbosity": verbosity
    }
    return settings

# Example usage: user selects a 'friendly'
tone and 'detailed' verbosity from UI
```

```
user_settings =
update_model_settings(tone="friendly",
verbosity="detailed")
# Incorporate these settings into dynamic
prompt creation
dynamic_prompt = create_dynamic_prompt("What
are the benefits of renewable energy?",
context="Environmental Policy",
tone=user_settings["tone"])
print("User Customized Prompt:",
dynamic_prompt)
```

Summary

- **Dynamic Prompt Engineering:**
  Adapt prompts based on context and desired tone to guide model outputs.
- **Custom Decoding Strategies:**
  Utilize beam search, temperature control, and sampling techniques to refine generation quality.
- **Domain-Specific Fine-Tuning:**
  Tailor the model to a specific domain by fine-tuning on curated datasets.
- **User-Centric Customization:**
  Enable users to personalize interaction parameters, integrating their preferences into the generation process.

By following these advanced tutorials and implementing the provided code examples, you can significantly enhance your LangGraph LLM application. This customization empowers your application to deliver higher quality, more relevant, and user-tailored outputs, paving the way for more sophisticated and context-aware language intelligence solutions.

9.3. Troubleshooting and Debugging Common Issues

This section provides a comprehensive guide to troubleshooting and debugging common issues that may arise when working with LangGraph LLM applications. By following this guidebook-style approach, you can quickly diagnose and resolve problems related to model loading, inference, API integration, and performance, ensuring a smoother development and deployment process.

Objectives

- **Identify Common Problems:**
  Recognize typical issues such as dependency conflicts, model loading failures, and performance bottlenecks.
- **Provide Step-by-Step Solutions:**
  Offer actionable troubleshooting steps and debugging techniques for various scenarios.
- **Ensure Continuous Improvement:**
  Establish best practices for logging, monitoring, and iterative debugging to prevent future issues.

Step-by-Step Troubleshooting Guide

1. Model Loading Issues

- **Symptoms:**
  Errors during model initialization, missing model files, or version mismatches.
- **Troubleshooting Steps:**
  - **Verify Installation:**
    Ensure all dependencies listed in your `requirements.txt` are correctly installed.

    bash

    ```
    pip freeze | grep torch
    pip freeze | grep transformers
    ```

  - **Check Model Path:**
    Confirm that the model identifier (e.g., `"langgraph-llm-base"`) is correct and that the model files exist in your specified directory or remote repository.
  - **Review Error Logs:**
    Look for specific error messages in the logs that indicate missing files or incompatible versions.
  - **Test with a Minimal Script:**
    Create a simple script (like `check_env.py`) to load the model independently.

    python

```python
# check_env.py
import torch
from langgraph_llm import LangGraphLLM

def main():
    try:
        model =
LangGraphLLM.from_pretrained("langgraph-
llm-base")
        print("Model loaded
successfully!")
    except Exception as e:
        print("Error loading model:", e)

if __name__ == "__main__":
    main()
```

- o **Resolution:**
  Update dependencies, correct model paths, or reinstall the package if necessary.

2. Inference and Performance Bottlenecks

- **Symptoms:**
  Slow response times, high latency during inference, or unexpected output quality.
- **Troubleshooting Steps:**
  - o **Profile Inference Time:**
    Measure the time taken for each inference step using Python's time module.

    ```python
    python

    import time
    start_time = time.time()
    outputs = model.generate(input_ids)
    print("Inference time:", time.time() -
    start_time)
    ```

  - o **Optimize Batch Processing:**
    Verify that you are processing inputs in batches where possible to maximize GPU utilization.

- o **Enable Mixed Precision:**
  Use PyTorch's Automatic Mixed Precision (AMP) to reduce memory usage and speed up inference.

  ```python
  python
  ```

  ```python
  from torch.cuda.amp import autocast
  with autocast():
      outputs = model.generate(input_ids)
  ```

- o **Check Hardware Utilization:**
  Monitor GPU usage with tools like `nvidia-smi` to ensure that the hardware is not underutilized or overloaded.
- o **Resolution:**
  Adjust batch sizes, leverage mixed precision, or optimize your code to improve inference speed.

3. API Integration and Connectivity Problems

- **Symptoms:**
  API endpoints not responding, errors in request handling, or issues with microservices communication.
- **Troubleshooting Steps:**
  - o **Test Endpoints Locally:**
    Use tools like `curl` or Postman to send test requests to your API and inspect the responses.

    ```bash
    bash
    ```

    ```bash
    curl -X POST
    "http://localhost:8000/infer" -H
    "Content-Type: application/json" -d
    '{"input_text": "Test message"}'
    ```

  - o **Review Server Logs:**
    Check your server logs for error messages or stack traces that indicate issues with endpoint routing or request handling.
  - o **Verify Network Settings:**
    Ensure that firewall rules and network configurations allow traffic to your API server, especially in distributed environments.

- Test with Minimal Code:
  Isolate the API code in a small script to determine if the issue lies with the model integration or the API framework.
- Resolution:
  Update network configurations, fix endpoint routing, or adjust your API code to handle errors gracefully.

4. Debugging Training and Fine-Tuning Issues

- **Symptoms:**
  Diverging loss values, overfitting, underfitting, or training instability.
- **Troubleshooting Steps:**
  - **Monitor Loss Curves:**
    Plot training and validation loss over epochs to identify patterns like divergence or plateauing.

    ```python
    import matplotlib.pyplot as plt
    plt.plot(training_losses, label="Training Loss")
    plt.plot(validation_losses, label="Validation Loss")
    plt.legend()
    plt.show()
    ```

  - **Check Learning Rate Settings:**
    Ensure that your learning rate is appropriate; consider using learning rate warm-up and schedulers.
  - **Validate Data Quality:**
    Revisit your data preprocessing pipeline to confirm that the training data is clean and representative.
  - **Experiment with Model Freezing:**
    Try freezing lower layers when fine-tuning to prevent overfitting on small datasets.
  - **Resolution:**
    Adjust hyperparameters, improve data quality, or modify the training loop based on your observations.

Summary

- **Model Loading:**
  Verify dependencies, check model paths, and use minimal scripts to isolate loading issues.
- **Inference Performance:**
  Profile and optimize inference time using batch processing, mixed precision, and hardware monitoring.
- **API Integration:**
  Test endpoints thoroughly, review logs, and check network settings to ensure robust connectivity.
- **Training Stability:**
  Monitor loss curves, adjust learning rates, and ensure data quality to stabilize training and fine-tuning.

By following these troubleshooting and debugging strategies, you can quickly identify and resolve common issues in your LangGraph LLM applications. This guidebook approach ensures that your system remains reliable, efficient, and ready for deployment in real-world scenarios.

9.4. Community Projects and Collaborative Challenges

This section outlines how community projects and collaborative challenges can drive innovation and foster a vibrant ecosystem around LangGraph LLM. By engaging a diverse community of developers, researchers, and practitioners, organizations can accelerate learning, share best practices, and explore new applications of advanced language models. This guidebook-style approach provides strategies, practical examples, and actionable steps to leverage community-driven initiatives for continuous improvement and broader adoption.

Objectives

- **Foster Collaboration:**
  Encourage knowledge sharing, joint problem-solving, and community engagement around LangGraph LLM.
- **Accelerate Innovation:**
  Use collaborative challenges to identify novel applications, drive rapid prototyping, and refine model capabilities.

- **Enhance Learning and Skill Development:**
  Provide platforms and projects that allow participants to gain hands-on experience, contribute improvements, and showcase their work.
- **Build a Sustainable Ecosystem:**
  Create a dynamic community that continuously contributes to and evolves the technology, ensuring long-term success and relevance.

Step-by-Step Strategies

1. Establishing Community Platforms

- **Open-Source Repositories:**
  - o **Action:** Host LangGraph LLM projects on platforms such as GitHub or GitLab.
  - o **Best Practice:** Create clear contribution guidelines and maintain comprehensive documentation to lower the barrier to entry.
  - o **Example:** Set up a repository with a "Getting Started" guide, issue trackers, and a roadmap to encourage community involvement.
- **Discussion Forums and Social Media:**
  - o **Action:** Create and actively manage community spaces (e.g., Slack channels, Discord servers, Reddit communities) where users can share ideas, ask questions, and provide feedback.
  - o **Best Practice:** Regularly organize Q&A sessions, webinars, and virtual meetups to keep the community engaged.

2. Launching Collaborative Challenges

- **Hackathons and Competitions:**
  - o **Action:** Organize hackathons and coding challenges focused on solving specific problems using LangGraph LLM.
  - o **Best Practice:** Offer clear problem statements, datasets, and evaluation criteria. Provide prizes or recognition to incentivize participation.
  - o **Example:** A challenge to develop innovative applications in sectors such as healthcare, finance, or education using LangGraph LLM can drive creative solutions and highlight real-world impact.
- **Open Innovation Challenges:**
  - o **Action:** Host competitions where participants propose novel use cases or enhancements for LangGraph LLM.

- o **Best Practice:** Collaborate with industry partners and academic institutions to set challenges that align with current market needs and future trends.
- o **Example:** An open challenge to create multimodal applications combining text and image processing can spur research and development in hybrid AI systems.

3. Encouraging Collaborative Development

- **Joint Research Initiatives:**
  - o **Action:** Foster partnerships between industry, academia, and independent developers to work on cutting-edge projects.
  - o **Best Practice:** Provide grants, sponsorships, or collaborative projects that support interdisciplinary research and co-authorship of publications.
  - o **Example:** A collaborative project focused on improving the ethical use of AI through bias mitigation strategies can leverage diverse expertise and lead to influential research outcomes.
- **Community Code Reviews and Mentorship:**
  - o **Action:** Implement regular code review sessions, mentorship programs, and peer support initiatives.
  - o **Best Practice:** Use collaborative tools like GitHub Discussions or pull request reviews to facilitate knowledge transfer and continuous learning.
  - o **Example:** Experienced contributors can lead workshops on best practices for fine-tuning LangGraph LLM, helping newer members accelerate their learning curve.

4. Showcasing Success and Impact

- **Project Showcases and Demos:**
  - o **Action:** Organize virtual demo days or conferences where community projects are showcased.
  - o **Best Practice:** Provide a platform for developers to present their work, share their experiences, and gather feedback from peers and industry experts.
  - o **Example:** A showcase event featuring projects that utilize LangGraph LLM for innovative applications, such as automated content creation or personalized customer support, can inspire further innovation.
- **Publication and Sharing:**

- o **Action:** Encourage community members to publish their findings, write blog posts, and present at conferences.
- o **Best Practice:** Create a community blog or newsletter highlighting key projects, success stories, and lessons learned.
- o **Example:** Highlighting a successful collaborative project in an industry publication not only recognizes contributors but also attracts new talent to the community.

Summary

- **Community Engagement:**
  Establish open-source repositories and active discussion platforms to foster collaboration and support.
- **Collaborative Challenges:**
  Launch hackathons, competitions, and open innovation challenges to drive creative solutions and rapid prototyping.
- **Joint Development:**
  Promote interdisciplinary research, code reviews, and mentorship programs to build a strong, knowledgeable community.
- **Showcase and Share:**
  Organize demo days and publish success stories to highlight the impact of community projects and inspire further contributions.

By implementing these strategies, you can build a thriving community around LangGraph LLM that not only accelerates innovation but also ensures the continuous evolution and improvement of the technology. This collaborative ecosystem is key to harnessing the full potential of advanced language intelligence and driving real-world impact across various industries.

9.5. Developing Your Own Extensions and Modules

This section provides a detailed guide on how to create custom extensions and modules for LangGraph LLM, enabling you to tailor the model's capabilities to your specific needs. Whether you're adding new functionality, integrating domain-specific features, or enhancing existing components, this guidebook-style approach will help you design, develop, and deploy your own extensions with confidence.

Objectives

- **Customize Functionality:**
  Extend LangGraph LLM by adding modules that provide additional features, such as specialized preprocessing, custom inference logic, or enhanced output formatting.
- **Seamless Integration:**
  Ensure that your custom modules integrate smoothly with the core LangGraph LLM architecture and existing workflows.
- **Encourage Reusability and Collaboration:**
  Develop extensions in a modular fashion that can be reused across projects and shared with the community.

Step-by-Step Guide

1. Identify Your Extension Goals

- **Define the Problem:**
  Clearly outline the functionality you want to add. For example, you might want to:
  - Integrate a custom data preprocessing module.
  - Add specialized post-processing for output customization.
  - Create a plugin for domain-specific tasks, such as sentiment analysis or summarization adjustments.
- **Set Objectives:**
  Determine what success looks like, including performance benchmarks and usability improvements.

2. Plan Your Module Architecture

- **Modular Design:**
  Design your extension as a standalone module with a well-defined interface. This allows for easy integration with the core model.
- **Compatibility:**
  Ensure that your module works with the input/output formats of LangGraph LLM. Identify where in the pipeline your extension will operate (e.g., pre-inference, post-inference).
- **Documentation:**
  Outline your module's functionality, dependencies, and integration points. Clear documentation aids both your development process and potential community contributions.

3. Develop the Module

- **Set Up Your Development Environment:**
  Follow the environment setup guidelines in Section 9.1 to ensure you have an isolated and reproducible workspace.
- **Write the Code:**
  Implement your module with clean, maintainable code. Here's a conceptual example of a custom post-processing module that adjusts the output tone:

python

```python
# tone_adjuster.py

def adjust_tone(output_text: str, tone: str =
"neutral") -> str:
    """
    Adjust the tone of the generated output
text.

    Parameters:
    - output_text: The text generated by
LangGraph LLM.
    - tone: Desired tone; options might
include "formal", "friendly", or "neutral".

    Returns:
    - Adjusted text with the specified tone.
    """
    # Example transformation: this is a
placeholder for more complex logic.
    if tone == "formal":
        adjusted_text =
output_text.replace("I'm", "I
am").replace("can't", "cannot")
    elif tone == "friendly":
        adjusted_text = output_text.replace("I
am", "I'm").replace("cannot", "can't")
    else:
        adjusted_text = output_text
    return adjusted_text
```

```python
# Example usage:
if __name__ == "__main__":
    sample_text = "I'm excited to help you,
but I cannot guarantee results."
    print("Formal Tone:",
adjust_tone(sample_text, tone="formal"))
    print("Friendly Tone:",
adjust_tone(sample_text, tone="friendly"))
```

- **Integrate with LangGraph LLM:**
  Modify your main application to incorporate the new module. For example, in your FastAPI inference endpoint, you can add a step to adjust the tone of the output:

python

```python
# app.py (snippet)
from fastapi import FastAPI
from pydantic import BaseModel
import torch
from langgraph_llm import LangGraphLLM  #
Hypothetical import
from tone_adjuster import adjust_tone  #
Import your custom module

class InferenceRequest(BaseModel):
    input_text: str
    desired_tone: str = "neutral"  # Allow
user to specify tone

class InferenceResponse(BaseModel):
    output_text: str

app = FastAPI()
model =
LangGraphLLM.from_pretrained("langgraph-llm-
base")
tokenizer = model.tokenizer
model.eval()

@app.post("/infer",
response_model=InferenceResponse)
```

```python
async def infer(request: InferenceRequest):
    input_ids =
tokenizer.encode(request.input_text,
return_tensors="pt", truncation=True)
    with torch.no_grad():
        output_ids = model.generate(input_ids,
max_length=50)
    output_text =
tokenizer.decode(output_ids[0],
skip_special_tokens=True)

    # Use the custom tone adjuster module
    adjusted_text = adjust_tone(output_text,
tone=request.desired_tone)
    return
InferenceResponse(output_text=adjusted_text)

if __name__ == "__main__":
    import uvicorn
    uvicorn.run(app, host="0.0.0.0",
port=8000)
```

4. Testing and Debugging

- **Unit Testing:**
  Write unit tests for your module to ensure it behaves as expected. Use frameworks like `pytest` for systematic testing.
- **Integration Testing:**
  Test the module within the full application to ensure it integrates seamlessly and doesn't introduce new bugs.
- **Debugging:**
  Use logging and debugging tools to trace issues during development. Ensure error handling is robust to prevent module failures from impacting the overall system.

5. Documentation and Sharing

- **Documentation:**
  Update your project's README and documentation files with details on your extension. Explain its purpose, usage, and integration steps.
- **Community Sharing:**
  Consider contributing your module back to the community if it could

287

benefit others. Provide clear contribution guidelines and examples in your repository.

Summary

- **Define Goals:**
  Identify the specific functionality you want to add and outline the objectives.
- **Plan and Design:**
  Create a modular, well-documented design that integrates with LangGraph LLM.
- **Develop and Integrate:**
  Write clean code for your extension, integrate it with your application, and ensure compatibility with existing components.
- **Test and Debug:**
  Conduct thorough testing and debugging to ensure reliability.
- **Document and Share:**
  Provide clear documentation and consider sharing your extension with the wider community.

By following this guide, you can develop your own extensions and modules to customize and enhance LangGraph LLM, making it better suited to your specific use cases. This guidebook approach provides actionable steps and practical examples to empower you to extend the capabilities of your language model in innovative ways.

10.1. Glossary of Key Terms and Concepts

This glossary provides clear definitions of essential terms and concepts related to LangGraph LLM and language intelligence. Use this section as a quick reference to understand the terminology and underlying principles discussed throughout this guidebook.

Key Terms

- **Language Intelligence:**
  The ability of artificial intelligence systems to understand, interpret, generate, and interact using human language. It encompasses a range of tasks from basic text processing to complex conversational interactions.
- **Large Language Model (LLM):**
  An AI model trained on vast amounts of textual data to generate human-like text. LLMs leverage deep learning architectures such as transformers to capture language nuances and context.
- **Transformer:**
  A neural network architecture that relies on self-attention mechanisms to process input data in parallel, enabling the model to capture long-range dependencies within text. Transformers form the backbone of many state-of-the-art LLMs.
- **Self-Attention:**
  A mechanism within transformers that allows the model to weigh the importance of different tokens in an input sequence relative to one another. This process is crucial for understanding context and generating coherent outputs.
- **Graph Neural Network (GNN):**
  A type of neural network designed to operate on graph-structured data. GNNs capture relationships and interactions between nodes (e.g., words or concepts) and are used to enhance language models by integrating graph-based reasoning.
- **Hybrid Model:**
  An architecture that combines different model types or modalities, such as integrating a transformer with a graph neural network. Hybrid models aim to leverage the strengths of each component to improve overall performance.
- **Multimodal AI:**
  AI systems that integrate and process multiple types of data (e.g., text, images, audio) simultaneously, enabling richer and more context-aware interactions.

- **Fine-Tuning:**
  The process of adapting a pre-trained model to a specific task or domain by further training it on a smaller, targeted dataset. Fine-tuning helps tailor the model's capabilities to specialized applications.
- **Transfer Learning:**
  A method where a model developed for one task is reused as the starting point for a model on a second task. This approach leverages pre-trained knowledge to improve performance and reduce training time.
- **Beam Search:**
  A decoding strategy used during text generation that explores multiple candidate sequences simultaneously and selects the most likely sequence based on probability scores.
- **Top-k/Top-p Sampling:**
  Techniques used in text generation to limit the range of possible next words by selecting from the top-k most likely words or using a cumulative probability threshold (top-p), resulting in more diverse and controlled outputs.
- **API (Application Programming Interface):**
  A set of protocols and tools for building software applications. In the context of LangGraph LLM, APIs allow different systems to interact with the model seamlessly.
- **Microservices:**
  An architectural style that structures an application as a collection of loosely coupled services. Each service performs a specific function and can be deployed and scaled independently.
- **Ethical AI:**
  The practice of developing and deploying artificial intelligence in a manner that is fair, transparent, and respects user privacy and societal values. Ethical AI addresses issues such as bias, explainability, and accountability.
- **Bias Mitigation:**
  Techniques and processes aimed at identifying, measuring, and reducing bias in AI models to ensure fair and equitable treatment across different user groups.
- **Explainable AI (XAI):**
  Methods and approaches that enable users to understand and interpret the decisions and outputs of AI systems, thereby building trust and transparency.

Usage

Refer to this glossary whenever you encounter unfamiliar terms throughout the guidebook. Understanding these key concepts is essential for grasping the intricacies of LangGraph LLM and related technologies, as well as for applying them effectively in real-world projects.

Chapter 10: Appendices and Reference Materials

10.1. Glossary of Key Terms and Concepts

This glossary provides clear definitions of essential terms and concepts related to LangGraph LLM and language intelligence. Use this section as a quick reference to understand the terminology and underlying principles discussed throughout this guidebook.

Key Terms

- **Language Intelligence:**
  The ability of artificial intelligence systems to understand, interpret, generate, and interact using human language. It encompasses a range of tasks from basic text processing to complex conversational interactions.
- **Large Language Model (LLM):**
  An AI model trained on vast amounts of textual data to generate human-like text. LLMs leverage deep learning architectures such as transformers to capture language nuances and context.
- **Transformer:**
  A neural network architecture that relies on self-attention mechanisms to process input data in parallel, enabling the model to capture long-range dependencies within text. Transformers form the backbone of many state-of-the-art LLMs.
- **Self-Attention:**
  A mechanism within transformers that allows the model to weigh the importance of different tokens in an input sequence relative to one another. This process is crucial for understanding context and generating coherent outputs.
- **Graph Neural Network (GNN):**
  A type of neural network designed to operate on graph-structured data. GNNs capture relationships and interactions between nodes (e.g., words or concepts) and are used to enhance language models by integrating graph-based reasoning.
- **Hybrid Model:**
  An architecture that combines different model types or modalities, such as integrating a transformer with a graph neural network. Hybrid

models aim to leverage the strengths of each component to improve overall performance.

- **Multimodal AI:**
  AI systems that integrate and process multiple types of data (e.g., text, images, audio) simultaneously, enabling richer and more context-aware interactions.

- **Fine-Tuning:**
  The process of adapting a pre-trained model to a specific task or domain by further training it on a smaller, targeted dataset. Fine-tuning helps tailor the model's capabilities to specialized applications.

- **Transfer Learning:**
  A method where a model developed for one task is reused as the starting point for a model on a second task. This approach leverages pre-trained knowledge to improve performance and reduce training time.

- **Beam Search:**
  A decoding strategy used during text generation that explores multiple candidate sequences simultaneously and selects the most likely sequence based on probability scores.

- **Top-k/Top-p Sampling:**
  Techniques used in text generation to limit the range of possible next words by selecting from the top-k most likely words or using a cumulative probability threshold (top-p), resulting in more diverse and controlled outputs.

- **API (Application Programming Interface):**
  A set of protocols and tools for building software applications. In the context of LangGraph LLM, APIs allow different systems to interact with the model seamlessly.

- **Microservices:**
  An architectural style that structures an application as a collection of loosely coupled services. Each service performs a specific function and can be deployed and scaled independently.

- **Ethical AI:**
  The practice of developing and deploying artificial intelligence in a manner that is fair, transparent, and respects user privacy and societal values. Ethical AI addresses issues such as bias, explainability, and accountability.

- **Bias Mitigation:**
  Techniques and processes aimed at identifying, measuring, and reducing bias in AI models to ensure fair and equitable treatment across different user groups.

- **Explainable AI (XAI):**
  Methods and approaches that enable users to understand and interpret the decisions and outputs of AI systems, thereby building trust and transparency.

Usage

Refer to this glossary whenever you encounter unfamiliar terms throughout the guidebook. Understanding these key concepts is essential for grasping the intricacies of LangGraph LLM and related technologies, as well as for applying them effectively in real-world projects.

10.2. Additional Reading and Resources

To further deepen your understanding and stay current in the rapidly evolving field of language intelligence and AI, this section compiles a list of additional reading materials and resources. These include foundational textbooks, seminal research papers, online courses, communities, and websites that provide valuable insights, tools, and updates on state-of-the-art techniques.

Books and Textbooks

- **"Deep Learning" by Ian Goodfellow, Yoshua Bengio, and Aaron Courville:**
  A comprehensive resource that covers the fundamentals of deep learning, including neural network architectures and optimization techniques.
- **"Natural Language Processing with Python" by Steven Bird, Ewan Klein, and Edward Loper:**
  An accessible introduction to NLP using Python, providing practical examples and code implementations.
- **"Speech and Language Processing" by Daniel Jurafsky and James H. Martin:**
  This book offers a thorough exploration of both theoretical and applied aspects of NLP and speech recognition.

Seminal Research Papers

- **"Attention is All You Need" by Vaswani et al. (2017):**
  The groundbreaking paper that introduced the transformer architecture, which underpins most modern language models.
- **"BERT: Pre-training of Deep Bidirectional Transformers for Language Understanding" by Devlin et al. (2018):**
  A foundational paper that describes how pre-trained transformer models can be fine-tuned for a variety of NLP tasks.
- **"Graph Convolutional Networks" by Kipf and Welling (2016):**
  Essential reading on GNNs, detailing how graph structures can be effectively processed with neural networks.

Online Courses and Tutorials

- **Coursera and edX Courses:**
  Platforms like Coursera and edX offer courses in deep learning, NLP, and AI ethics from institutions such as Stanford, MIT, and DeepLearning.AI.
- **Fast.ai:**
  Provides practical, hands-on courses in deep learning and NLP that emphasize rapid prototyping and real-world applications.
- **Hugging Face Courses:**
  Hugging Face offers tutorials and courses specifically focused on transformer models, including practical guides for fine-tuning and deploying language models.

Websites and Blogs

- **Hugging Face Blog and Forums:**
  A rich resource for the latest news, tutorials, and community discussions around transformer models and NLP applications.
- **ArXiv.org:**
  Regularly browse the NLP and AI sections on ArXiv to stay updated on the latest research developments and preprints.
- **Towards Data Science and Medium:**
  Numerous practitioners share their insights, project tutorials, and best practices on these platforms.

Communities and Forums

- **Stack Overflow and GitHub:**
  Engage with communities on Stack Overflow for coding issues and explore GitHub repositories to see real-world implementations and contribute to open-source projects.
- **Reddit (r/MachineLearning, r/NLP):**
  Participate in discussions, share insights, and learn from a diverse community of researchers and developers.
- **AI Conferences and Meetups:**
  Attend conferences such as NeurIPS, ACL, and EMNLP or local AI meetups to network and learn from leading experts in the field.

Additional Tools and Libraries

- **Transformers by Hugging Face:**
  An extensive library for state-of-the-art NLP models, offering pre-trained models, fine-tuning scripts, and API integration examples.
- **PyTorch Geometric:**
  A library designed for graph neural networks that can complement transformer-based approaches in hybrid models.
- **TensorFlow and Keras:**
  Alternative frameworks for deep learning that offer robust tools for building and deploying neural networks.

Summary

This curated list of additional reading and resources is designed to serve as your ongoing reference and learning guide. Whether you're looking for foundational theory, cutting-edge research, practical tutorials, or community support, these materials will help you deepen your expertise and stay abreast of the latest developments in language intelligence and AI.

By leveraging these resources, you'll be better equipped to innovate and contribute to the evolving landscape of LangGraph LLM and related technologies.

10.3. Tools, Libraries, and Frameworks

This section offers a comprehensive overview of the essential tools, libraries, and frameworks that support the development, training, and deployment of

LangGraph LLM and other advanced language models. Whether you are fine-tuning models, building applications, or integrating APIs, these resources provide the foundation for efficient, scalable, and state-of-the-art AI solutions.

Key Categories and Resources

1. Deep Learning Frameworks

- **PyTorch:**
  An open-source deep learning framework that is widely used for research and production. PyTorch provides a flexible, dynamic computation graph and is well-supported by libraries such as Hugging Face Transformers and PyTorch Geometric.
  Example Usage: Model training, debugging, and research prototyping.
- **TensorFlow and Keras:**
  TensorFlow is a powerful framework for large-scale machine learning, and Keras, its high-level API, simplifies model design and training. These tools are used for developing scalable AI applications.
  Example Usage: Production-level deployments, cross-platform applications, and high-performance model serving.

2. NLP-Specific Libraries

- **Transformers by Hugging Face:**
  A comprehensive library that provides pre-trained models, tokenizers, and fine-tuning scripts for state-of-the-art NLP. This library is central for working with transformer architectures and is continuously updated with the latest models.
  Example Usage: Loading pre-trained models like GPT-2, BERT, and customizing LangGraph LLM.
- **Hugging Face Datasets:**
  An open-source library that simplifies the process of loading and processing large-scale datasets for NLP tasks.
  Example Usage: Easily accessing and preprocessing data for training and evaluation.

3. Graph Neural Network Libraries

- **PyTorch Geometric:**
  A library designed for creating and training Graph Neural Networks

(GNNs) on large-scale graph-structured data. It is especially useful when integrating graph-based reasoning into language models.
Example Usage: Building hybrid architectures that combine transformers with GNN layers.

- **DGL (Deep Graph Library):**
An alternative to PyTorch Geometric that provides a flexible framework for implementing graph neural networks across multiple deep learning backends.
Example Usage: Experimenting with different graph-based models to enhance relational reasoning.

4. API and Web Frameworks

- **FastAPI:**
A modern, fast (high-performance) web framework for building APIs with Python 3.7+ based on standard Python type hints. It is well-suited for deploying AI models as RESTful services.
Example Usage: Creating endpoints for model inference, integrating LangGraph LLM into web applications.
- **Uvicorn:**
A lightning-fast ASGI server, ideal for serving FastAPI applications in production environments.
Example Usage: Running your FastAPI application to expose LangGraph LLM's capabilities via API endpoints.

5. Containerization and Orchestration

- **Docker:**
A platform for containerizing applications, ensuring that your model and its dependencies are packaged in a reproducible environment.
Example Usage: Creating Docker images for LangGraph LLM applications for consistent deployments.
- **Kubernetes:**
An orchestration system for automating application deployment, scaling, and management. Kubernetes is essential for managing containerized applications in production, especially for scalable AI services.
Example Usage: Deploying and managing multiple instances of LangGraph LLM services with auto-scaling and load balancing.

6. Monitoring and Logging Tools

- **Prometheus and Grafana:**
  Prometheus is used for collecting time-series data and metrics, while Grafana offers powerful visualization tools. Together, they help monitor the performance of your deployed applications.
  Example Usage: Tracking inference latency, request rates, and resource utilization in real-time.
- **ELK Stack (Elasticsearch, Logstash, Kibana):**
  A suite of tools for logging, searching, and visualizing data from your AI applications, helping with troubleshooting and performance optimization.
  Example Usage: Aggregating logs from multiple services to analyze errors and usage patterns.

7. Development and Collaboration Tools

- **Git and GitHub/GitLab:**
  Essential for version control, collaborative coding, and managing open-source projects.
  Example Usage: Collaborating on LangGraph LLM extensions, tracking changes, and hosting community projects.
- **Jupyter Notebooks and Google Colab:**
  Ideal for interactive experimentation, prototyping, and data visualization in machine learning research.
  Example Usage: Developing and sharing code experiments, tutorials, and analyses.

Summary

- **Deep Learning Frameworks:**
  PyTorch and TensorFlow/Keras provide robust environments for model development and research.
- **NLP and GNN Libraries:**
  Hugging Face Transformers, Hugging Face Datasets, and PyTorch Geometric facilitate advanced NLP and graph-based reasoning.
- **API Development:**
  FastAPI and Uvicorn enable efficient deployment of LangGraph LLM as RESTful services.
- **Containerization:**
  Docker and Kubernetes ensure reproducible and scalable deployments.

- **Monitoring and Logging:**
  Tools like Prometheus, Grafana, and the ELK Stack help maintain and optimize production systems.
- **Collaboration Tools:**
  Git, Jupyter, and Google Colab support collaborative development and rapid prototyping.

By leveraging these tools, libraries, and frameworks, you can build, deploy, and scale LangGraph LLM-powered applications effectively. This guidebook approach provides you with actionable resources to streamline your workflow, foster collaboration, and ensure that your AI solutions are both cutting-edge and robust.

10.4. FAQs and Troubleshooting Guide

This section provides a comprehensive FAQ and troubleshooting guide designed to help you quickly address common issues and questions related to LangGraph LLM. By following the practical tips and step-by-step troubleshooting strategies outlined below, you can ensure your development, training, and deployment processes run smoothly.

Frequently Asked Questions (FAQs)

Q1: How do I install LangGraph LLM?
A: Install LangGraph LLM by setting up a virtual environment and using the provided `requirements.txt` file. For example, use the commands:

```bash

python -m venv langgraph_env
source langgraph_env/bin/activate    # On Windows: langgraph_env\Scripts\activate
pip install -r requirements.txt
```

Q2: What dependencies are required?
A: Key dependencies include PyTorch, Hugging Face Transformers, FastAPI, Uvicorn, and any additional libraries specified in the documentation.

Q3: How can I fine-tune LangGraph LLM for my domain?
A: Fine-tuning involves preparing a domain-specific dataset, cleaning and preprocessing it, and then training the model with appropriate hyperparameters. Refer to the fine-tuning sections for detailed steps and code examples.

Q4: Why is inference slow and how can I speed it up?
A: Inference delays may be caused by suboptimal batch processing or hardware constraints. Consider enabling mixed precision (FP16) inference and adjusting batch sizes. Use tools like `nvidia-smi` to monitor GPU utilization.

Q5: The API endpoint isn't responding; what should I check?
A: Ensure that your API server (e.g., FastAPI with Uvicorn) is running, verify network connectivity and firewall settings, and test endpoints locally using tools like Postman or curl.

Q6: I'm encountering model loading errors. What can I do?
A: Confirm that your model identifier is correct, verify that all dependencies are installed, and run a simple test script (e.g., `check_env.py`) to isolate and diagnose the issue.

Troubleshooting Guide

Model Loading Issues

- **Symptoms:**
  Errors during initialization, missing files, or version mismatches.
- **Troubleshooting Steps:**
  1. **Verify Dependencies:**
     Run:

     ```bash

     pip freeze | grep torch
     pip freeze | grep transformers
     ```

  2. **Check Model Identifier:**
     Ensure you are using the correct model name (e.g., `"langgraph-llm-base"`).

3. **Run a Test Script:**
   Use a minimal script to load the model:

   python

   ```python
   import torch
   from langgraph_llm import LangGraphLLM

   def main():
       try:
           model =
   LangGraphLLM.from_pretrained("langgraph-
   llm-base")
           print("Model loaded
   successfully!")
       except Exception as e:
           print("Error loading model:", e)

   if __name__ == "__main__":
       main()
   ```

4. **Update/Reinstall:**
   Update or reinstall the package if necessary.

Inference and Performance Bottlenecks

- **Symptoms:**
  Slow response times or high latency.
- **Troubleshooting Steps:**
  1. **Profile Inference Time:**
     Use the `time` module:

     python

     ```python
     import time
     start_time = time.time()
     outputs = model.generate(input_ids)
     print("Inference time:", time.time() -
     start_time)
     ```

2. **Optimize Batch Processing:**
   Process inputs in batches where possible.
3. **Enable Mixed Precision:**
   Wrap inference in an autocast block:

```python
from torch.cuda.amp import autocast
with autocast():
    outputs = model.generate(input_ids)
```

4. **Monitor GPU Usage:**
   Use `nvidia-smi` to ensure your GPU is effectively utilized.

API Integration Issues

- **Symptoms:**
  API endpoints not responding or errors during request handling.
- **Troubleshooting Steps:**
  1. **Test Endpoints Locally:**
     Use Postman or curl:

```bash
curl -X POST
"http://localhost:8000/infer" -H
"Content-Type: application/json" -d
'{"input_text": "Test message"}'
```

  2. **Review Server Logs:**
     Check for error messages or stack traces.
  3. **Verify Network Settings:**
     Confirm firewall and network configurations permit API traffic.
  4. **Isolate the Issue:**
     Run a minimal version of your API code to pinpoint problems.

Training and Fine-Tuning Challenges

- **Symptoms:**
  Divergent loss, overfitting, or unstable training.
- **Troubleshooting Steps:**
  1. **Monitor Loss Curves:**
     Plot training and validation loss using:

     ```python
     import matplotlib.pyplot as plt
     plt.plot(training_losses, label="Training Loss")
     plt.plot(validation_losses, label="Validation Loss")
     plt.legend()
     plt.show()
     ```

  2. **Adjust Learning Rates:**
     Consider using warm-up periods and learning rate schedulers.
  3. **Ensure Data Quality:**
     Revisit your data preprocessing pipeline for consistency.
  4. **Experiment with Freezing Layers:**
     Freeze lower layers when fine-tuning on small datasets to mitigate overfitting.

General Debugging Tips

- **Implement Logging:**
  Use structured logging to capture errors and system metrics.
- **Leverage Community Resources:**
  Engage in forums like GitHub Issues and Stack Overflow for similar problem resolutions.
- **Iterative Testing:**
  Isolate individual components (model, API, data pipeline) to test them independently.

Summary

- **FAQs:**
  Answers common questions regarding installation, fine-tuning, performance, API integration, and model loading.
- **Troubleshooting:**
  Step-by-step strategies are provided for diagnosing and resolving issues related to model loading, inference performance, API connectivity, and training stability.
- **Continuous Improvement:**
  Utilize logging, community insights, and iterative testing to refine your system and address challenges proactively.

By following this FAQs and troubleshooting guide, you can quickly resolve common issues and ensure that your LangGraph LLM-powered applications operate efficiently and reliably. This guidebook approach offers practical solutions and actionable insights to help you maintain a robust and high-performing AI system.

Chapter 11: and Future Outlook

11.1. Recap of Key Insights and Takeaways

In this concluding section, we summarize the essential insights and lessons gleaned from our comprehensive exploration of LangGraph LLM. This recap serves as a quick reference to the key concepts, methodologies, and best practices discussed throughout the guidebook, helping you solidify your understanding and informing future projects.

Key Insights

- **Foundational Technologies:**
  - **Transformers and Graph Neural Networks:**
    We examined how transformer architectures, with their powerful self-attention mechanisms, form the backbone of modern language models, while graph neural networks add a layer of relational reasoning that enhances context understanding.
  - **Hybrid and Multimodal Approaches:**
    The integration of multiple modalities—text, images, audio—through hybrid architectures can unlock richer representations and support a wider range of applications.
- **Training and Fine-Tuning:**
  - **Data Preparation:**
    High-quality, clean, and representative data is critical for training robust models. Emphasis on domain-specific fine-tuning can significantly boost performance for targeted applications.
  - **Optimization Techniques:**
    Techniques such as mixed precision training, distributed learning, and adaptive learning rate scheduling are vital for efficient model training and resource utilization.
  - **Continuous Improvement:**
    Feedback loops and iterative testing are essential to refine model behavior and maintain performance over time.
- **Practical Applications:**
  - **Industry Use Cases:**
    From healthcare and finance to marketing and customer service, LangGraph LLM has proven its value in automating

tasks, enhancing user experiences, and driving operational efficiencies.
- o **Integration Strategies:**
  Leveraging APIs, microservices, and containerization enables seamless integration of LangGraph LLM into real-world systems, ensuring scalability and reliability.
- **User Interaction and Ethical Considerations:**
  - o **Conversational Interfaces:**
    Best practices in UI/UX design for AI emphasize clarity, context, personalization, and transparency, which are crucial for building trust and engagement.
  - o **Ethical AI:**
    Mitigating bias, ensuring fairness, and maintaining data privacy are non-negotiable elements of responsible AI deployment. Transparency and user empowerment are central to building ethical AI systems.
- **Community and Future Trends:**
  - o **Open-Source Contributions:**
    Engaging with the open-source community and participating in collaborative projects accelerates innovation and broadens the impact of language intelligence technologies.
  - o **Future Developments:**
    The field is poised for rapid evolution with advances in hybrid models, multimodal AI, and energy-efficient techniques, setting the stage for next-generation applications.

Takeaways for the Future

- **Embrace Innovation:**
  Continuously monitor emerging trends and integrate new technologies to maintain a competitive edge.
- **Foster Collaboration:**
  Leverage community insights, open-source contributions, and interdisciplinary partnerships to drive further advancements.
- **Prioritize Ethics and Transparency:**
  Maintain a strong focus on ethical practices, user privacy, and explainability to build systems that are trustworthy and socially responsible.
- **Iterate and Improve:**
  Use feedback and rigorous testing to refine your models, ensuring they evolve in line with user needs and technological progress.

This recap encapsulates the core concepts and practical strategies presented in the guidebook, providing you with a solid foundation to harness the full potential of LangGraph LLM in your projects. As you move forward, remember that the landscape of language intelligence is dynamic—staying informed, agile, and ethically committed will be key to your success.

11.2. The Impact of LangGraph LLM on Industry and Society

LangGraph LLM has emerged as a transformative tool, influencing a wide range of industries and bringing significant societal benefits. In this section, we examine how its advanced language intelligence capabilities have reshaped business processes, enhanced decision-making, and contributed to broader societal change.

Industry Impact

1. **Healthcare:**
   - **Enhanced Clinical Efficiency:**
     LangGraph LLM has been leveraged to automate the summarization of electronic health records and clinical notes, reducing the administrative burden on medical professionals and enabling faster, more accurate patient care.
   - **Improved Diagnostic Support:**
     By integrating advanced language understanding with medical data, the model assists in extracting key insights from vast amounts of clinical literature, supporting diagnostic decisions and personalized treatment plans.
2. **Finance:**
   - **Streamlined Market Analysis:**
     Financial institutions use LangGraph LLM to analyze market trends, earnings call transcripts, and news articles, leading to faster and more informed investment decisions.
   - **Automated Reporting:**
     The model's ability to generate coherent summaries of complex financial data reduces manual labor, minimizes errors, and accelerates reporting cycles.
3. **Marketing and Customer Service:**
   - **Personalized Customer Engagement:**
     In marketing, LangGraph LLM enables the creation of tailored content and dynamic campaign strategies that

resonate with target audiences, boosting engagement and conversion rates.
- o **Intelligent Virtual Assistants:**
  By powering chatbots and virtual assistants, the model has revolutionized customer service, delivering rapid, context-aware responses that enhance user satisfaction and reduce operational costs.
4. **Technology and Software Development:**
   - o **Code Assistance and Documentation:**
     Developers benefit from AI-driven code suggestions and automated documentation, leading to increased productivity and improved code quality.
   - o **Innovation in Product Development:**
     The model supports idea generation and research by summarizing technical literature and identifying emerging trends, thereby driving faster innovation cycles.

Societal Impact

1. **Increased Productivity and Efficiency:**
   The automation of repetitive tasks and enhancement of decision-making processes have led to significant productivity gains across industries. This efficiency not only saves time and resources but also fosters innovation and competitive advantage.
2. **Democratization of Knowledge:**
   LangGraph LLM makes advanced language processing accessible to a wider audience, from small businesses to large enterprises. By lowering the barrier to entry, it empowers organizations and individuals to harness the power of AI without requiring deep technical expertise.
3. **Improved Access to Information:**
   With its ability to quickly process and summarize vast amounts of data, LangGraph LLM facilitates better access to information. This is particularly impactful in fields such as education and public health, where timely and accurate information can have life-changing effects.
4. **Ethical and Responsible AI:**
   The emphasis on fairness, transparency, and ethical design in LangGraph LLM has set a benchmark for responsible AI development. By integrating bias mitigation strategies and promoting explainability, the model contributes to a more equitable deployment of AI technologies.

5. **Job Transformation and Skill Development:**
   While the automation capabilities of LangGraph LLM may reshape certain job functions, they also create opportunities for new roles in AI management, data analysis, and model fine-tuning. This shift encourages ongoing skill development and adaptation in the workforce.

Summary

- **Industry Transformation:**
  LangGraph LLM has redefined processes in healthcare, finance, marketing, and technology by automating complex tasks, enhancing decision-making, and driving innovation.
- **Societal Benefits:**
  The model contributes to increased productivity, democratized access to information, and the promotion of ethical AI practices, thereby fostering a more informed and equitable society.
- **Future Outlook:**
  As LangGraph LLM continues to evolve, its impact on both industry and society is expected to grow, offering new opportunities and challenges that will shape the future of work and communication.

By integrating advanced language processing with practical, real-world applications, LangGraph LLM has proven to be a catalyst for change, delivering tangible benefits across multiple sectors and contributing to the broader advancement of society.

11.3. Vision for the Future of Language Intelligence

Looking ahead, the future of language intelligence promises to be transformative, not only in advancing technology but also in reshaping the way we interact with information and each other. As we project into the coming years, several key themes and trends are set to define the evolution of language models like LangGraph LLM.

Integrated Multimodality

Future language systems will increasingly integrate multiple forms of data—text, images, audio, and video—into a unified framework. This convergence will lead to richer contextual understanding, enabling applications that can, for instance, describe visual content, analyze multimedia news stories, or support cross-modal interactions in virtual reality environments.

Enhanced Personalization and Adaptability

As models become more sophisticated, they will offer unprecedented levels of personalization. Future systems will dynamically adapt to individual user preferences, learning from continuous interactions and tailoring their responses accordingly. Imagine conversational agents that not only understand your language but also adjust their tone, style, and content to match your unique context and needs in real time.

Ethical, Transparent, and Responsible AI

With growing concerns around bias, data privacy, and accountability, the future of language intelligence will place a premium on ethical design and transparent operations. New methodologies will be developed to detect and mitigate biases, while robust explainability features will allow users to understand how decisions are made. This commitment to ethical AI will build greater trust among users and set industry standards for responsible innovation.

Hybrid and Adaptive Architectures

The integration of graph-based reasoning with advanced transformer architectures will continue to evolve, leading to hybrid models that are not only more efficient but also better at capturing complex relationships within data. These adaptive architectures will be able to learn continuously from new data streams, reducing the need for frequent retraining and enabling AI systems that evolve alongside changing environments and user needs.

Democratization and Broad Accessibility

The future of language intelligence is not just about technological breakthroughs—it's also about broadening access to AI capabilities. As models become more cost-effective and easier to deploy, smaller businesses and individuals will have the opportunity to leverage cutting-edge AI, fostering innovation across all sectors. Open-source contributions and community-driven research will play a critical role in democratizing access, ensuring that the benefits of advanced language processing are shared widely.

Convergence with Emerging Technologies

The next wave of innovation in language intelligence will likely converge with breakthroughs in other areas, such as quantum computing, neuromorphic engineering, and Internet of Things (IoT) connectivity. These intersections will open up entirely new paradigms for how AI processes and interacts with data, offering possibilities that today may seem like science fiction.

A Collaborative Ecosystem

Finally, the future vision of language intelligence is deeply rooted in collaboration—across disciplines, industries, and geographies. By fostering interdisciplinary research, encouraging open-source development, and engaging diverse communities, the collective intelligence of global experts will drive continuous improvement and ensure that language models remain adaptable, ethical, and impactful.

Summary

- **Multimodality:** Future systems will seamlessly integrate text, image, audio, and video data for richer, more contextual interactions.
- **Personalization:** AI will adapt dynamically to individual user preferences, leading to more engaging and effective interactions.
- **Ethical AI:** Transparency, bias mitigation, and robust privacy practices will be integral, ensuring responsible and trustworthy systems.
- **Hybrid Architectures:** The fusion of transformers with graph-based and adaptive models will enhance efficiency and relational understanding.
- **Accessibility:** Democratization of advanced language technologies will empower smaller organizations and individuals, broadening the reach of AI.
- **Technological Convergence:** Integration with emerging technologies like quantum computing and IoT will open new frontiers in AI.
- **Collaboration:** A global, interdisciplinary ecosystem will drive continuous innovation and refinement of language intelligence.

This vision for the future of language intelligence sets a roadmap for how technology can continue to transform industries and improve our daily lives. By anticipating these trends and embracing collaborative, ethical, and innovative approaches, organizations and developers can ensure that the next generation of language models not only advances technical capabilities but also contributes positively to society as a whole.

11.4. Final Thoughts and Call to Action

As we conclude this comprehensive guidebook on LangGraph LLM, it's clear that the journey through advanced language intelligence has been both enlightening and transformative. Throughout these chapters, we have explored the theoretical underpinnings, practical implementations, and real-world impacts of integrating state-of-the-art language models into various domains. The insights gained—from hybrid architectures and multimodal capabilities to ethical AI practices and community collaboration—highlight the immense potential of LangGraph LLM to drive innovation and reshape industries.

Final Thoughts

- **Embrace Continuous Learning:**
  The field of language intelligence is rapidly evolving. Stay curious, keep exploring new research, and be willing to iterate on your projects as technologies advance.
- **Innovate Responsibly:**
  As you leverage LangGraph LLM and similar models, remember that ethical considerations—such as bias mitigation, transparency, and data privacy—must remain at the forefront. Responsible innovation ensures that the benefits of AI are realized in ways that are fair, accountable, and beneficial to society.
- **Collaborate and Share:**
  The open-source community and interdisciplinary collaborations are powerful catalysts for progress. Contribute your insights, share your successes, and engage with peers to drive collective innovation. Your contributions can help shape the future of language intelligence and make these advanced technologies accessible to a broader audience.

Call to Action

- **Experiment and Build:**
  Take the practical projects, tutorials, and strategies outlined in this guidebook and apply them to your own initiatives. Whether you're

developing a cutting-edge application or refining existing systems, use LangGraph LLM as a springboard for innovation.

- **Engage with the Community:**
  Join online forums, attend conferences, participate in hackathons, and contribute to open-source projects. Your engagement not only enriches your own expertise but also accelerates the collective advancement of AI technologies.
- **Champion Ethical AI:**
  Advocate for transparency, fairness, and user-centric design in all your AI endeavors. Lead by example, and help establish best practices that ensure AI continues to benefit all segments of society.
- **Stay Informed and Adaptive:**
  Keep abreast of emerging trends, such as multimodal integration, adaptive learning, and hybrid models. As the landscape evolves, be prepared to adapt and integrate new advancements into your projects, ensuring that your work remains at the cutting edge.

Together, by embracing continuous innovation, fostering collaboration, and upholding ethical standards, we can drive the next generation of language intelligence and make a lasting impact on industries and society. Now is the time to take action—experiment, share, and lead the way into a future where advanced language models empower us to communicate, create, and innovate like never before.

www.ingramcontent.com/pod-product-compliance
Lightning Source LLC
LaVergne TN
LVHW080113070326
832902LV00015B/2558